MIGHTY WOMEN

MIGHTY WOMEN

*Stories of
Western Canadian Pioneers*

GRANT MACEWAN

GREYSTONE BOOKS
Douglas & McIntyre
Vancouver/Toronto

Copyright © 1975 by Grant MacEwan

First Greystone edition 1995

95 96 97 98 99   10 9 8 7 6

This book was published originally by Western Producer Prairie Books, a publishing venture owned by Saskatchewan Wheat Pool.

All rights reserved. No part of this book may be reproduced, stored in a retrieval system or transmitted in any form by any means, without the prior permission of the publisher or, in the case of photocopying or other reprographic copying, a licence from CANCOPY (Canadian Reprography Collective), Toronto, Ontario.

Greystone Books
A division of Douglas & McIntyre Ltd.
1615 Venables Street
Vancouver, British Columbia
V5L 2H1

Canadian Cataloguing in Publication Data

MacEwan, Grant, 1902–
    Mighty women

    (Grant MacEwan classics)
    Previously published as: And mighty women too.
    "Greystone Books."
    ISBN 1-55054-416-0

    1. Women — Canada, Western — Biography. 2. Frontier and pioneer life — Canada, Western 3. Canada, Western — Biography. I. Title. II. Title: And mighty women too. III. Series: MacEwan, Grant, 1902–. Grant MacEwan classics.
FC3208.M33 1995   971.2'0922'2   C95-910057-1
F1060.3.M33 1995

Cover design by Jim Skipp
Cover illustration by Michael J. Downs
Printed and bound in Canada by Best Book Manufacturers
Printed on acid-free paper ∞

To the memory of a pioneer mother

FOREWORD

Somebody will say that I was bullied into writing this. It is not so, although after writing *Fifty Mighty Men* some years ago, there were reminders that such a book embracing men only should not stand alone. Of that I was very conscious because I had the opportunity of knowing many of the pioneer women and to know them was to admire them and love them.

Fifty Mighty Men, a collection of biographical sketches of frontier figures in Western Canada, was in some respects an experiment. It met with an encouraging response and survived through rather many reprintings to bring satisfaction to both the author and the publisher, *The Western Producer*. But always there were the questions: Why only men in that collection? Where were the pioneer women? The answers should have been forthcoming; true, men outnumbered women in homestead and other frontier communities — sometimes five to one — but the role of the latter was in no way less important. It was always the author's intention that *Fifty Mighty Men* would have a companion volume. The companion was started long ago but there were delays; and circumstances dictated a change in the form. Instead of adhering rigidly to a uniform chapter size, it was thought better to be guided by the volume of material considered pertinent. The total number of sketches would be reduced but many of them would be longer and more complete in treatment.

It seemed most appropriate that the publisher that brought out *Fifty Mighty Men* and kept the volume alive and gay, would produce the companion. Needless to say, I was happy to find my friends at The Western Producer eager to publish. My thanks to them and others who helped to bring this series into the mainstream of a rapidly growing Canadiana.

Grant MacEwan
(1975)

CONTENTS

1. Marie-Anne Lagimodière: The Indians Called Her Ningah 1
2. Jane Carruthers Trimble: A Thousand Miles by Covered Wagon 18
3. Henrietta Muir Edwards: The Lady and the Law 26
4. Kate Simpson Hayes: Alias Mary Markwell 33
5. Elizabeth Boyd McDougall: First in the Southwest 42
6. Mary Drever Macleod: Brought a Kindly Dignity 51
7. Jessie Turnbull McEwen: The Lady of Tullichewen 59
8. Pauline Johnson: Princess 67
9. Lucy Margaret Baker: With the Brave Heart of a Bullfighter 76
10. Mary Ellen Andrews: Caught Milking the Wrong Cow 84
11. Elizabeth Scott Matheson: A Lady Doctor on the Frontier 91
12. Cora Hind: Voice of the Agricultural West 100
13. Martha Louise Black: Wedded to "My Beloved Yukon" 110
14. Caroline "Mother" Fulham: The Lady Kept Pigs 119

15 Emily Murphy: Captain of the Famous Five......127
16 Louise Crummy McKinney: Death on Booze 138
17 Irene Parlby: The Voice of Farm Women 146
18 Nellie McClung: "Loved and Remembered".....159
19 Miriam Green Ellis:
   The Lady with the Notebook 169
20 Violet McNaughton: The Mighty Mite 175
21 Emily Carr: Artist Ahead of Her Time.............181
22 Victoria Callihoo: Granny 190
23 Dora Alice "Ma" Brainard:
   House by the Side of the Road.......................200
24 Julia Scott Lawrence: Granny of the North 207
25 Margaret Newton:
   Tracking Down the Stem Rust 214
26 Edna Jaques: 3,000 Poems Later 220
27 Mary Barter Cody:
   To Nurse Cody "With Love" 229
28 Ellen Foster: Friend of God's Wild Children 238
29 Hilda Neatby: A Plea for Love of Learning 246
30 Margaret "Ma" Murray:
   Spearing for the Truth 253
31 Lydia Gruchy: A Long Wait for Ordination 261
32 Anahareo: The Screams of Suffering Animals 267

MARIE-ANNE LAGIMODIÈRE: THE INDIANS CALLED HER NINGAH

Who was the first white woman to become a permanent resident of the West? She was Marie-Anne Lagimodière. Who had the first legitimate white baby to be born in what is now Manitoba? Marie-Anne Lagimodière. Who had the first white baby in what is now Saskatchewan? Marie-Anne Lagimodière. Who had the first white baby in what was to become Alberta? The answer is the same, but unfortunately for the record, the lady and her famous husband, Jean-Baptiste Lagimodière, did not go on to country now identified as British Columbia.

The Saulteaux Indians called her Ningah, meaning "Mother," and no woman had a better claim to the lovely name than this frontier personality who gained further distinction by becoming the grandmother of Louis Riel. Her association with the western fur country began with her arrival in 1807, five years before the coming of the Selkirk settlers, and ended at her death in 1875, five years after the birth of the province of Manitoba. The intervening years were crowded with frontier adventures, dangers and joys such as few if any other women experienced.

With less courage, she would never have seen the lawless West when "fur was king," but she vowed that where her husband went, she would go. It was not exactly the way he wanted it but he discovered quickly the sinew in his wife's determination.

Jean-Baptiste Lagimodière and Marie-Anne Gaboury were born and raised at Maskinongé, close to the St. Lawrence River, where French Canadian settlers occupied long, narrow farms. It was a quiet community in which there was rarely anything more exciting than a wedding or funeral. Boys were expected to become farmers and family men, and girls had no future except in the roles of wives and mothers of big families. But Jean-Baptiste, who could outrun, outfight and outpaddle any young fellow of his age, was one of the exceptions. His resolve was to join one of the North West Company canoe brigades going far west. It had all the marks of a reckless decision but the young man, twenty-four years old in that spring of 1801, had a reputation for being wild and reckless and nobody was surprised. Neighbors gathered to say "farewell" and join in hoping he would be spared from drowning in river rapids, freezing in a western winter, and scalping at the hands of prairie Indians.

Unafraid, Jean-Baptiste took his place in one of the big Montreal freight canoes loaded with trade goods for the far Northwest. He knew what was expected of him; as one of twelve voyageurs in the canoe, he would do his share of paddling — fifty strokes per minute — through long days. He would eat cornmeal mush and fat pork and sleep under an overturned canoe or under a pine tree. At Grand Portage, a sort of midcontinent divisional point, there would be the first major pause for rest and celebration, and then, after carrying freight over the longest and most difficult portage of all, he would face more weeks of paddling before reaching Red River and the buffalo country.

For the next four years, Jean-Baptiste trapped, traded and lived the wild, free life afforded by the lawless land. And then he joined an eastbound brigade of canoes loaded with ninety-pound bales of fine furs and returned to Maskinongé. There he was welcomed with undisguised surprise by people who thought he would be dead. He was like a hero home from the wars and men who had never been more than a day's drive from their farms plied him with questions and girls peeked admiringly. Marie-Anne, now twenty-five years old and employed as assistant housekeeper at the home of the parish priest, attended a house party in his honor. She had seen him a few times before he went to the West, the last being at a taffy party in the sugar-maple woods. Although they had never spoken to each other, she recalled how their glances met several times that day and a restrained attraction seemed to tear at her heart. Now he was back, looking more tanned, more muscular and more manly. She was not beautiful but she was trim and refreshing and sweet, and to her delight, his special attention was for her. During the next months, he found many excuses to call at the priest's house and on April 21, 1806, Marie-Anne and Jean-Baptiste were married and moved to a small cabin where, as any bride would expect, they would farm modestly and raise a big family.

But it was not to be. Jean-Baptiste loved his wife, but growing within him day by day was a longing to be back in the West. The spring season made him realize more than ever that he could not settle to live quietly on a little farm in the valley. The great spaces, the wild freedoms, the reckless hunting companions of that far country were tugging at his heartstrings. Much as he hated the necessity of doing it, he confessed the awful compulsion to his wife.

"You won't understand, my dear," he said gently, "but the longing to be back is more than I can endure. I have to go. But you'll be all right. You can go again to work at the priest's place. Anyway, I'll come back. Please, Marie-Anne, try to understand."

His words cut like a knife in her flesh and she had no answer. Suddenly all the joy of making a home and having children vanished, leaving an awful void. She collapsed in a chair and sobbed and said nothing. But she caught a wild idea and that night she prayed for guidance. She consulted her priest and, with fresh courage, she faced her husband again, this time with dry eyes and firmness in her voice.

"Jean-Baptiste, you listen to me. If you are going to that faraway West, I go too."

Now it was for her husband to be stunned and he shouted, almost hysterically, "Don't be a fool. You can't do that. You don't know what you're talking about. No white woman has ever entered that country. Not one. It wouldn't be safe for you and you would hate it. Now forget the damned nonsense."

She fixed him with a defying gaze and spoke slowly, "Jean-Baptiste, you heard me. I am your wife. Where you go, I go. Now say no more."

He was coming to know the fiber in her determination. He heaved a sigh and walked away with his problem. He knew the agents of the North West Company wanted him for one of their spring brigades but they could change their minds if they knew he was taking his wife. "Curses on women," he repeated, running his agitated fingers through his hair.

The reaction of the Company men was exactly as he expected. "Preposterous. It never happened before but if she is determined to take the risks and hardships, we'll give her a place in a canoe. But, remember, she can't expect a lot of favors and special treatment!"

At the appointed day in that spring of 1807, the Lagimodières with personal belongings limited to what could be packed in two bags of forty pounds each, went to Montreal and then to Lachine, the head of western navigation. An air of excitement gripped the riverside. Men moved hurriedly and cursed loudly as they completed the loading of canoes. Marie-Anne had misgivings. Perhaps it was a mistake, but she banished the thought and took her place on the floor of the canoe, with bales of freight piled all around her and ten paddlers eager to be going. She waved a last farewell to friends on the shore, and with a lump in her throat, wondered when she would see them and her native countryside again. The answer would have been "Never," and it was better that she did not know it.

The voyageurs sang gaily as their paddles dipped in perfect unison. People along the shore cheered and the steersman, trying to be humorous, called to Marie-Anne, "Only another thousand miles to Grand Portage, Madame."

Marie-Anne was not expected to paddle but she could be useful. She took charge of the food supplies and mended clothes for the men. To her surprise, the voyageurs accepted her as a legitimate member of the team, even going to the length of helping to gather spruce boughs to cushion her bed; but the monotony became awful. Apart from changes of scenery, about the only variations in routine were the all-too-numerous portages and the occasional shot from the gun of an Indian sniper on the bank. For the men, the "carrying places" meant shouldering the big canoe and every bundle of freight. For Marie-Anne, they meant carrying her forty-pound bag of personal belongings and having a walk. She kept count — thirty-six portages before they reached the broad waters of Lake Superior.

Before going far on the big lake, the voyageurs sighted a fleet of canoes coming toward them. As it drew near, it was recognized as an eastbound brigade loaded with furs and on its way to the St. Lawrence. Paddlers in both groups steered close enough to exchange greetings and inquire about the state of affairs at Grand Portage and Montreal, respectively. And Jean-Baptiste, still nursing his protest about his wife's determination to make this long and dangerous journey, found courage to speak once again on the subject, whispering quietly, "You know you could go back with those fellows if you've had enough of this. Sometimes they exchange passengers or paddlers when they meet like this. It's the last chance to get back to Maskinongé."

She eyed her husband coldly. "Yes, it would be easy to go back — and safer — but don't you remember what I said? Where you go, I go. If you turn back, I turn back. If you continue this way, so do I."

Grand Portage offered a few fresh experiences, not all

good. The pemmican-eating voyageurs from the West and the corn-and-pork eaters from the East celebrated together, drinking, singing, arguing and fighting. But to help sober them up, there was the trying nine-mile portage, enough to confirm for anyone the harsh realities of life. Marie-Anne was glad to be traveling again and after more weeks of paddling, portaging and fighting flies, the party crossed Lake Winnipeg, paddled up the Red River, passed the mouth of the Assiniboine River where there was no sign of human life, and came at length to a collection of misfit shacks where the Pembina River joined the Red.

"This is the end of the trail for the present," Jean-Baptiste announced to his wife, obviously delighted to be back where he knew the hunters, the traders and Indians, all of whom he greeted as old friends. Marie-Anne was subdued, unimpressed by these rough people.

"No church here, Jean-Baptiste?" she inquired and he replied, "No church."

"Who makes the laws?" was her next question. "No laws," he answered, "but don't be afraid. They're not such bad people and you just stay close to me."

But Marie-Anne was not safe and the warning came awkwardly. "Better take your wife away from here at once," one of the traders told Jean-Baptiste. "That Indian girl, Little Weasel — you know the one you lived with when you were here before — well, she intends to kill your wife. When she heard you arrived back she came to claim you again for her tipi but when she saw you had brought a white squaw, she vowed to kill. She may seem friendly but she is just waiting her chance."

Jean-Baptiste was instantly worried. He had not told Marie-Anne about that affair. Not that he saw much wrong with it; it was just the custom in the country, something which resulted from convenience and necessity. But Marie-Anne would never understand. His friend Bertrand confirmed the necessity of moving without delay and he informed his wife that they were going on a hunting expedition, just the two of them. With tent and blankets and gun and ax, they would paddle up the Pembina to some favorable location.

"Why are we doing this?" she inquired, seriously. He realized that he had to explain, however much he might wish to avoid doing it. There was no escape and it was better that the story come from him than from another. "You know I was here before," he began, "lived like all the other white men, and that Indian girl, Little Weasel, was my servant and, well, like a wife I suppose. Now she wants to get rid of you and have me back."

Marie-Anne became pale. She was shocked as never before in her life and she slumped on a buffalo robe on the floor. Jean-Baptiste tried to comfort her but she pushed him away. She longed for Maskinongé and the ear of her priest; she longed for sleep but for most of the night she stared into the darkness, arguing with herself. Finally, she wondered why she was so agitated and, awakening her husband at an early morning hour, said: "Jean-Baptiste, listen to me. I've been thinking all night and I've made up my mind. You should have told me sooner but, anyway, you told me and I was upset. But I love you and now I think I'm ready to regard that affair as something which is sealed tightly in your past and I can forget it. You told me you were sorry and now I'm sorry to have been so disturbed about it. Now let's go on from here as if the talk of this night were just a dream."

Jean-Baptiste, still wondering why her little speech had to be delivered in the middle of his sleeping hours, kissed her and mumbled: "You're a good woman; that's what you are. I hoped you would see it that way. Tomorrow morning we go west."

When they pitched their tent on the following evening, they were in a wooded area offering shelter, fuel, good hunting and natural beauty. For what remained of the autumn, that was the Lagimodière home. Then, as winter began to fix its icy grip upon the countryside, there was a double reason for returning to Pembina. Marie-Anne was expecting her first baby and guessing it would come soon. She longed for the attention of someone in whom she could have confidence. Even an Indian woman who knew about babies would be better than a rank amateur like Jean-Baptiste. They decided to pack and return to the motley community beside Red River.

At Pembina, Jean-Baptiste found a log shack for their use and arranged with Chalifou's Cree Indian woman to remain near to help his wife. Happily, the girl who threatened to kill the white wife of the man with whom she had lived and traveled, was no longer there and Marie-Anne and Jean-Baptiste lived in peace for the following weeks, waiting for the baby. And then the hour came and Chalifou's squaw, good as her word, was present with extra buffalo robes, moss, and herbal tea. Marie-Anne prayed and her confidence was bolstered. "Don't worry," she said to her husband. "I was worried but I'm not worrying any more. It's going to be all right."

And it was all right. A baby girl was born on January 6, 1808, and after being made dry with wood ashes, was introduced to her warm moss-lined cradle-bag. Marie-Anne held the little one tenderly, christened the child herself with the name Reine, and smiled joyfully.

"Do you suppose our little girl is the first white baby in this new land?" she asked and her husband nodded with a grin of satisfaction. "You are the first white woman and Reine is the first white baby." But as the new parents were to learn later, this distinction to which they were laying claim did not really belong to them. As written in the journal of Trader Alexander Henry on December 29, 1807 — eight days before wee Reine's arrival — "one of Mr. Henry's Orkney lads" had a baby. The circumstances were strange indeed. As Henry explained, the Orkney "lad" employed in the fur trade was overcome by sudden illness and given a bed in Henry's house. But this was no ordinary illness and in a very short time the sick person gave birth to a healthy baby. The new parent then confessed to hiding her true sex in order to accompany her lover from Scotland to Rupert's Land. After dressing and working as a male for more than two years, she now needed pity. Deserted by the man with whom she had crossed the ocean, she had nobody to whom she could turn for assistance. It was arranged, however, that she and her baby would be sent back to the Old Country. And if Marie-Anne was not the first white woman in the West and the mother of the first white baby, she was certainly the first white woman to become a permanent resident and mother of the first legitimate white baby.

With the coming of spring and a million freshets carrying water to the swollen Red River, Jean-Baptiste talked about traveling westward on the Saskatchewan. Alexander Henry's brigade would be leaving soon after the ice was out and Jean-Baptiste and his friends, Belgrade and Chalifou, could add their canoe and travel with greater safety from Indian attack than if going by themselves. Jean-Baptiste told his wife that she and the baby would remain at Pembina and he would return in the autumn. The country away west was too primitive and too savage for a white woman. But he should have known better.

"Do we have to debate that question again?" she inquired impatiently. "If I didn't intend to live with you, I wouldn't have married you. Maybe it isn't a safe place for a woman and baby but neither is Pembina entirely safe. If you go, we go too. I'll look after Reine and you'll look after me. When do you think we will go?"

The Indian wives of Belgrade and Chalifou were accompanying them and now it would require two additional canoes in the brigade. Alexander Henry did not mind but he was surprised at Marie-Anne's decision and observed that she would be dead before the summer ended. The departure was exactly a year after Marie-Anne left her St. Lawrence River community and again she was about to travel into territory where no white woman had been known to travel before. The canoes were smaller than those used on the eastern route but members of the party paddled and sang and camped at night very much as voyageurs were expected to do. They crossed Lake Winnipeg and entered the broad Saskatchewan. They halted at Cumberland House and remained longer than intended. It happened that the Indians were in the midst of a summer celebration, feasting upon everything from roast dog to boiled buffalo tongues. They wanted the people in Henry's party to join them and they became increasingly fascinated by the white woman and her baby. They had never seen anything like these and the chief came forward with a formal proposition for the white woman. He and his people had heard of the white man's Queen living far across the big ocean but the Indian people had never had a queen. They should have a queen and his proposal was for Marie-Anne to stay and accept such high office. They promised to be good and serve her well.

Marie-Anne blushed when the chief's words were interpreted for her. Looking at him, she smiled in queenly fashion but asked Alexander Herny's interpreter to thank the Indians and explain the necessity of her continuing westward with her husband.

Jean-Baptiste's little group left the brigade at what was known as Isaac's House, an aging post sometimes called Fort des Prairies, about due north of where the town of Melfort was located later. The men wanted to hunt and they pitched their tents a short distance from the old fort. There Marie-Anne saw proof of the dangers her husband had warned about. On a pleasant afternoon, a few days after arriving, she and Reine and Belgrade's wife were alone when they heard the rumble of horses' feet. In an instant, a party of mounted Indians, dressed and painted for war, rode directly to the tent and halted. Although instantly frozen with fear, the young mother's first thought was for Reine, but without waiting for instructions, Belgrade's squaw grabbed the baby and disappeared into the nearby woods, leaving Marie-Anne entirely alone. The Indian leader or chief dismounted and advanced, mumbling words of surprise and pleasure. Surely, a white woman, alone, was a prize he had never thought of winning and he seized the girl by the upper arm, grinning with a wicked possessiveness. Trembling and pale from fright, she tried to brush his hand away but she was unable to release the giant grip. She wanted to scream but closed her eyes in prayer instead. If ever she needed divine help it was now. The seconds seemed like hours as she tugged to break away and then she heard a voice saying: "Madam, what you doing here?"

As she opened her eyes she saw another man standing in front of her, likewise decked in feathers and paint. Having recognized her as a white woman, he rode forward and stood beside the chief. "You are French?" he asked in words she could understand. She nodded in her surprise and he responded, "I, too, was French until I became an Indian. I did not know there was a white woman in the country and you are very brave to be here. I will talk to this chief and persuade him to leave you alone."

The Frenchman-turned-Indian addressed the leader and what followed was a heated debate in Cree. It was evident that the chief did not want to forfeit his claim to a young woman with white skin but, finally, with a scowl on his face, he relaxed his hold, mounted his horse and led his warriors away at a defiant gallop.

Marie-Anne breathed deeply and offered a prayer of thanks. As soon as the visitors were out of sight, Belgrade's wife emerged from the forest of willows with baby Reine. Everybody was safe, and when Jean-Baptiste came back in the evening, his wife told him that she had never seen prayer answered so promptly.

Every day brought fresh adventures, some more dangerous than others. She was expecting another baby and trying to avoid needless exertions but they came unexpectedly. Jean-Baptiste wanted to travel overland for a while and exchanged the canoes for Indian horses and tried carrying his pregnant wife and the baby on a travois. But it was rough and Marie-Anne thought she would prefer to ride on a horse. "All right," Jean-Baptiste said, "Which horse do you choose?" A brown mare with sleek coat and friendly face was the one she wanted, and with Reine in her moss-lined bag, she rode quietly and well for several days. But there was trouble ahead. Her mare had been trained to chase the buffalo and loved to do it. The Lagimodières were traveling peacefully one afternoon when a small herd appeared, and in spite of the woman's attempts to hold her, the mare raced away at a gallop, determined to overtake the animals. Marie-Anne screamed for help and Jean Baptiste on his horse gave chase, which only made the mare run faster. At every stride, Marie-Anne expected to be dashed to the ground. But, amazingly enough, she was not thrown, and when the mare became fatigued, she slackened her pace and stopped. Jean-Baptiste caught up and called, "Are you all right?" to which the reply was muttered feebly, "I don't know. I think I'm sick."

He made camp at once and before the next sunrise, Marie-Anne's second baby, a boy given his father's names, was born there on the Prairies, somewhere within the bounds of the present province of Saskatchewan.

This blue-eyed boy baby was the one which seemed to fill the Indians with envy and evil designs. A chief tried to barter for him, offering at first one horse, then two horses and, finally, five horses. And at Fort Edmonton, where the Lagimodières were camping in the following year, a squaw attempted to steal the boy. But the kidnapper did not succeed; in a frenzy, Marie-Anne pursued, fearlessly attacked the squaw and tore away the blanket used to hide the baby. In an instant the child was back in his mother's arms and the squaw knew something of the fury of which white women were capable.

It was in the same vicinity of Fort Edmonton that Marie-Anne gave birth to her third baby, Josette, the first of the kind to be born on what is now Alberta soil.

"I've got news," Jean-Baptiste said one day in 1812. She listened attentively. "James Bird at the fort told me — a farming settlement to be started at Red River. A Scottish earl called Selkirk is backing it. What do you say about going back and seeing what's happening. I'll bet it won't work out but we could watch it anyway."

Marie-Anne's face brightened and her first question was spontaneous: "Do you suppose there will be white women?" It was now five years since she had seen a white person of her own sex and her husband knew the longing she felt. "Yes," he replied, "white women but not French. Most of them from Scotland."

She was ready to return and with nothing to complicate the departure, Jean-Baptiste announced: "We'll leave in the morning, as soon as I pack our tent in the canoe."

Marie-Anne was about as busy looking after her three children as her husband was handling the paddle. But the current helped and their rate of travel was better than they might have expected. Along the great length of the Saskatchewan and at Lake Winnipeg nothing of consequence had changed since the upstream journey, but where the Assiniboine River joined the Red, many changes were in evidence. Men of the North West Company had built a fort on the south of the confluence, calling it Gibraltar, and a short distance downstream, some rough shacks appeared. The Scottish settlers were there, but bewildered and disorganized. It was now autumn and the newcomers, many speaking only Gaelic, were without proper shelter and food supplies for the winter months. Their leader, Highlander Miles Macdonell, recognized the seriousness of the situation. He knew there was buffalo meat on the plains but the immigrants, having never hunted the buffalo, needed assistance if they were to escape starvation. He was relieved to meet Jean-Baptiste and learn that he would be willing to hunt meat for the months ahead. As it turned out, Jean-Baptiste's gun had a lot to do with saving the colony in the first two winters. Macdonell sent most of the settlers to Pembina for the first winter and Marie-Anne, although separated from the Scottish women by language, was happy to be among them and able to help them.

Then came the most dangerous adventure in Jean-Baptiste's career and scarcely less dangerous for his wife who was left behind. It was late in 1815. The settlers had been at Red River for three troubled years. Men of the North West Company, bitter rivals of the Hudson's Bay Company, resented the establishment of an agrarian colony which would be a threat to the fur trade. The colony was especially irritating because it was situated right on one of their river lifelines. They succeeded in convincing the Métis that these newcomers were their enemies and attacks followed. The settlement lacked the strength to fight back and Colin Robertson, who was then in charge, saw the necessity of an immediate appeal to Lord Selkirk, then in Montreal, for military aid. But Montreal was at least 1,500 miles from Red River and with winter coming and snow on the ground, the transmittal of a message would call for a daring courier. Who could and would undertake such a difficult and dangerous journey? Jean-Baptiste said that if somebody had to go, he would do it but would expect the Company to look after his family.

Robertson was elated and told the daring fellow to bring his family to Fort Douglas, adding, "You must start as quickly as possible. The survival of this colony may depend on you." Marie-Anne and the children moved into the shelter of the post, to enjoy the best security the community could afford, while her man, with blankets, snowshoes, gun and ax — and Robertson's message tucked in his cap — slipped away as inconspicuously as possible. It would be a hazardous undertaking, to be sure, but if anybody could get through, Marie-Anne reminded herself, "my man will do it." She would miss him, but in knowing the importance of his mission, she was proud.

Jean-Baptiste experienced the varied difficulties he might have anticipated but he reached Montreal in what was considered to be record time and delivered the message. Impressed by the achievement and grateful to the man from Red River, Lord Selkirk invited him to remain and rest for a few weeks but Jean-Baptiste had more desire to get back to his family than to holiday in Montreal and announced that he was returning at once.

The last half of that historic trip was even more dangerous than the first part and Jean-Baptiste was captured by men of the North West Company and taken as a prisoner to Fort William. Marie Anne wondered why he did not return and became discouraged. At the same time, she and all the residents of the colony had other worries.

The Indians Called Her Ningah • 15

The harassment by Nor'Westers became more intense and there was the awful climax when, on June 19, 1816, Governor Robert Semple — wisely or unwisely — led a little group of armed men to intercept a mounted troop riding in a northeasterly direction close to the fort. There were sharp words between the Selkirk men and the Métis led by Cuthbert Grant. A shot was fired and then another and the ensuing battle left Semple and twenty of his followers dead on the field.

Those who remained at Fort Douglas knew that the victors would now return to destroy the post and Marie-Anne was worried for the safety of her children. But before the battle ended, the old chief of the Saulteaux, Peguis, crossed the river to instruct her to come with her children to his camp. She might have questioned his motives but she believed it was his respect for Jean-Baptiste that led him to make the proposal. She followed him to the river and his canoe. Understandably nervous, she upset the chief's canoe as she entered it and plunged with her children into the shallow water. But there was no lasting ill effect and they arrived as guests at the chief's tipi, there to receive the best care the Indian and his wife could provide.

A year passed from the time of Jean-Baptiste's departure and no word of him reached Red River. It was to be presumed that he was dead. But close to Christmas, a tired man with ragged whiskers opened the door of the cabin Marie-Anne was occupying and stumbled in. Almost hysterical in her glee, Marie-Anne embraced her husband and the children climbed over him. It was like having a loved one return from the grave and there was a joyful reunion. A few days later, Lord Selkirk's paid soldiers arrived and promptly recaptured Fort Douglas. The settlers were invited to return to rebuild their homes. And Jean-Baptiste's gallant effort on behalf of the colony was not overlooked because Lord Selkirk saw to it that a substantial piece of choice land on the east side of the river was set aside as a grant to him, an expression of appreciation.

Marie-Anne had more babies, the seventh being Julie who was destined to marry Jean-Louis Riel, respected "Miller of the Seine," and become the mother of the famous Métis leader, Louis Riel. Jean-Baptiste died on September 7, 1855, and his widow went to live with her son, Benjamin. And remaining bright and active, she watched the rapidly changing scenes, the coming of the first steamboat on the Red River in 1859, the disappearance of the buffalo, the transfer of Rupert's Land from the Hudson's Bay Company to Canada, the Métis revolt under her grandson, the birth of the province of Manitoba, the incorporation of the city of Winnipeg and the coming of the Mounted Police.

Oh, yes, the Grand Old Lady of the Frontier was saddened to see the Red River Insurrection of 1869-70 and even more saddened by the circumstances which made it necessary. But she had faith in her grandson, Louis Riel, and believed he was sincere and right. Riel, at the same time, had faith in and affection for his grandmother and may have consulted her more often than the writers of history knew. She tried to watch every move he made in seizing Fort Garry and setting up a provisional government. He was a good boy, she repeated, and she was proud of him. She was proud that he could and would speak firmly in support of his people, proud of the respect he had for her. And then her pride knew no bounds when she saw that grandson, although branded a rebel, rallying to the defense of the Red River community when Fenian and Indian raiders from south of the boundary threatened attack. She was there to see the new Lieutenant-Governor, Adams G. Archibald, cross the river expressly to thank and congratulate Louis Riel for his loyal support when the province was facing that danger. Descendants believe that Riel, after thanking the Lieutenant-Governor, added, "I'd like you to meet my grandmother. She's one of the greatest people you'll ever meet."

Marie-Anne Lagimodière, surrounded by children, grandchildren and great-grandchildren, died on December 14, 1875, at the age of ninety-five years, leaving behind an unparalleled record for courage and fortitude. Terese Lagimodière, proud of her great-great-grandmother's place in the annals of Canadian history, told me about it.

JANE CARRUTHERS TRIMBLE: A THOUSAND MILES BY COVERED WAGON

A light in the Trimble window west of Portage la Prairie was for some years the last that Edmonton-bound travelers on the Saskatchewan Trail would see until nearing their destination. The tallow candle placed there unfailingly by Jane Carruthers Trimble glowed compassionately and tired and hungry and chilled travelers turned in, especially at mealtime or bedtime. It happened so often — a stranger arriving at mealtime — that Mrs. Trimble's formula in setting the table was always the same: plates to match the members of her own family, "plus one."

Although some settlers on the Portage Plains were worried about night-prowling Indians, the Trimble door was never locked and when members of the family arose in the mornings, they never knew how many unfamiliar figures they might see emerging from blankets spread on the kitchen floor. But whoever the guests might be, they knew they were invited to stay for breakfast.

Mrs. Trimble's pioneer hospitality was matched only by the frontier experiences she could recall. Had there been an Honor Roll for those who really traveled a thousand miles or more by covered wagon, Mrs. Trimble would have been among the first to qualify. And nobody could recount the long trail from Missouri to Manitoba — all strange country to the travelers — with more vivid detail and clearer recollection of the brushes with danger than Mrs. Trimble.

For William and Jane Trimble, the search for farm land began in Ontario and took them to the Western United States before it led to Portage la Prairie where they and their children and children's children were to find contentment. William Trimble, born in Durham County, September 26, 1840, and Jane Carruthers, born in the same part, November 14, 1847 — both from Irish immigrant parents — were married at Gorie in April, 1867. The young couple intended to farm but not necessarily in the home district where the struggle with big hardwood trees and stumps was discouraging.

At the time of their marriage, the federation of four provinces, to be known as the Dominion of Canada, was nearing fulfillment but the big country far to the west — Rupert's Land and Indian Territory — was still the exclusive responsibility of the Hudson's Bay Company. That ancient trading corporation had consistently discouraged land settlement and if young easterners wished to farm in the West, the only practical hope was in the Western United States where land was available but where reported Indian hostility was sufficient to frighten all but the bravest souls. William Trimble was interested in what the American plains had to offer and even before he was married, he and his lifelong companion and neighbor, Richard Craig, made a trip to Missouri. But the Civil War was raging and the climate for settlement was unfavorable. They returned to cut more big trees and sell more potash and timbers for masts on British Navy ships, and cultivate around the unyielding stumps. When the Civil War ended, however, Trimble and Craig renewed their interest in the American West and in 1868, they, with Jane Trimble and nine-months-old daughter Jennie accompanying, were venturing toward that remote Missouri Plains country, traveling via Chicago and St. Paul.

As it turned out, Missouri was a four-year experiment with more disappointments than successes. One of the two Trimble children born there died from the familiar baby fever and Mrs. Trimble, caught in a typhoid epidemic, almost died too. While her husband broke prairie ground and planted four crops — all more or less failures — her premonition told her they should be moving again. Chinch bugs, those ill-smelling, black and white insects with huge appetites for crops and unbelievable capacity for reproduction, became the principal influence in the decision to move again.

Actually, the Trimbles had never lost completely their interest in settling to farm in the British Northwest, somewhere west of Fort Garry or Winnipeg as the place was coming to be called. Since their departure from Ontario, the situation in that part had changed completely. Just a year after they went to Missouri, the new Canada had acquired the Northwest by purchase and in 1870 the insurrection at Red River ended and the province of Manitoba was created. William and Jane Trimble and Richard Craig talked it over and decided to inquire about land policies in the new province. To their satisfaction, they discovered that the new Dominion Land Act, providing for free homesteads and millions of acres from which to choose, was soon to come into effect. and although Manitoba had experienced grasshoppers, at least it appeared to be free of chinch bugs.

"How do we get there and when do we start?" Jane asked the men and was told that the new Land Act was to become effective on July 1, 1872. "And get there?" William repeated, "there's no railroad into that country or near it yet. I suppose we'd have to go by wagon." Turning to Craig, he added: "As a bachelor, you wouldn't have much of a problem in moving to Manitoba but I have Jane and the two children to think about. However, if Jane is agreeable, I think we should start without much delay, and hope to get to Winnipeg soon after that land office opens for filing on homesteads."

The diminutive Jane, with a good Methodist face and

lots of courage, was nodding approval and Craig was making some estimates with pencil and a piece of board: "We'd have to drive to St. Paul in Minnesota and then north to Winnipeg. It would be over a thousand miles, I figure, and we'd have those disagreeable Sioux Indians to think about too. Pretty rough on a lady with two kids, spending most of the summer in a wagon. But I'm in favor of it. We'd take two wagons — covered wagons — and we'd be sure of some shelter anyway. Likely take us between two and three months on the trail."

Early in May, 1872, with essential belongings packed on two wagons and tenting canvas stretched over hoops to afford some protection for contents and riders, the Trimbles and Craig were waving a farewell to the Buckland community in Missouri. Craig had two cows tied behind his wagon and the Trimbles had one tied behind theirs. The cows would furnish milk along the way and be useful on the homesteads at journey's end. And as insurance against a setback caused by loss of a horse or horses, the cows were shod with iron shoes such as those sometimes used on oxen. The cows were uncooperative at first but soon accepted the necessity of traveling with the wagons and followed along whether tied to the vehicles or not.

In addition to furnishing fresh milk for the two Trimble children, the cows supplied butter along the way. It was discovered that when a container of cream was hung high on the wagon, the constant jolting over the faintly marked prairie trails was enough to produce a churning of butter.

The Trimbles appreciated the company and aid given cheerfully by their friend of many years and a growing number of adventures, Richard Craig. On this journey, the two wagons were never separated by more than a few rods and for night camps the wagons were drawn side by side, except on those occasions when the Trimbles and Craig fell in with other travelers and there were enough wagons to make a defensive circle at night. Inside a circle of wagons it would be easier to fight off a band of attackers. The fear of attack from Sioux Indians, who believed they had good reason for their belligerence against the white intruders, increased as the travelers came closer to St. Paul and then drove north from St. Paul. When it came time to retire at night, one member of the party remained on duty to watch and listen for possible attackers. Jane Trimble, though small of stature and midway through another pregnancy, insisted upon taking her turn as a sentry. For eyes capable of penetrating the darkness, she would have presented a picture of pioneer courage, sitting high on one of the wagons, a repeating rifle lying across her knees, and humming an old Wesleyan hymn.

River crossings presented ordeals, especially in the months of May and June when many streams were running full and fast. Bridges were almost unknown in this particular area and travelers had only two choices: They could ford or swim their horses, or they could turn back. It might not have seemed so serious if the Trimbles had full knowledge of the rivers they faced. As it was, every river was an experiment but their true friend, Dick Craig, insisted always upon being the "tester" and the first to cross. "I have no wife and children to suffer if I drown," he would say as he chained his wagonbox to the running gear to prevent the top part from parting company with the wheels and floating away. When the river proved too deep for fording, the horses had to swim and take the floating wagon with them. There were some really treacherous crossings and some worried travelers but good fortune rode with them and there was no mishap.

It was ever more apparent that covered wagons were not built for comfort. Not only were they without springs but they seemed to magnify every irregularity on the trail. Jane Trimble, sitting on the wagon seat through long days, exposed constantly to the jerking and jolting, might well have wondered if picking potatoes would be any more tiring. The canvas cover gave a parasol protection against hot sun but it did not offer much shelter in the wind. Although the canvas was gathered and tied at the back, "bonnet fashion," the front remained open to the wind. It was open also to the cool night air unless a quilt or blanket was hung loosely from the foremost hoop. It was not sufficient to mislead many mosquitoes. Beds were made by placing feather ticks on the trunks in the wagon.

It was easy to curse the wagon but it was home for much of that summer and Mrs. Trimble washed clothes and baked bread and prepared meals with reasonable regularity. Only on Sundays was it not in motion. Twice a week the lady of the wagon had bread dough ready to go into pans when the evening campfire burned down to leave a bed of hot coals sufficient to complete the baking operation.

It was a happy moment when on July 29 the two wagons reached Portage la Prairie. All concerned were in good health and when William Trimble counted his money he found that he had exactly the same amount as when he started on the long trip, exactly fifteen dollars. How could it have happened after a one-thousand mile journey? Along the way a Manitoba-bound traveler with an overloaded wagon offered to pay reasonable freight rate on a part that Trimble could take on his wagon and the five dollars earned in this way matched the cash expenditures made for extra flour, tea, sugar and bacon. Now he would have to reckon with a ten-dollar homestead fee.

A few days after arrival, William Trimble filed on a homestead on section 21, township 12, range 7, west of the 1st meridian. It was a short distance northwest of the village of Portage la Prairie. And the good Richard Craig filed on an adjoining quarter. For a time Mrs. Trimble and children lived at the old fort while buildings were being erected on the family land. And twenty-four days after arrival, she gave birth to another baby, this one to be called Joseph and destined to an important role in leadership in agricultural and exhibition circles on the Prairies.

For horses as well as humans it was good to be through with the long trail but the cows found it difficult to revert to the sedentary life; after walking with the covered wagons day after day for months, they seemed to become attached to the idea and, as Mrs. Trimble recalled, every time they saw a covered wagon they wanted to follow it.

To prevent them from leaving home, they had to be tethered.

The Trimbles and Craig were not the first to homestead on the Portage Plains but they were among the first. The honor of being the very first in the entire West went to a Trimble neighbor, Scottish Jock Sanderson who happened to be at the front of the line when the land office opened at Winnipeg a few weeks before the Trimble arrival. Some other notable figures were nearby on that productive Portage soil, among them John McLean who was the first farmer in the area even though he was not the first to make formal application for a homestead, and Kenneth MacKenzie at Rat Creek and Walter Lynch and Hugh Grant and Donald Stewart, all people with qualities of leadership. And the unfailing neighbor and friend, Richard Craig, who finally abandoned bachelorhood, had to be numbered among the stalwart Portage pioneers.

The area had grasshoppers in disaster numbers in the year of the Trimble arrival and had them for several successive years. It had frozen crops some years, too much rain in some seasons and not enough at other times. But the soil was excellent and the Trimbles knew they were in a good part of the world. They were there to stay. Mrs. Trimble became a community worker as well as a homemaker. Largely as a result of her efforts, Bell Plain School District was organized. She opened her homestead home to be used for community church services until the West Prospect Methodist Church was built. She was available at any time she was needed by sick neighbors or when someone nearby was having a baby. Smallpox and diphtheria epidemics found her working where the need appeared to be greatest, forgetting the dangers to herself.

As one of the well-deserved rewards, Jane Trimble saw her family grow in numbers and in service to the Portage la Prairie district. And in 1921, after almost fifty years as a Manitoba resident, her son, Joe, took her on a motor trip, back over the long route on which she had traveled by covered wagon in 1872. She followed the course with eager interest, recognizing many of the landmarks, the scenes of difficult river crossings, the places where they experienced delays because of colic in horses or cows straying away during nights, camp grounds marked in her memory by Indian scares, and the spot where the wagons bogged down in soft ground. The trip made in a few days by car filled her with wonder and thankfulness. It was a fitting climax in the life of a pioneer and she died just a few months later, March 26, 1922.

Those who attended the Trimble Farm Centennial in 1972, wished, of course, that William and Jane Trimble, the founding parents of the clan, could have been present to see the numerous members, the prominent sons and daughters, the old homestead being farmed by a fourth generation Trimble on Manitoba soil, with a fifth generation coming up to the time when one of its members could take over. The pioneer Trimbles would have been proud.

Glenbow-Alberta Institute, Calgary, Alberta

HENRIETTA MUIR EDWARDS: THE LADY AND THE LAW

"Henrietta Edwards belongs to us," said the mayor of Fort Macleod with justifiable pride. "We're rich in western history."

Any district which could lay claim to the invincible bucking horse, Midnight, and the riding champion of 1912, Tom Three Persons, would be sure of a place in history. But Fort Macleod, nestling beside the Oldman River and commanding a preferred view of the Canadian Rockies, never lacked for distinctions. After being the scene of the earliest North West Mounted Police activities in the Far West, the town was the self-proclaimed Capital of the Cowboy Country. There the frontier statesman, Frederick Haultain — later Sir Frederick — began his notable career in politics, and it was there on one election occasion that candidates for office were so numerous that no eligible male remained to be a returning officer and it became necessary to place a hurried call for one to be sent from Lethbridge.

If more were needed to give Fort Macleod people a proud sense of individuality, they could certainly claim Henrietta Muir Edwards, one of Alberta's "Famous Five

Women," one whose influence both within and beyond the National Council of Women, reached across Canada. Throughout her mature years she was one of the front-line fighters for women's rights. The source of her greatness was not so much in the high offices she held as in her tenacious ways which brought lasting benefits for Canadian women and children.

The Henrietta Edwards crusades began in her home city of Montreal, long before she saw the West, and ended only at her death at age eighty-two. There in Montreal where she was born on December 18, 1849, and christened Henrietta Louise Muir, she and her sister founded the Working Girls' Club, something quite new and offering meal services, reading rooms and study classes. Such an organization emerging in 1875 had to be recognized later as a forerunner of the Young Women's Christian Association. Together, the same two sisters edited and published a periodical known as *The Working Women of Canada,* mainly to direct attention to some urgent social needs. By depriving themselves of all personal luxuries and by selling miniature paintings of their own making, the girls carried much of the cost of publication. Sir Wilfrid Laurier and Lord Strathcona were Henrietta's favorite painting subjects and her creations were popular.

One of Mrs. Edwards' treasures in later years was a set of China dishes she painted at the request of Canadian government officials for inclusion in the Canadian exhibit at the World's Fair in Chicago in 1893. This she was permitted to retain after the fair.

Henrietta Muir, in 1886, married Dr. Oliver Cromwell Edwards and before very long the doctor was accepting a government position as medical health officer to the Blood Indians, south of Fort Macleod, and members of the family were moving to make their home on the reserve. The town of Fort Macleod, clinging stubbornly to the character of the Old West, could display a rare collection of frontiersmen, the like of Kamoose Taylor who was operating the famous Macleod Hotel and subjecting it to the most unusual set of hotel rules in the world; the like of half-breed Jerry Potts whose native talents brought the Mounted Police to this place; Fred Kanouse who had a first-hand knowledge of how the whisky trade should be conducted, and various well-educated remittance men who had difficulty in staying sober. Mrs. Edwards formed a friendly acquaintance with Frederick Haultain, Premier of the Territories, and they exchanged views on many serious matters. Then her scope of acquaintances broadened to include Emily Murphy, Nellie McClung, Irene Parlby and Louise McKinney, and with them she was ready to do battle on behalf of the women seeking the franchise or anything else they might need to bring them a better measure of security and comfort.

When women in these so-called Prairie Provinces obtained the right to vote, Nellie McClung, acting within the framework of the Council of Women, called a meeting to consider how the new democratic power could be used most beneficially. There was agreement for the formation of a Provincial Laws Committee, and Mrs. Edwards was asked to become the chairman. Having started in 1908 to compile legal information with special application to women and children, she was already an authority. Irene Parlby became the vice-chairman of the new committee.

This added responsibility furnished the incentive needed and Mrs. Edwards embarked at once upon a more intensive analysis of federal and provincial laws concerning women, laws touching upon marriage, divorce, adoption, property rights, dower rights, protection of children, minimum wages, widows' allowances and anything else which might appear pertinent in the light of the newly gained franchise.

It was a task to consume many years of tedious work and to involve numerous conferences with legal authorities near and far. Her summarization of the law served to show areas of gross inadequacy, where new legislation was needed. Those compilations of laws touching or failing to touch women and children were ultimately published and distributed widely. The first edition of *The Legal Status of Women in Alberta* was published in 1916

— the very year in which women of the West were granted the right to vote — and the second edition, in 1921, was introduced with the brief statement: "Compiled by Henrietta Edwards, Issued by and under authority of the Alberta Attorney General." It was a compliment to an author who was totally outside of the civil service and, also, outside the legal profession. A short time later, in 1924, her *Legal Status of Women in Canada* followed into publication.

Having prepared the "Legal Handbook" for women, she kept it up to date and became an unchallenged authority. She had no legal training but was so knowledgeable and so widely known that lawyers and judges came to her for opinions. One of her friends complained that Mrs. Edwards was obliged to pay the lawyers when she needed their advice but they never considered paying her for the help and information she provided.

Her record included the chairmanship of the Committee on Law in the National Council of Women for more than thirty-five years. It was a marathon performance.

But her contributions extended far beyond the Law Committee of the Council of Women. Single-handedly when necessary, she tried to render services of the kind normally offered by a Y.W.C.A. In war years she became a Red Cross leader. She was born to lead, it seemed. Late in the period of the First World War, when allied resources were being taxed to their limit and workers, food and money were needed urgently, the Government of Canada hoped to invoke stricter conservation measures. Seeking greater public support, Ottawa officials called selected individuals to assist in an advisory capactiy. Mrs. Edwards was among those invited by the War Committee and it was the first time in Canadian history that a woman had been called for a review of public policy with the government.

The appropriate advice was given — perhaps more than was anticipated or invited. Government representatives were told that, war or no war, there should be a Department of Public Health and a Department of Child

Welfare. These innovations, it was said, would constitute progressive conservation at any time. Those attending the conference agreed that women were capable of doing more of the farm work which was at that time begging for helpers, and Mrs. Edwards demanded that the women who turned their hands to such duties should be employed at the same wage rates as men of equal experience. Some special training programs would be needed for the females entering the "Land Army," but as Mrs. Edwards was quick to observe, an expenditure for education and training was never a bad investment.

On the National Subcommittee to which the subject of thrift and economy in Canadian homes was assigned, Mrs. Edwards was named secretary and brought to it her customary vigor. She was called upon to bring the Committee's message to many wartime and postwar meetings. At such a meeting at Lethbridge on May 30, 1920, she said: "The world is almost at the point of starvation and it is still the homemaker's duty to reduce waste and needless luxury in food, dress and entertainment. Let's forget about jewelry for the time being," she urged. "Let's practice economy in the homes, use wheat and meat substitutes where possible, make use of leftover foods, minimize waste in cooking, and refuse to place bread on our tables until it is twenty-four hours old." It sounded like the message of an environmentalist speaking fifty-five or sixty years later. She believed that with so many hungry people in the world, waste was criminal. There should be inspection of garbage cans and fines levied where proof of waste was found. Probably she would use about the same words today.

When Dr. Edwards retired from service on the Blood Reserve, the family moved to live in Fort Macleod, in a rather long, story-and-a-half house still standing in the 400 block on 121st Street. Mrs. Edwards' sister, remembered for her work in the Presbyterian church and Sunday school while the others went to the Anglican church, continued to be part of the household. The pioneers who might have relaxed at this time, seemed to have as many

The Lady and the Law • 31

interests as ever. Mrs. Edwards was drawn to civic challenges. As a new town library was being opened in 1975, a citizen remarked: "It is something of a monument to Mrs. Edwards who, as a leader in the Council of Women, was one of the moving spirits in getting the first library for this place."

Henrietta Edwards died at Fort Macleod on November 10, 1931. The tributes took many forms. A plaque at the entrance to the Senate Chamber in Ottawa bears the names of Mrs. Edwards and the four others who fought long and effectively for women's suffrage and then to make it possible for women to be admitted as members to the Senate.

Another plaque to her memory was placed at the entrance to the Post Office in her hometown of Fort Macleod and officially unveiled on July 18, 1964, conveying the following information:

"Henrietta Muir Edwards
1849 — 1931

A crusader for social and legislative reform, she devoted herself to these causes throughout her lifetime and was a member of 'The Group Of Five' whose efforts led to recognition of women as persons eligible for appointment to the Senate of Canada, October, 1929.
Erected by the Government of Canada,
Historic Sites And Monuments Board."

Mr. Richard Secord, of the Historic Sites and Monuments Board, was the chairman for the occasion and many public figures, including Senator James Gladstone, were present. And invited to deliver the address was Mrs. Ryder Davis who could speak as one who knew Mrs. Edwards well and tell authoritatively of her zeal for the betterment of conditions affecting women and children in Canada. As Mrs. Davis noted, Henrietta Edwards was indeed one of the Mothers of the Women's Suffrage Movement in the West and a dominant force behind the passing of the Dower Act in 1917, "a cornerstone in protective legislation for women."

Speaking at Calgary a few days after Mrs. Edwards' passing, Nellie McClung *(Calgary Herald,* November 21, 1931) pleaded that the record of the lady "who for 40 years was convener of laws for the National Council of Women" should not be forgotten.

KATE SIMPSON HAYES:
ALIAS MARY MARKWELL

Kate Simpson Hayes had the distinction of being the author of the first book to be both written and printed in the new West. It was *Prairie Pot Pourri,* printed by Stovel Company of Winnipeg in 1895. In addition to being a writer of prose and poetry and plays, she was a librarian, a business woman, an organizer, an orator and said to be the most glamorous woman in Regina. She also managed to raise some Regina eyebrows.

Somebody observed that if the early West had had half a dozen elected representatives like Nicholas Flood Davin, the Canadian capital would have been withdrawn from Ottawa to be relocated somewhere on the Prairies. In the same sense it might have been noted that if the frontier town of Regina had had a few more men like Davin and a few more ladies like his friend Kate, it might have become the acknowledged cultural capital of the continent as well as the political capital of the Northwest Territories.

The arrival of a striking and vivacious lady at Regina, slowly becoming accustomed to the change of name from Pile of Bones in 1885 — rebellion year, did not go unnoticed either by the males who turned to look again or by the females who wondered why a person of her talents and tastes had passed Montreal and Toronto. Nor was it overlooked that a lady of her cut could be a threat to domestic equanimity in the town.

Understandably, she remained something of a conundrum about Regina. Anyone with her face and figure and manner would be a prime topic for conversation and questions. Why would she choose Regina? How did it happen that a pretty woman, with two children and separated from her husband, was now breaking boldly into a man's world of endeavor? And what was to be made of this alleged "affair" with the local publisher and Member of Parliament, of all things? There was some shaking of heads, of course.

The more benevolent conversation soon turned to the lady's surpassing literary talent and the cultural leadership she was capable of providing — and did provide. Clearly she was pointing the way to a bigger and better role for members of her sex, doing it far ahead of her time. And whatever the relationship between Kate and Davin, they would have to be recognized as the most scholarly and creative pair or team to appear on the entire western scene.

Kate's life of challenge and excitement began at Dalhousie, New Brunswick, in 1856. When twenty-six years of age she married C. Bowman Simpson, of Bowmanville, Ontario, and in the next three years she was pregnant exactly half the time and mothered two children, son Burke and daughter Elaine who was commonly called Bonnie. But there was domestic incompatibility and Kate, taking her two children, set out for some place in the Territories where she could start a new life. It took courage when there was no guarantee that a woman could find work and no assurance that the recent rebellion trouble on the South Saskatchewan would not erupt again. As a destination, one point on the map looked about as good as another and Kate bought tickets for Prince Albert of which she knew nothing except that it was at the extreme northern end of a new branch line.

How was she to support herself in a frontier town where she was a total stranger? She had no answer for the question but with typical pioneer faith, she was sure she would find it. And sure enough, somebody out there needed a governess or just a household helper and she applied and was hired. It was all right for a short spell but she had a hunch that Regina, which had just been named to be the Capital of the Northwest Territories, was likely to be rich in opportunity. She moved and found the new capital to be little more than a shack town occupied by optimists ignoring the unkind remarks the Winnipeg editors were making about the folly of choosing this dismal prairie site for capital purposes.

She knew at once that Regina would suit her, and Regina residents were no less aware immediately that a woman of unusual natural endowments had moved in. At the end of her first week she was opening a millinery shop and aiming to fill Regina ladies with desire for big new hats with great flowing plumes. Unfortunately for business, women were scarce but that peculiar sex balance would change, she was sure. At the end of her second week in the community, she was being appointed to play the organ in the Roman Catholic church, and at the end of the third week, she was organizing Regina's first Literary and Musical Association and bringing increasing amazement to the town's people who had not seen her kind before.

She was now thirty years of age, graceful and forceful, and sure to arrest the attention of both men and women. She enjoyed meeting people, especially those who could and would converse freely but she had to make it clear to the numerous bachelors that she was not on a husband-hunting expedition. She had a husband from whom she was separated and was in no position to consider another union, even if she wanted it.

But Kate's meeting with Regina's most eligible bachelor, Nicholas Flood Davin, founder and editor of the *Regina Leader* and soon to become Member of Parliament for Assiniboia West, had a special quality about it. Almost at once they seemed to need each other and the reasons were not difficult to find. She was the attractive type capable of arousing the interest of any normal male and her cultural leanings, her familiarity with music and good literature, and her admiration for fine oratory would add to the attraction for a man like Davin.

Her interest in this Tipperary-born Irishman who started the *Leader* in 1883, just about the time the upstart town was named to become the capital of the Territories, may have begun with a sort of academic curiosity. He was forty-three years old, balding, rather nervous in mannerism, not very handsome but already recognized as an ingenious editor and literary giant. One of his most recent successes was in circumventing the official ruling which prevented a newspaper representative from interviewing the condemned Louis Riel who was occupying a death cell at Regina jail. Davin, believing the press had a right to obtain Riel's views on certain matters, outfitted himself with false beard, cassock, a clerical hat and big silver crucifix and presented himself at the jail as Riel's Father Confessor. Readily enough he was admitted and closeted with Riel long enough to obtain the information he wanted and left without arousing suspicions.

Regina was not the place where a man like Davin would be expected to be found. As a writer he was versatile as well as extremely skillful; he could compose a scholarly article which the best magazines would be eager to publish and he could bring the same master touch to the composition of poetry and editorials. And as an orator, he had no peer. Nova Scotia's Joseph Howe may have won more public acclaim for orations and D'Arcy McGee was regarded as Howe's equal in debate, but it is doubtful if either could bring finer workmanship or more classical style to the platform. And as for endurance, it is doubtful if anybody could hold an audience for three or four hours as well as Davin.

For Kate, it was a ten-year friendship and it rocked Regina to its foundations but regardless of what the gossips said, she and Davin, with similar talents and convictions, inspired each other and helped each other. During part of those years, she worked for the *Regina Leader* and then became the first legislative librarian in the Northwest Territories. By this time, her own ability to write prose and poetry and plays was demonstrated, just as Davin's literary output was winning wider recognition. Unquestionably, they motivated each other and the reciprocal influence could be seen. When Davin, on May 8, 1895, introduced his famous motion in the House of Commons to extend voting rights to women, his critics were quick to comment, "Kate talked him into that one." The motion as presented, stated: "That in the opinion of this House, the privilege of voting for candidates for membership thereof should be extended to women possessing the qualifications which now entitle men to the electoral franchise."

The debate was solemn and long and as seen by more modern observers, it was highly entertaining. That the motion would not be popular was quickly apparent and those who opposed it argued that voting women would magnify political differences and disrupt homes. Arguing righteously against the motion, most honorable members were sure that equal voting rights would have a degrading effect upon women and rob them of their "moral purity and sweetness."

One of the honorable cynics considered it ridiculous that any mature Member would attempt to show "the female portion of humanity" as having a natural right to vote. "To invite the fair sex to take part in our political contests," he shouted, "seems to me to be as humiliating and as shocking a proposition as to invite her to form part of the militia battalions for the defence of the country . . . Woman might be "the queen of the home," "the guardian angel of society," but fellow members were implored to safeguard her, shield her purity, "by refusing to . . . degrade her" through the exercise of the franchise.

To nobody's surprise, Davin's motion was defeated soundly, 47 votes in favor, 105 opposed.[1]

[1]House of Commons Debates, June 5, 1895

The political analysts could reason that it had been Kate Simpson Hayes' idea from the beginning. Perhaps it was, but other forces were at work and just thirty days after the motion was defeated, the Member for Assiniboia West, very much to the astonishment of friends and acquaintances, married twenty-one year-old Eliza Jane Reid in Ottawa.

The marriage of fifty-three-year-old Davin might bring surprise to many; to Kate Hayes it could bring only disappointment and heartache and she did not hide her feelings. A few weeks later, the *Regina Leader* — no longer owned by Davin — carried verses over the name of Mary Markwell, which Regina people recognized as the pen name adopted by Kate Simpson Hayes. They knew, also, that the "death" to which the poetess alluded, was simply a dead love affair and she was hurt:

When you died, I thought I too must die;
How could I live without your word and smile?
How meet the morrow and alone? when thou and I
Together long had planned and dreamed; the while
You held my hand the hill of life,
    care-strewn, was sweet,
And thorns to roses turned beneath my tired feet.

When you died, I said, 'I too must die.'
But spite of grief and spite of woe and tears,
I could not blind the sunshine of the sky;
And some sweet tinge of hope upheld my fears.
And looking back upon the path we walked, I see
Where your feet failed — the day you died for me.

The sun still circles and the clouds drift;
The prairie's blossoms bud and bloom and die;
Sunshine and rain alternate through clouds' rift,
And tears and gladness come as I pass by,
The same old pathway where sad memories bide,
And linger in my heart, because you died.[1]

[1]*Regina Leader*, Oct. 10, 1895

Six years later, the news concerning Kate's old friend was still more surprising and far more shocking. After losing the election of 1900 to Walter Scott, the young man to whom he sold the *Leader,* he was despondent in failure to understand the defeat. He was drinking heavily and experiencing financial difficulties. Late in 1901, he went to Winnipeg to keep an engagement at a public meeting and while in that city bought a revolver, returned to his hotel room and ended his life.

But that year of Davin's marriage was one of triumph as well as grief for Kate because it saw the publication of her first book, *Prairie Pot Pourri,* the first publication of book proportions to be produced in total in the West. Regina was in that year the scene of the Territorial Exhibition, most ambitious thing of its kind the West had seen. Opening on July 29, it was trumpeted across the far-flung homestead land as a sort of miniature World's Fair and the Dominion Government as well as the Territorial Government supported it generously. Color and pomp were not lacking and Governor General Lord Aberdeen came to open the event. Agriculture was featured prominently, of course, and homestead resourcefulness was demonstrated clearly in the exhibits. There were games and music and dancing and a fine arts display with sketches and paintings by local artists. And although printed some months earlier, Kate Hayes' *Prairie Pot Pourri* was making its official appearance, a 186-page book containing both short stories and poems — and a Christmas play for children, *Slumberland Shadows,* written mostly in verse. The book, the best possible souvenir, was being sold from a tent on the grounds at $1.00 per copy with the author's autograph when requested. A verse of dedication was another hint of the depth of her friendship with Davin. The book was:

> *Gratefully inscribed*
> *To the early days and the weary ways*
> *Enshrined in the sunset land;*

> *To a kindly voice that bade grief rejoice*
> *And the clasp of a friendly hand.*
> Mary Markwell, Regina, N.W.T., July, 1895.

Canada's literary community was hearing about Mary Markwell and expressing surprise that one of her great talent would be writing from Regina. But there she was, writing fiction based on current western events, poetry which appeared in *Songs of the Great Dominion* published in London, England, in 1889, and plays and operettas for Canadians of all ages. What was said to be the first three-act play presented to the Regina public appeared in 1892 and was Kate Simpson Hayes throughout; not only did she write this one but she directed its production and even acted a part. Another operetta which she wrote for children, saw her own daughter, Bonnie, taking the leading part. And the leading story appearing in *Prairie Pot Pourri,* entitled "The Light of Other Days" — based on the Northwest Rebellion — brought calls for more of similar kind.

Later in Canadian history, writing might have been her career and her name would have been familiar to all readers. As it was, writing had to be a pastime, something for idle hours. She had to make a living, but being creative and dynamic, she demanded change in her ways of life. After a few years as legislative librarian, she taught school and worked for a time as clerk in the Territorial Department of Agriculture. Then, as the century drew to a close, she left Regina to take a position with the *Free Press* in Winnipeg and still later with the Canadian Pacific Railway. It was a time when Canada was making a special effort to attract immigrants from overseas, and Kate Hayes, as an employee of the railway company, was frequently in England, Scotland and Ireland on colonization missions. Her success led John Hawkes to write of the "splendid work" she did for Canada "among the women of England."[1]

[1] Hawkes, John, *The Story of Saskatchewan and Its People,* p. 678, 1924

Among other skills, she had the gifts of an organizer and left a trail of new clubs and associations with the vigor to survive. The Literary and Musical Association which she promoted before she was completely settled in Regina, was not only the first motivating force for local culture but it proved to be effective beyond the fondest hopes at the time. Before long, having talked the Mounted Police into furnishing music, she was announcing Saturday night programs for children, admission ten cents. The Regina list of organizations would be long and after leaving that city she was one of the founders of the Canadian Women's Press Club. Fourteen Canadian writers and reporters were returning from the World's Fair at St. Louis in 1904 when two members of the group, Kathleen Coleman known as Kit, and Kathleen Hayes known as Kate, advanced the idea of forming a national body. Almost at once, Kit Coleman was named to be the first president and at the next annual meeting at which officers were being elected, Kate Hayes was elevated to the president's chair, thus becoming the second president in the history of the illustrious organization.

Kate Simpson Hayes' life was not all sunshine but it was a life of action and when she died on Vancouver Island in 1945, age eighty-eight, she was acclaimed as one of Canada's leading figures in raising women to a more independent and prominent role in the life of the country. Her series of careers was an excellent demonstration of something in which she believed, service, independence, work and creativeness.

Glenbow-Alberta Institute, Calgary, Alberta

ELIZABETH BOYD McDOUGALL: FIRST IN THE SOUTHWEST

A woman with less fortitude might have bolted from the frontier as she found it and gone screaming back to Grey County, but Elizabeth Boyd had just taken the well-known Methodist missionary, Rev. John McDougall "for better or for worse" and she was taking the new West of 1872 exactly the same way. Certainly her initiation on the trail to Fort Edmonton, which included prairie fire, Indian intimidation, river crossing in icy water and winter blizzards, would have been considered rough by any standard.

After starting from Winnipeg with the intended luxury of her own horse and buckboard and the false assurance of Indian summer skies, traveling conditions grew steadily worse until a picture of the dismal scene during the last weeks would have shown the bride of a couple of months bundled in buffalo robes on the floor of a horse-drawn toboggan while her husband on snowshoes struggled ahead leading or dragging the animal as it plunged through the drifts. For an Ontario girl who had never seen the buffalo country, it should have paralyzed her with fear. But instead of surrendering to dismay, she accepted each new hardship and brush with danger philosophically, as if it were an invention for her edification.

She found reassurance, of course, in the knowledge that her new husband, known to the Indians as Praying John, was a seasoned westerner, having been in the country for twelve years. In that time he had become an expert buffalo hunter and a resourceful traveler. He knew how to lash a couple of carts together to devise a raft for a river crossing; he knew how to talk to hostile Indians and understood the technique of making a night camp in the snow. He knew how it felt to be pursued by a wounded buffalo bull when his own ability to outrun the brute was untested, and he could relate privations necessitating the boiling of his moccasins for supper. The fact was that John McDougall was naturally resourceful and if his wife did not know it, somebody should have told her of her fortune in having one of the most versatile of outdoor men as her teacher.

If he was a good teacher, she was a good pupil and from this point forward, the husband and wife story became so interwoven that it was difficult to relate about one without talking about the other. He was thirty years of age; she was nineteen. He saw Fort Edmonton in 1862 and helped build a home for his father's family at Victoria, ninety miles northeast of Edmonton. His first wife was the Indian girl, Abigail Steinhauer, who died during the smallpox year of 1871, leaving three small children. But as a dedicated Wesleyan missionary, he could not relax long, any more than he could hold his breath.

As it happened, the Conference of the Methodist Church was being held at Winnipeg for the first time in 1872 and many notable leaders were attending, Dr. William Morley Punshon, president of the Canadian Conference; Dr. Enoch Wood, secretary of missions; Rev. George McDougall, John's father, and Rev. Henry Steinhauer, father of John's late wife. As for John, he had been a most active churchman for twelve years but had never been ordained, not at least until Sunday morning during the Conference when the Hudson's Bay warehouse was requisitioned to accommodate the crowd and John McDougall became the Reverend John McDougall. At the same Conference, it was recommended that an effort be made to take the Church to the Stoney Indians back against the Rockies.

Sessions over, John McDougall accompanied the church leaders eastward. If it could be called a holiday, it was the first since coming to the West. But he had another purpose: Hoping to improve his academic qualifications, he requested leave of absence to allow for a full year of study. To his surprise, however, he was told that he could not be spared from the field and, anyway, it would be better if he spent his time in the East looking for a wife. Dr. Wood knew a young lady who would make an admirable partner for him. The fact was that the idea of matrimony had not escaped him but he felt quite capable of conducting his own search.

Before many weeks in Ontario, Elizabeth Boyd, of Cape Rich, Grey County, had been courted and won for a lifetime partnership and was getting ready for a late-September marriage and an immediate departure for the West thereafter.

The journey to Chicago and St. Paul by rail, and to Winnipeg by riverboat was pleasant and the McDougalls had the company of Dr. George and Mrs. Bryce, traveling for the laying of a cornerstone for Manitoba College. The autumn days under Manitoba skies were lovely but John McDougall knew that time was important and after only two days at Winnipeg, the necessary provisions were assembled and the McDougalls were starting over the long trail. It was October 15 and the bride, ensconced on the bench-like seat of a one-horse democrat, was handed the reins, with instruction, "keep that nag jogging most of the time." John would be riding horseback and watching for trouble, especially on the horizon.

Almost at once, Elizabeth McDougall was made aware of the hazards of prairie travel. Not far from Winnipeg, she saw billowing clouds of smoke which John told her was from a grass fire. "It may pass us," he said optimistically. But it didn't pass; it swept in upon the trail faster than the travelers could get ahead of it. "Whatever do we do now?" she asked, praying as she made her inquiry. Instead of taking time for a reply, John was directing the horse and democrat to the center of a nearby creek, then setting a new fire intended to burn back from the stream to meet the oncoming flames. The smoke was intense but the strategy worked perfectly and the fire went around, allowing the travelers to continue over freshly blackened grass country.

The next test came in the form of a band of mounted Indians, members of the Sioux tribe blamed for the extensive massacres on the Minnesota side. They were painted hideously, suggesting a mission of war. Breathlessly, Elizabeth watched John ride forward to meet the leader and greet him with words the native probably did not understand. What he did understand was the present of a piece of bacon, apparently enough to satisfy the Chief because he wheeled and led his braves away at a gallop.

The weather turned cold and the girl from Ontario had reason to wonder if any vehicle in the world offered less protection against freezing winds than a buckboard. Bravely, however, she drove on, day after day. Then there was the ordeal of the river crossing at the South Saskatchewan, made more frightening by the presence of floating ice. "We've no time to lose," John remarked as he went to work to lash some dead wood together to make a raft big enough to carry the democrat and camping material and themselves. "We'll swim the horses behind the raft."

The loaded raft was pushed out into the current, the unwilling horses following. Elizabeth watched the floating ice crash against the raft, pondering again those unanswered questions: Why would anybody exchange life in Grey County for something like this? How does anybody survive for long in this vengeful land?

Again she took her place at the center of the buckboard seat and drove on as if she had no misgivings whatever, until a little farther along, when crossing a partly frozen creek, one democrat wheel came off and the resulting jolt was enough to break an axle. John saw it happen and heaved a sigh. By some means he would have to make a repair, even though he had no repair material except a piece of rope. He needed all his ingenuity but managed to effect a splice with a willow sapling and was soon back on the trail.

Still the bride had not seen all the varieties of frontier cussedness. Snow began to fall and became heavier until the horse in harness was working hard to merely keep the wheeled vehicle in motion. "Are we close to Edmonton?" Elizabeth asked, hopefully, and John replied: "No. We should be nearing Fort Pitt and there we'll be a couple of hundred miles from home." It was discouraging but John added something of comfort, "Fort Pitt will give us a chance to get thoroughly warmed and reorganized. We should see it tomorrow." Little did he know what that last night before Pitt held for them.

They made their evening camp much as usual, except for the inconvenience of the snow falling heavily and gently. The snow in itself was not so serious but after they had retired, a gale came out of the northwest with sudden and savage fury. Without warning, the countryside was wrapped in a winter blizzard. The tent covers rattled and threatened to blow away. The trouble was more than driving snow because the cold became intense and John McDougall knew they were in for a troubled night. It would take willpower on his part to stir from the blankets and robes but by midnight, with no abatement in the storm, he knew he would have to move the tent or be resigned to losing it. He remembered the grove of tall spruce trees close by. The only hope for protection was in moving the tent to the leeward side of those trees. How he wished he had made his camp there in the first place! Every fresh gust of wind was like a greater heave to tear the tent apart and John disclosed to Elizabeth that he would be forced to rebuild the tent and might as well move it at the same time. "Now you hang on to me," he warned, "because if you became separated, you could easily become lost and frozen."

He thought he could recall the direction of the spruce trees and got ready to move. The tent by this time was flat on the snow anyway and he believed that between them they could carry tent and poles and bedding at one time. "If we're lucky, we'll strike the big trees at about a couple of hundreds yards and have their shelter while we get set up."

With arms full of blankets and other things and almost numb from cold, they were ready to move. "You stay close behind me," John said again as they staggered through the fresh drifts and, as luck would have it, came to the protected side of the trees. Any degree of relief from that wintry blast was welcome, and using spruce boughs, John was able to start a fire. While Elizabeth added more wood to the fire, John erected the tent and felt confident it would remain secure. The McDougalls brushed surplus snow from their clothing and again retired to bedrolls. John was nearly exhausted and Elizabeth, although almost perished, made it her responsibility to keep wood on the fire. The fact was that she, too, was nearly exhausted.

What a night! If the friends in Grey County could have seen this nineteen-year-old girl now, they would have been shocked and pessimistic about her chance of living very long in such a country. But as John MacLean remarked in the book, *McDougall of Alberta*, "Love and duty laugh at storms."

Came morning and the travelers remained in camp until the storm subsided next day. By that time the drifts were deep and the unfortunate democrat horse could hardly move the vehicle. But happily, they were close to Fort Pitt and reached the place before sunset.

The fort beside the North Saskatchewan River gave Elizabeth a chance to relax and John a chance to make a change in their way of travel. Leaving the democrat behind, he took possession of a toboggan and devised a means of hitching his wife's faithful horse to it. For his own conveyance, he exchanged his horse and saddle for a pair of snowshoes and hitched the horse to pull a second toboggan to be under the charge of a new helper, Sandy by name.

Reclining on the bottom of her toboggan and bundled like a parcel of laundry, Elizabeth now felt helpless but secure. "Don't worry," John called as they were moving again, "wiggle your toes if they are cold. We'll be home in about another week."

The snow was now both soft and deep and there was no alternative to simply inching their way toward home, one step at a time. Finally the reward: on New Year's day, after two and one-half months of travel from Winnipeg — 300 miles through fresh snow — the McDougalls were at home at Victoria where shelter and warmth awaited them, also a welcome to a new step-mother who had displayed such admirable grit and cheerfulness on the trail.

Getting to know her husband's character better, Elizabeth probably inquired: "What next?" The answer would have been: "Bow River." It was a McDougall idea in the first place to establish a mission among the Stoney people and the Winnipeg Conference had endorsed it. Now it was up to John to carry out the plan. He traveled south to determine how the Stoney tribesmen were likely to receive the proposed mission, taking with him Dr. Lachlin Taylor, church official from the East. He liked the Stoney people but failed to find a lot of enthusiasm for Taylor who was said to be a complainer and who brought long delay to the trip by losing his false teeth. The important point was that the Indians along the Bow were ready to take the McDougalls among them.

Elizabeth McDougall might have remained comfortably at Victoria or Edmonton or Woodville but she was determined to move and be active in John's work. When the cavalcade set out from Edmonton on October 1, 1873, she was the driver in charge of a team of horses and a wagon loaded with supplies. John and his brother David, exercising general supervision, were mounted and so was John's little daughter, Flora, who appointed herself to herd the twelve cows and a bull which would constitute the first herd of domestic cattle to graze in the Bow Valley, just as Elizabeth McDougall was to be the first white woman in that vast southwestern area.

The initial problem was to take carts, wagons, horses, cattle and humans across the North Saskatchewan. It required patience but it was accomplished and Elizabeth McDougall was again traveling day after day through country which she had never seen before and country which had never before seen a white woman. The trip was enlivened by the occasional halt for a buffalo hunt or the necessity of conducting a search for the herd bull exercising his masculine prerogative of straying to fraternize with buffalo cows. From those sorties, the bull invariably returned bloodied and bruised but never wise enough to shun the next similar temptation.

At a point a couple of miles back from the Bow River — later called Morley — the wagon stopped and John McDougall announced: "This will be the location of our home." There was still no building or evidence of a building but John and David began at once to gather logs and incorporate them into the walls of a log cabin. Seven days later, the big log shack was roofed with sods and its windows were fitted with deerskin parchment or rawhide, and Elizabeth McDougall moved from tent to house. "We leveled the ground in the kitchen end," she explained, "and put up the cookstove." The other part of the shack was treated to a wood floor made from whipsawed or handsawed lumber. This was the frontier of frontiers. Surplus fat was collected for candles; furniture was made from lumber whipsawed on the spot; buffalo fat took the place of butter and pemmican was like a "staff of life." Wild duck eggs were popular foods in their season and the prevailing fear was in the form of angry Indians. There was that day when two painted natives appeared at the McDougall door and made signs that they expected gifts and would not be leaving until they received them. Mrs. David McDougall was with Mrs. John McDougall at the time and both had grown knowledgeable of native character and while one of the ladies engaged the men in conversation, the other picked up John's musket and, confronting the visitors with it, recommended that they depart. They departed.

Elizabeth was becoming involved in numerous ways. She gathered sick Indians and some orphans around her Morley home and cared for them; she helped to provide a school, the first one; she had a welcome for the Mounted Police making their initial appearance in the area; she was present at the signing of Blackfoot Treaty No. 7; she was given much of the credit for the early Morley Church which stood beside the Banff Highway of later years; she gave a president's leadership to the Southern Alberta Pioneers' and Old Timers' Association; she was largely responsible for the building of the first Protestant church in Calgary; she and her distinguished husband were present to see the approach of the first Canadian Pacific train and as they thought of the long-awaited termination of isolation, they paused and sang "Praise God From Whom All Blessings Flow."

Elizabeth McDougall's good works were indeed interwoven with those of Reverend John but while he died in January, 1917, the lady whose life seemed to be so often in danger during her early years that her expectancy was considered short, lived for another twenty years and died in Calgary in March, 1940, age eighty-seven. It was the passing of one of The First Ladies Of The Land, the passing of the lady who led men to say: "Love and duty laugh at storms."

Glenbow-Alberta Institute, Calgary, Alberta

MARY DREVER MACLEOD: BROUGHT A KINDLY DIGNITY

Commissioner James F. Macleod of North West Mounted Police fame earned an undisputed place of honor in Canadian history; scarcely less deserving was his wife, Mary Drever Macleod, who shared the hardships of life and travel in a land so recently shedding its cloak of lawlessness. The new force needed her influence and young police officers far from home admitted they needed her motherly interest. In her unpretentious way, this tall, graceful and energetic lady, graying early, brought a kindly and priceless dignity to the frontier force.

The fact was that the Red River Drevers had been drawn into the weave of western history long before the Mounties made their appearance and before James Macleod, as a member of Col. Garnet Wolseley's Expeditionary Army saw the country in 1870. Indeed, Miss Mary, by her own actions during the period of the Riel Insurrection, came to be remembered as a sort of "Laura Secord of the West." She did not drive a milk cow through enemy lines to disguise the real reason for being abroad, as the Upper Canada woman did in the War of 1812, but setting out on a similarly secret and dangerous mission when

Louis Riel's forces held Fort Garry, she drove a horse and cart from Lower Fort Garry to the riverboat landing near the Upper Fort and carried out her purpose.

Yes, the Drevers were long in the country. Mary's father, William, an Orkneyman, came to Rupert's Land to work for the Hudson's Bay Company in 1821 — the year of its union with the North West Company — and after eighteen years at and around York Factory, moved to Red River Settlement where he met and soon thereafter married the Aberdeenshire girl, Helen Rothnie, whose coming to these parts was for household duties in the home of pompous, severe and unpopular Adam Thom, Recorder of Rupert's Land.

For William Drever, Red River presented a totally new world of opportunities, like meeting and marrying Miss Helen. He bought a house, called it Clova Cottage, and there daughter Mary Isabella was born in 1852. When his family became bigger, Drever built a bigger and better house, Rothnie Cottage, and as if he had a prophetic vision of Winnipeg growth and development, he bought property and built a general store very close to the intersection of two trails later identified as the city's lifelines, Portage and Main.

The Drevers were leading citizens, which only added to their problems when insurrection gripped the area. They were loyal to principles and loyal to the West. They attended St. Andrew's Church and the girls were pupils at the private boarding school conducted by Mathilda Davis. Two of the girls married prominent churchmen, Margaret becoming the wife of Rev. J. A. Mackay, and Jean the wife of Rev. W. C. Pinkham — later Bishop Pinkham.

When Louis Riel and his Métis followers seized local control in 1869, the Drevers were among those caught up in the trouble. It was a critical time for the West, an anxious time for all its people. In taking over Rupert's Land and the Northwest Territories from the Hudson's Bay Company, the Government of Canada had moved in a clumsy manner, even to the point of failing to confer with the dominant group in the area, the half-breeds. These people, with the best of native claims, recognized a growing threat to their way of life and were hurt and angry. With Louis Riel as their leader, they were ready to take a stand. And take a stand, they did. They halted and turned back Hon. William McDougall who was coming to assume the office of Lieutenant-Governor. Waxing still bolder, they seized Fort Garry on November 2 and set up a provisional government which many prominent Red River residents refused to support. Mary Drever's father and many of her friends were arrested and imprisoned at the Fort.

Riel's biggest error was in ordering the shooting of Thomas Scott, after which fear gripped the community and anger gripped the East. By midsummer, a strong force of regulars and militiamen under Col. Garnet Wolseley was on its way to restore order and it was at this point that a dashing young Irish officer, Lieut. William Francis Butler, appeared briefly on the western scene. Riel's scouts riding hard ahead of the incoming riverboat, *International,* reported a mystery man on board, one to be watched.

The boat arrived as darkness was settling over Fort Garry and as it was using the mouth of the Assiniboine River to gain turning space and came close to the north shore, two men leaped to land and scrambled up the bank and disappeared. Riel's men searched the ship before hearing that two passengers had jumped and got away. They turned to pursue the escapers and caught one who was found to be William Drever, Junior, Mary's brother. The other who was William Francis Butler, walked all night as Drever had advised, and found himself in friendly surroundings near Lower Fort Garry. He found shelter at a home where Mary Drever was well known and she came that way and heard Butler tell about the guidance he had received from her brother. Butler admitted that he was there to conduct intelligence work for Wolseley and would leave to join him as soon as he had time to make an assessment of the local situation. In the meantime, he wanted to dispatch a message to Ottawa and Wolseley in the care of officers on the *International* but the bearer of a letter would run the risk of being intercepted and he did not know how to deliver the packet at the boat.

The story has been told with rather wide variations but it seems that seventeen-year-old Mary Drever said she knew how Butler's packet could be delivered: She would take it. Her friends protested, warning that if she were caught carrying messages to those Riel considered as enemies, she might be executed. But the girl showed no fear and said she would hitch an old mare to her buggy and be on her way.

Accepting the important communication, Miss Mary placed it in the bosom part of her dress and drove away, looking as unconcerned as if her only object were to deliver a dozen eggs to a customer. Those who watched her leave breathed a prayer for her safety.

Sure enough, when close to the ship's landing and the Upper Fort, she was stopped and an armed man searched her buggy. But he didn't think to look further or lacked the nerve to look further and Miss Mary drove on toward the boat and after tying her horse, went aboard and placed the packet in the hands of an officer who promised to carry it to a reliable point for mailing.

Butler in the days that followed, moved from place to place and, to his surprise, was overtaken by an invitation to meet Riel for discussion. The half-breed leader had changed his mind; instead of capturing Butler, he now wanted to learn something of Wolseley's advances. Butler replied that he would be available for a meeting if Riel released Drever and took down the New Nation's flag. Strangely enough, Riel agreed and the meeting was held, revealing Riel's hope of avoiding a clash with Wolseley.

Butler vanished to make his way eastward by any means possible and report to Wolseley concerning the Fort Garry situation. The possibility of a gun battle had to be anticipated but on August 24 the Wolseley force reached the settlement to find the Fort gates open and the stockaded premises deserted. Riel had decided against armed resistance and disappeared.

The province of Manitoba was born on July 15 and Adams Archibald arrived about a week after Wolseley's troops, to become Lieutenant-Governor. The troubled time seemed to have ended and the Imperials or Regulars in Wolseley's following could return eastward. The men of the Canadian Militia would remain for the winter, and among them was Brigade Major James Farquharson Macleod whose mother was a Mackenzie, whose birthplace was the Isle of Skye, whose B.A. degree was from Queen's University and whose diploma in law was from Osgood Hall. Soon after his arrival, Jim Macleod met the winsome Mary Drever with brown curly hair and a delicate air, and a mutual interest was kindled. They saw much of each other during the winter and when the time came for the troops to leave Fort Garry, the parting was sorrowful but the young officer said he would be back.

Perhaps it was the memory of Mary at faraway Fort Garry that brought James Macleod into the new North West Mounted Police so promptly after recruitiing was authorized. Since leaving Fort Garry he had visited his native Scotland and then tried to settle down to the practice of law but was having difficulty in overcoming an indifference toward the very idea of a legal career. Moreover, he was exactly the type of young man the new force wanted and needed, and before the end of 1873, he was the Assistant Commissioner and traveling west with a detachment of recruits to drill and study and winter at Lower Fort Garry.

Again the officer and Mary Drever saw much of each other and the winter passed pleasantly. By late spring when the men of the NWMP were about to leave for some point unknown in the far West, they were engaged but in view of the extremely heavy demands upon the Assistant Commissioner, marriage would have to wait. It waited for two years, or until July, 1876, the very month in which the Assistant Commissioner became the Commissioner. On his way back from Ottawa, the new Commissioner stopped briefly at Winnipeg and he and Mary were married. But still it wasn't like an ordinary marriage; with the pressure of duties arising from a new treaty to be negotiated with the Cree Indians at Fort Carlton and Fort Pitt, and the possible impact of the Custer Massacre across the border, the Commissioner could not stop for a honeymoon holiday. It would have to wait. There was another tearful farewell, but he would be back soon, he promised.

Before the end of the year, the Commissioner was leaving Fort Macleod to attend as an appointed representative on the new Council of the Northwest Territories, called to meet at Fort Livingstone. To get to that place on Swan River, he traveled to Fort Benton with police horses, then to Helena by stagecoach and from Corrine in Utah territory to Chicago by Union Pacific Railway. At Chicago he met his bride of five months earlier and their honeymoon began. But even then it could not be totally separated from official duties. Livingstone, which was officially the headquarters of the Mounted Police, was still the Commissioner's destination and to reach there, the Macleods traveled by rail to Fargo, Dakota, stagecoach to Winnipeg and Portage la Prairie and dogsled for the remaining 300 miles to Livingstone. The "train" of four dogsleds gliding across the snow would have made an attractive picture, but nobody got it.

Departure from Livingstone at the end of the Council meetings was much like the arrival, by dogteam, but the Macleods were now scheduled to journey to Ottawa. There they were received by Governor General and Lady Dufferin and the new First Lady of the NWMP made a fine impression. With her grace and dignity and western friendliness, she was enriching the image of the Force. Most of the men in the Mounted Police were easterners; the first lady was all-western and the point was noted with approval.

Now the Commissioner and his wife were traveling westward to Fort Macleod — and home. Mary Macleod would be seeing the Oldman River and the Blackfoot Indians and the Rockies for the first time. And to be sure, the men in the Force at Fort Macleod were as much interested in seeing this lady as she was in seeing her new home surroundings.

She would not be the first white woman to be seen at Fort Macleod, but she would be one of the first. The *Daily Free Press* of Winnipeg, on June 22, 1876, quoted from a letter written so recently by a Mounted Police constable at Fort Macleod. The letter recorded "as the event of the day, the arrival of a white woman, the first that ever came this far west. She had more spectators the first few days than a circus would have. Every man was anxious to have a peep, most of us not having seen a white woman for two years. This is the place for girls in search of husbands."

Mary Macleod recognized it as her new duty to make a home, but not to stay there continuously. She traveled much with the Commissioner, traveled to Blackfoot Crossing for the important negotiations in September, 1877, and was one of those to sign Treaty No. 7. From there she returned home to prepare for the birth of her first baby to come in the following February.

Mary was a source of strength to the Commissioner and he valued her judgment and counsel. A surviving letter written from Fort Walsh in October, 1877, hinted at his need for her ear:

My Dearest Mary,
I have just got to this place with Sitting Bull and a lot of his Chiefs. It was quite a job getting them this far, they are so very suspicious. However, here they are, safe within the Fort, about 25 of them. I expect General Terry at the Boundary on Sunday and am going to meet him myself. I hope to get through with them on Tuesday or Wednesday and then, if possible, I shall start for home. How I do look forward to getting there, day and night. Winder writes by Mr. Powers that you were not well. I seriously hope it was only that cold you spoke about. Perhaps you will see me before

> you see this. The messenger is waiting for my dispatches so good bye my own darling.
> I am as ever, your own,
> Jim.

Colonel Macleod was finding his duties as a magistrate taking more and more of his time and at the end of October, 1880, Col. A. G. Irvine became Commissioner and the Macleods moved to make their home at Pincher Creek. Then, appointment to the high office of Judge of the Supreme Court of the Northwest Territories necessitated more moves, back to Fort Macleod and then in 1894, to Calgary where Mr. Justice Macleod died later in the year.

The country had lost one of its more effective and respected public servants. But although he had served Canada well, he did not serve his own ends as well and savings and assets at his death were trifling, making for a greater burden upon his widow, but courage never failed Mary Macleod and she managed. And regardless of the state of her finances, she remained rich in friendships and public gratitude. She outlived her famous husband by thirty-nine years and did not lose the right to be remembered as the woman who conveyed to the all-male Force an intangible quality which only a woman could bring. And as one of the very first strictly western personalities connected with the Mounted Police, she helped to give westerners a proper sense of possession and belonging. Perhaps what Mary Macleod did was not spectacular, but it was important.

JESSIE TURNBULL McEWEN: THE LADY OF TULLICHEWEN

Had she lived a generation later, Jessie Turnbull McEwen[1] would have been pressed into a career in politics, probably to occupy a seat in the House of Commons and be addressed as the Honorable Member for Brandon, possibly to be elevated to cabinet rank and discharge the high office of a minister in charge of an important branch of government. It would be easy to see her making parliamentary history similar to that made by Agnes Macphail, Ellen Fairclough, Grace MacInnis and Judy LaMarsh. She was the dignified little lady with the talent and resolve to make her conspicuous in any generation. She was the kind who could be the perfect hostess when the Governor General paid a visit and then pitch in to help do the farm chores when necessary.

It was the judgment of Lillian Baynon Thomas, well known in western writing circles, that in shaping "the finer destiny of this Canada of ours, it is doubtful whether any name would stand higher than that of Jessie Turnbull McEwen."[2] She was not particularly robust but, unfail-

[1] No relation to the author
[2] Thomas, Lillian Baynon, "Early Culture on the Red River," *The Farmers' Advocate*, p. 1001, June 30, 1927

ingly, the recognition of a social need — especially if it touched members of her own sex or little children — aroused this Brandon lady's determination and the list of her accomplishments became long, like an Elton municipality voters' list.

After Mrs. McEwen's death in 1920, Lillian Thomas wrote: "Her body is gone but she lives in numerous institutions and organizations and in the lives of many people who do not know to whom they owe their happy surroundings."

When Donald and Jessie McEwen, in 1884, turned their backs upon Toronto and the East to cast their lot with the opening West, a railroad train was still a novelty in Manitoba and a buggy with rubber tires was the ultimate in luxurious country travel. The McEwens, like their neighbors in the Brandon district of their choosing, endured frontier hardships but graduated from them rather rapidly. The heavy-set Donald, with Scottish accent and an air of composure, was at ease in any company. He could recite "Tam O' Shanter" or the "Address to the Haggis on Burns' Night"; he could and did make more noise on the curling ice than any other contestant, and with some varied business connections, he prospered. As the Canadian representative of a Scottish manufacturer of woolen goods, he traveled extensively between Halifax and Vancouver but his greatest joy was in returning to the home farm known as "Tullichewen," section 14, township 11, range 19, west of the 1st meridian, where he and his wife built the big house, completing it in 1893.

It took most of the first summer, 1891, to excavate for the "Big House," and then to complete the massive stonework foundation, "built for eternity." The first framework for the mansion fell a victim to a summer tornado, and the wreckage, which was scattered half way to Carberry, raised doubts about reconstruction. But the McEwens were not quitters and Donald, on returning from business travels in the East, said firmly: "We will not let a tornado stop us."

When the Big House was being built, it came to have a

rival of similar proportions just a few miles away. It, too, was completed in 1893, the property of the eccentric John Sandison who aspired to be the biggest farmer in Manitoba, also the most elegant. His extravagant tastes included fancy Hackney horses, expensive clothes worn on all occasions, the latest in farm machinery, and a fastidiousness about the way his shirts were ironed. Unhappy with local laundry service, he, it was said, sent his weekly washing to Scotland for what he considered proper attention. But when creditors began to hound him in 1893, the Manitoba Wheat King disappeared, leaving behind a wife, many workers, about 2,500 acres of crop and the new house he had never occupied. The McEwens, by contrast, were building for the future and bringing good sense and good judgment to everything they did. The Tullichewen house remained a showpiece in the North Brandon community, destined to stand for at least the best part of a century. Neighbors were somewhat overwhelmed and there was the danger that this new symbol of affluence might force the McEwens into a position of isolation. There was no such separation, however, even though the Tullichewen home required the services of two servants and two gardeners to keep the premises constantly ready for visitors.

The official opening of the new home came in the month of June, with the first two evenings for city friends and the next two for farm neighbors. The city guests marveled at finding such elegance on a Manitoba farm. The rural neighbors came with some misgivings because they were not sure how to measure this unusual lady. With her grace and compassion was a scholarly reserve which fellow farmers did not fully comprehend. They were pretty sure that she would always be "Mrs. McEwen," never "Jessie," no matter how close they might live. But they discovered quickly that her heart was big, just as her mind was active, and she was ready for any worthy challenge. She could be forgiven for some slight reserve.

Another point was soon established: When the city of Brandon had distinguished visitors from Ottawa or overseas, the local itinerary planned for their enlightenment was not considered complete unless it included a visit at Tullichewen. If it was a nice afternoon, the guests could expect to ride in a stylish Colquhoun and Beattie carriage drawn by a pair of prancing roadsters, with the first stop at the Experimental Farm and the second for tea at the McEwen home.

When Bertha Krupp, heiress to the internationally famous munitions works in Germany, stopped at Brandon, she was accorded the Number One Welcome, presented with a flowery address and given a chance to reply with high-sounding expressions of good will from Kaiser Wilhelm, then taken over the route which the livery horses knew so well. So it was when Lord and Lady Aberdeen toured Canada in 1907, and the Duke and Duchess of Devonshire came in 1916. In the latter year, there was trouble on every hand; Canada was involved in war and western wheat crops were suffering seriously from a strange new pest, stem rust, and even Donald McEwen was feeling the pinch of financial reverses. But the Big House and its Chatelaine continued to dispense western hospitality with undiminished charm.

Most memorable — and in some ways most important — was that Vice-Regal visit of June, 1907, when the McEwens received and met Lord and Lady Aberdeen for the first time. The display of ceremony was the most unusual and glittering the local frontier had witnessed. Farm neighbors, seeing the gay cavalry escort, the gleaming brass mountings, the prancing horses, the servicemen attending to security, and the reception carried out with flawless protocol on the McEwen lawn, agreed with the remark of one of their number: "Golly, I always figured I'd have to go to Ottawa or London to see anything like that."

The distinguished visitors of that day were as much impressed as the farm neighbors. They were eager to know more about Donald and Mrs. McEwen and a lasting friendship was born. Lady Aberdeen and Mrs. McEwen found they had many interests in common and

The Lady of Tullichewen • 63

agreed upon the need for more women's organizations. They agreed to correspond, and strengthened by each other's resolves, both were the means of furthering the fortunes of the Council of Women. While Lady Aberdeen was encouraging the National Council, Jessie McEwen organized a local branch and became its president, an office she was to fill for the next twenty-one years.

Public service came naturally to the little lady. Before leaving Ontario she had been active in the campaign to gain for women the right of admission to Canadian colleges and universities; and soon after coming to Brandon, she started the first Women's Missionary Society within the Presbyterian Church of Western Canada. Translating her convictions to action, she furnished the drive to obtain a Y.W.C.A. hostel at Brandon, and rather many other institutions of related kind. It was largely through her efforts that domestic science and manual training were offered in the public school system in the area, and then there was the drive to obtain library services and travelers' aid. No citizen in that part had more to show from dedication and public service.

It added to the respect she commanded that she could and would do so much without any neglect of her duties as mother and homemaker. Daughters May and Grace and sons Mortimer and Gordon had all the benefits a devoted mother could bestow and they in turn became leaders in the respective areas in which they chose to live and serve.

Motherhood was the highest of all callings, she believed, and the responsibilities could not or should not be delegated. "To be worthy of the sacred name of Mother, no woman could, for the sake of amusement or self-gratification, commit her precious little ones to the care — or more frequently the carelessness — of hirelings. Can any condemnation be too strong for such women?"[1]

Her personal dedication to family duties and her success added weight to her messages. For years she contributed to the Home Magazine Section of the *Farmer's*

[1] McEwen, Jessie, *Farmer's Advocate*, July 6, 1902

Advocate, commonly messages with a high moral tone and just about as commonly, with a recognition of the might of the home influence in shaping the destiny of the new West. Her character as well as her convictions came through clearly.

"Children," she wrote, "should be trained both by precept and by example to be careful in making a promise, and then to be as careful in the fulfilling of it. There is much evil done in the world by those who lightly esteem their promises, and set at naught their most sacred pledges. Were this regard for one's word taught in our homes as it should be, there would be fewer delinquents in public life, fewer who for the sake of place and power stoop to make promises and give pledges they never intend to keep."[1]

On the same theme she wrote later: "To this integrity and uprightness of character let us seek to add the grace and charm of true courtesy. Our age has made rapid advancement in science, in discovery, in invention, but it certainly lags far behind in reverence and in courtesy. We must look to the mother of our homes and to the teacher in our schools to correct this defect in the manners of the majority of our young people.

"Mothers should see that every possible opportunity is given to their children to become familiar in their homes with good books and magazines, with music and with pictures of an elevating character. . . . The love of the beautiful in Nature and in art should be more cultivated and encouraged in our rural homes and schools. What scope and opportunity are about us on the prairie for the pursuit of nature study! But alas! Where one soul is to be found with a clear and appreciative outlook, there are ten or it may be twenty, blind and unconscious to the grand and ever-changing panorama spread before them."[2]

In her same motherly manner, she tried to befriend the lonely wherever they might be. The immigrants, flocking in thousands through the prairie "gateway" at Winnipeg

[1] McEwen, Jessie, *Farmer's Advocate,* July 6, 1902
[2] McEwen, Jessie, *Farmer's Advocate,* Dec. 14, 1904

to fan out from there, captured her feeling. She tried to reach them to offer a message of comfort. Among the newcomers were many mothers with shawls on their heads, babies in their arms and looks of despair on their faces. When a Brandon neighbor met Mrs. McEwen on Portage Avenue in Winnipeg, there was the usual question: "What brings you here?" Her reply: "I just wanted to spend a few days meeting these newcomers from Europe; they're so lonely and frightened."

Still concerned about the immigrants, she wrote: "We women pioneers of the West will not easily forget our own experience of homesickness and isolation from friends and former interests. Shall we not then extend to these women from other lands our kindly good will?"[1]

With her enthusiastic approval, the International Council of Women raised a sum of money with which to provide the incoming Doukhobor women with materials for their home industries — spinning, weaving, knitting, embroidery and work on linen, partly to keep them occupied during the first winter. Reporting, Mrs. McEwen could say that the gesture was "welcome and sweet to these women who are themselves so gentle and kindly one to another and to their children."

The lady of Tullichewen died in 1920, and as might have been expected, the tributes were many and splendid. The *Farmer's Advocate,* under the caption "The End Of A Beautiful Life," captured the message in Jessie McEwen's years most successfully and sounded it in words of wisdom which all citizens should have paused to read:[2]

> *If you could choose what your life will be in the quiet evening of your day, what sort of life would you plan? You would never dream of deliberately planning a lonely, friendless old age, with no interests, a mere living from day to day, perhaps puttering on little tasks that you know to be unimportant, a mere onlooker at the busy life of the*

[1] McEwen, Jessie, *Farmer's Advocate,* March 20, 1902
[2] *Farmer's Advocate,* June 23, 1920

younger generations. Yet many of us lay the foundation of just such a regime for the closing years of our lives, and when the time comes to live them, it is too late to alter the plan.

There are men and women in their seventies, their eighties and even their nineties, who are an inspiration to the rest of us, and we say how we wish we may be like them when we have passed as many milestones. Almost any friend with the gift of frankness can tell us now whether we will get our wish. If we are living to ourselves alone, concentrating only on the material advancement of our fortunes, lacking interest in other people, and caring nothing for the welfare of the race or even the neighbors, bored by mental pursuits, and with zest only for the more physical exercises that mean so much to the vigor of youth, we cannot expect to store up treasure for the delight of our declining years. The people who will have a happy, useful old age are the people who now in their youth and their middle years are alert mentally and physically, with the habit of right thinking, and with some interests outside their own families and the four walls of their homes, storing up happy memories, cultivating a delight in good reading, building friendships that will last.

A life we may well envy has just ended, and many a man and woman in the West is thinking with tender regret of Mrs. Jessie McEwen of Brandon. How wonderfully fine a use she made of the life that was given her. She was a real pioneer of the West, and her deeds live after her. In the Council of Women and in many an organization that works for the good of the people, her wise and kindly presence will be sadly missed.

We are losing them one by one, those wonderful pioneer women to whom we owe such a tremendous debt in that they laid so truly and well the foundations of a fine and upright national life here on the prairies. The finest memorial we can offer them is to keep alive the traditions they established.

Provincial Archives, Victoria, B.C.

PAULINE JOHNSON: PRINCESS

Without Pauline Johnson, the Gay Nineties would not have been the same. Canadian poetry would have been poorer by the absence of one of the country's most gifted authors. Public school readers would have been different with a substitution for "The Song My Paddle Sings," and Canada's native people would have been denied their proud claim to the girl who became known as the Mohawk Princess.

For two decades Canadians found no better entertainment than attendance at public performances at which Pauline Johnson sang Indian songs and recited her verses ranging from gentle to ferocious. It was a favorite trick when her listeners seemed tranquilized by her poetic lullabies, to jolt them with sudden war whoops. In Edmonton when she was performing in Robertson Hall in 1904, her premeditated war cry was followed immediately by an unpremeditated scream from an emotional woman, loud enough to silence the author's best effort.

Half Indian and half white, half Easterner and half Westerner, Pauline Johnson was proud of her heritage. She had every reason to be. Nobody had a better claim to the Canadian title and people across the country responded with affection for the girl whose verses brought delight and whose public appearances captivated audiences at home and abroad.

No, she was not of pure Indian breeding and she admitted this with a hint of apology. Overhearing somebody attending a reception in her honor remark, "She's just like a white woman," Pauline snapped angrily, "Is that intended to be a compliment?"

Her father was George Henry Martin Johnson — in the Indian tongue, Onwanonsyshon — full-blooded Mohawk and Head Chief of the Six Nations Indians on the reservation beside the Grand River, south of Brantford, Upper Canada. As a young man, this Johnson was placed in the position of interpreter for an Anglican missionary, Rev. Adam Elliott. What might have been a dull job took on fresh interest when Johnson discovered that Mrs. Elliott had an unmarried sister, Emily Howells, staying with her. The young Indian and the strictly English girl born at Bristol were instantly attracted and there was a romance which brought prompt disapproval from members of both families. But true love is difficult to arrest and George and Emily were married and settled down to serious homemaking on the reserve. The young wife, with cultural tastes, brought — of all things — a piano to her reservation home. Her husband was no less determined to make the marriage succeed and built a handsome two-story house overlooking the river, about twelve miles from Brantford. Known as "Chiefswood," it was for long the biggest and finest house on the reserve and destined to receive many notable visitors from Canada and abroad.

There at Chiefswood Pauline was born on March 10, 1861, the second daughter and the youngest of four children in the family. In the Mohawk tongue, her name was Tekahionwake, which meant "smoke from many campfires." Her playmates were young Mohawks but from total parental influence came a dual loyalty. Perhaps she was more aware of the bonds which held her to the

Mohawk tribe of her father, reaching back to Hiawatha's Brotherhood of Five Nations which the French called Iroquois. Traditionally there was Iroquois friendliness with Britain, sufficient to bring members of the tribal group into conflict with both the French and the Colonial revolutionaries. The same loyalty resulted in the allocation of the reservation lands on the Canadian side. The loyal feeling toward Britain was something Pauline Johnson never lost, and it was reflected clearly in her poems.

Schooling for the girl presented problems and was limited to two years tutoring at home, three years at a grade school on the reservation and two years of school in Brantford, a total of seven years. There was no opportunity for attendance at high school or university but the girl possessed natural gifts of creativeness and the desire to use them. Also, she was athletic and could rival any of the boys in handling a canoe.

Even at the age when children are normally starting to school and still unable to write, she was composing simple verses about dogs and horses and other animals she regarded as friends. Her mother encouraged the little girl to read the works of great writers as soon as she was able, and she devoured everything she could get of Scott and Longfellow and Tennyson in a relatively short time.

Pauline's fondness for poetry grew and when she was only thirteen years of age, a New York magazine, *Gems of Poetry*, accepted and published some of her verses. This initial success was followed by acceptance from *Toronto Saturday Night*, *The Week* and other magazines published in Canada, the United States and England. It did not follow that monetary reward was high; actually it was low. For that poem, which was to become universally popular, "The Song My Paddle Sings," she was paid three dollars and was glad to have the money. For another accepted for publication, she received seventy-five cents and had the good humor to return it to the publisher with the comment that in his apparent state of poverty, she could not conscientiously take the money.

Chief Johnson died in 1884 and his widow and children left Chiefswood to reside in Brantford. Pauline was then twenty-three years of age but a career on the stage was not something the girl had seriously considered. When she left home the first time in 1892 to accept the invitation for a public appearance in Toronto and was gone for three days, she was homesick and vowed she would not repeat such an adventure. The invitation came from the Young Liberal Association of Toronto of which Frank Yeigh, with a Brantford connection, was the president. It was to be a program of readings by Canadian authors, and the young lady with dusky complexion, long, black hair hanging in braids, flashing Indian eyes, and native costume enhanced by a necklace made from bears' claws, was unable to hide her nervousness. But contrary to all expectations, she was the hit of the evening. As critics related it, the earlier items on the program proved to be dull and men trying to hide their yawns wished they were at home. Nor was there any reason to suppose the girl from Brantford would change the dismal tenor of the evening. But she did change the tone of things by reciting "The Cry Of An Indian Wife," inspired by events in the Northwest Rebellion; listeners heard the young wife instructing her Brave to "Go forth, nor bend to greed of white man's hands."

The audience was loud in approval and there was almost an immediate call for the girl's return with more of her poetry. Not being overwhelmed by the attractions of the big city, she might have chosen to cling to the calm and obscurity of her home but she was instantly caught up in the mainstream of public demand and within a few weeks she was back in Toronto, this time at Massey Hall for an entire evening devoted to her poems. Members of Toronto's scholarly set were talking about her. At thirty years of age she was being seen as an author with great promise.

Prepared expressly for that recital was the poem which was to become familiar to millions of school children and others across Canada, "The Song My Paddle

Sings," one with the throb and rhythm of beating tom-toms.

One who knew her said that because she had composed this poem so recently, she failed to carry all of it in her memory and forgot some of the lines. But instead of giving up and fleeing from the stage as a frustrated girl might have done, she stood firm and swung to verses from an entirely different poem which her audience seemed to appreciate to the full.

The Toronto recital led to a cross-country tour of performances, and then to one in England where, in 1895, the first collection of her poems, *The White Wampum,* was published in book form. Almost at once the Mohawk girl became an international figure. Londoners loved her poems and her personality and the reviewers were high in their praise of her work — at least most of them. Phonies have never been uncommon among literary critics, and a reporter trying to be sophisticated wrote that the Canadian lady pretended to know something about Indians but it was doubtful if she had ever seen a real one. He must have been embarrassed by the truth but he had the goodness to print a retraction. A few years later, 1903, a second book of poems, *Canadian Born,* appeared and her poetic character showed more sharply. In all her writing there was the spirit of patriotism and love of the land.

Rather quickly she became a professional trouper, almost constantly on tour in Canada, the United States and England, appearing on all kinds of platforms, from the highbrow to the lowbrow. In fashionable circles she could carry off her part with perfect poise, and in a barroom or poolhall or place of rowdy entertainment, she seemed no less at ease. Often in later years she appeared wearing two human scalps suspended from her belt, one of them having been taken from a Huron killed by the Iroquois, the other being of Cree origin and presented to her by an admiring Blackfoot chief in Alberta. Western Canadians saw her occupying a church pulpit for the presentation of her program and they saw her mounting an empty whisky barrel in a hotel barroom for the same purpose. Commonly they saw her appear for the first part of her presentation wearing native costume, then coming to the second half in an expensive, imported gown. When on tour she traveled by train, by stagecoach and on at least one occasion by the transportation she loved most, namely, canoe. She recalled a trip north from Ashcroft, British Columbia, in a stage coach chartered for the exclusive use of herself and traveling companion, and driven throughout the journey by a local character known as "Buckskin Billy." It was an unusual tour in all respects. The advance arrangements and advertising had been unsatisfactory and at those points where there had been no prior notice whatever, it fell to Buckskin Billy to conduct last-minute publicity by any means at his command. As soon as he had stabled his horses, Billy would take to the street and become the Town Crier announcing the concert, then install himself for the purpose of selling tickets. On that series of performances, the admission was set at one dollar per person for white customers and fifty cents for Indians; apparently when Buckskin Billy recognized a half-breed, he compromised judiciously and charged seventy-five cents.

After overcoming her initial timidity, the mood of the Nineties suited Pauline Johnson perfectly and she played the demanding circuits tirelessly. She continued to write poetry, not voluminously but with no departure from that drum-beat pace which Canadians loved. Her voice was sweet and clear and her listeners recognized the music in her words, and responded to the metaphors exuding imagination and beauty. She wrote impartially about Halifax and Regina and Calgary and Vancouver, as though conscious of the need to promote Canadian unity. Her Muse caught so completely the spirit of nature and her Indian people. With rare simplicity she brought that bouncing rhythm to her lines, demonstrating a very special talent. She could and did bring protest and unmistakable anger to verses in which she spoke for fellow natives, as in "The Cattle Thief." And in "A Cry From An Indian Wife" she reminded those of the invading race of their aggressions.

Her arrows could penetrate and hurt but Pauline Johnson seemed to reach her best with a paddle. For prairie people, however, a favorite poem had to be "The Legend of Qu'Appelle," partly because they knew something of the story long attached to the valley but mainly because of the poet's inimitable presentation of the tragedy, the Indian male returning to the valley to claim his wife and arriving in time to hear her voice but not in time to see her alive.

Pauline Johnson did not marry but had numerous male admirers and a number of serious romances. While appearing at the old Winnipeg Theatre in 1903, she met an Ontario entertainer, Walter McRaye, who was distinguishing himself in giving habitant recitations from the poems of Dr. William Henry Drummond, and they became almost constant traveling companions. In the years following, they appeared together on Canadian, United States and English stages. At times they were on Chautauqua circuits, becoming well known as a "team." McRaye was younger than Pauline by fourteen years but was a constant admirer and his loyalty remained constant to the time of her death.

Advance notices of the Johnson and McRaye performances would describe the lady as "the Indian author and entertainer, bringing laughter and humor and stirring patriotism," and present McRaye as "a humorist delightfully portraying the French Canadian habitant characters." In 1904, the notices carried an extract from a letter from Dr. Drummond to McRaye: "I congratulate you on your great success because from all quarters of Canada I hear you have achieved a triumph."

By 1910, the years of almost constant travel were telling and Pauline Johnson was tired — and, at times, ill. She was advised to quit the road and accept semi-retirement in Vancouver, the place of her choice. Although the revenue from the entertainment circuits had been substantial, she failed, in her devil-may-care manner, to save much and she realized too late that she must continue to work or endure the pain of poverty. She began writing prose, wrote a novel, *The Shagganapi.* She was also collecting West Coast legends of Indian origin. A few years earlier she had met Chief Joe Capilano of the Squamish Reserve and they had become staunch friends. Patiently he had repeated legends and lore told around coastal campfires and she had recorded the most interesting parts. From this material, with the help of concerned friends — many of them members of the Women's Canadian Club of Vancouver — she compiled articles which were published as *The Legends of Vancouver.*

Pauline Johnson's health was deteriorating but she remained philosophical. Addressing her friend, Jean Stevinson, who lived at a later date in Alberta, she inquired: "Do you know what I would do if I had only two dollars and knew they would be my last? I'd spend half on my body and half on my soul. With one dollar I'd buy a whacking good meal and with the other a dozen cut carnations. Then I would die happy looking at my lovely flowers."[1]

Unfortunately she did not live to reap reward from the major publication of her poetry, *Flint and Feather,* which the Musson Book Company, Toronto, published in 1917. Fifty-five years later the book was in its twenty-eighth edition or impression, with sales far in excess of 50,000.

As it was, this lady who cared little for money and spent it as it came, died in poverty. A short time before her passing, she confided in a friend that her income from writing would probably bring her ten dollars for the week and might total sixty dollars for the month. Such privation, however, was not entirely new in her life; she told of becoming ill when on tour and finding it necessary to sell her jewelry in order to buy food, all her jewelry except the treasured ring given to her by the city of Brantford.

By 1912, Miss Johnson was an invalid. She had cancer and knew it. The pains were severe but her friends rallied to her bedside and cheered her. Sometimes they would convey her to Stanley Park and pause to view Siwash

[1] *Calgary Herald,* March 5, 1932

Rock, which she loved. In the next year she accepted the care of a nursing home and it was public knowledge that she was dying. Her friend from years on the entertainment circuits, Walter McRaye, returned to be near her. Death came on March 7, 1913, as she was approaching her fifty-second birthday.

In keeping with her expressed wish, Pauline Johnson's remains were buried in Stanley Park. The simple stone marker placed there presented a carved profile and carried the only message needed, just "PAULINE." What more needed to be said of the lady whose full name and poetic talents were known to all Canadians?

One of the many people paying tribute to her after her death said she was most distinctly "a daughter of the soil." It might have been added that she was most distinctly Canadian, one who was at home in any part of Canada, one who was equally at ease in a canoe, a drawing room and a theater. Everybody in the country could mount some claim to her and just about everybody tried to do it.

Happily, the centenary in 1961 of the poet's birth did not pass unnoticed. The city of Vancouver honored her memory in a rededication ceremony at the memorial stone standing where her ashes were deposited; it was the spot dignified by what she called "The Cathedral of Trees," those trees, which, according to her comment, "are the acme of Nature's architecture . . . she will never originate a more faultless design, never erect a more perfect edifice."

A student recited "The Song My Paddle Sings" and Vancouver's nine o'clock gun boomed from Brockton Point. And, then, recognizing Pauline Johnson as a great national figure, the Federal Post Office issued a commemorative stamp; it was the first such honor to be directed at a Canadian author, first for a Canadian woman, first for a Canadian Indian. At about the same time, her book of prose, *The Legends of Vancouver,* published in the first instance to raise money for the ailing poet, was reprinted. Pauline Johnson was not to be forgotten.

Courtesy James Studio, Prince Albert, Saskatchewan

LUCY MARGARET BAKER: WITH THE BRAVE HEART OF A BULLFIGHTER

Lucy Baker had the gentle ways of a model nurse and the brave heart of a bullfighter. She was the Girl from Glengarry who became one of the unforgettable Saskatchewan teachers who brought added distinction to the frontier community of Prince Albert. Her arrival there was two years after the famous Custer Massacre south of the border and coincided exactly with the alarming appearance at Prince Albert of a hostile band from Sitting Bull's 5,000 refugee Sioux. It was a time of grave danger and uncertainty.

Prince Albert, oldest city in Saskatchewan and one of the oldest settled communities in the West, attracted none but courageous men and women. Rev. James Nisbet, in 1866, arrived with a party of settlers and founded the place, and women like that remarkable little teacher, Lucy Baker, came with a similar sort of dedication to the uplift of fellows and unwillingness to let surmountable obstacles stand in the way.

Nisbet, with missionary zeal, accepted a proposal from senior churchmen to establish a settlement and mission at some distant point on the North Saskatchewan

River. From Fort Garry it was a fifty-day journey by Red River cart to the place of his choice, which he called Prince Albert, honoring the Prince Consort of that time. There at the new site, Nisbet and his friends, including the well-known buffalo hunter, John McKay, and teacher, Adam McBeth, built a mission and school and started a farm, mainly for the benefit of the Indians in the area. Work began on July 26 with an urgency prompted by the need to recover winter fodder for the animals, build shelters for both humans and animals, and break and prepare land for the next season's planting.

The response on the part of the Indians — mainly Cree — was encouraging and at the end of the first year Nisbet's school had twenty-six children, fourteen of them as resident pupils. Nisbet and his wife were apparently overworked but they remained until 1873 when, worn out physically, they went back to Red River where they died within a few months of each other in 1874.

It was an appeal for help for Nisbet's school that brought Miss Lucy to Prince Albert. As old-timers remembered her there, she was a little person with gray hair, an impish grin and a fondness for satin and lace. But appearances do not tell all; this five-foot-three lady who lived to serve, faced dangers which would have induced most people to flee. She went among the angry Sioux Indians loitering nearby as though they were children attending a Sunday School picnic.

Born in Glengarry County, she received part of her schooling at nearby Summertown, part in Montreal and part in the United States, then enriched an already excellent command of French by a stay in France where she happened to be while caring for a sick relative. Back in Canada she taught school in the province of Quebec. With her excellent qualifications she might have had schools of her choice almost anywhere.

At this time an interest was awakened in the work of the Presbyterian church and she became active in Sunday schools and Women's missionary societies. James Nisbet at faraway Prince Albert heard about her and just before his death, requested that she or somebody with similar dedication and talents be obtained to teach at the Prince Albert mission school.

The proposal aroused her interest but her friends felt compelled to discourage the idea of an unmarried girl venturing into that remote part of the world. As it happened, Dr. Donald Ross was appointed by the Home Mission Board of the Presbyterian Church to a post at Prince Albert and he and Mrs. Ross were about to start on the long journey, thereby affording Lucy an opportunity to make the trip with female companionship. She agreed to go and was becoming quite excited about the challenge when, close to the date set for departure, both Dr. and Mrs. Ross became ill and felt obliged to cancel their traveling plan. Miss Lucy could have canceled out also but her decision was to go.

Of course, respectable young ladies did not make such long trips alone and she set about searching for another lady who might be traveling westward and who might be glad of companionship. Not many women were going to the Northwest Territories in those years but Lucy was in luck and located a lady whose traveling destination was Fort Edmonton. It suited both to travel together and Lucy Baker said "farewell" to relatives and friends and set out by train to Chicago and St. Paul. From the Minnesota city she would travel by stagecoach and riverboat to Fort Garry, and from the latter point to Prince Albert, her mode of conveyance would be a two-horse wagon tented over to give it the covered wagon effect.

As the autumn days grew colder, the canvas cover offered scant protection but there was nothing to be gained by complaining. An early season snowstorm brought the wagon to a stop for a couple of days and the Girl From Glengarry must have considered the danger of being snowbound at a desolate prairie location for the winter. But the weather moderated and the wagon wheels were turning again, and on arrival at Prince Albert late in October, 1878, Lucy Baker stood as the first Canadian woman to represent the Presbyterian Church in the Northwest.

Lucy's arrival at Prince Albert created no excitement, except among the bachelors who were eager to improve their domestic status. She offered no encouragement because she was there to teach and knew the magnitude of the responsibilities resting upon her. She knew she could have continued to teach in the East but here was a brand new challenge and she was determined to succeed. There were some surprises and disappointments on the first day at school and she was exhausted at nightfall.

Already there had been a full compliment of pupils at the church school, about as many as could be accommodated. After her first day at school, attendance dropped, especially among the boys. The idea of a lady teacher was not attractive to the young males, but Lucy Baker persevered and when her worth both as a teacher and a citizen became better known, attendance increased until the school was much overpopulated. The lady teacher was a success.

Beyond the school, however, there were distractions, serious dangers presented by the visiting Sioux Indians. Most residents of the community — including the local Cree — were visibly worried. Lucy Baker should have been worried too. Friends warned her before leaving the East that prairie Indians were not to be trusted and unless she managed to evade them she might lose her scalp.

The Prince Albert people were not worried about the Sioux who had fled to Canada sixteen years earlier to escape United States vengeance after the Minnesota massacres, but these recent arrivals, members of Sitting Bull's warrior band encamped at Wood Mountain, had the blood of the recent Custer Massacre on their hands and everybody on the Canadian side wished they would return to the United States and take their hatreds with them. But Sitting Bull resisted all pleas to return, knowing he would almost certainly be involved in a continuing war with the United States forces. Sioux bitterness toward the white man grew no less. The Canadian Government refused to grant Sitting Bull's people a reserve and in their frustrations they were inclined to greater defiance and more roaming. Some arrived at Prince Albert where a remnant of the refugees from the trouble in Minnesota in 1862 had finally gained grudging acceptance.

The *Saskatchewan Herald,* published at Battleford — the only paper published in the Territories, reported just two weeks after Miss Lucy's arrival, that seventy lodges of Sioux of various bands were camping at Prince Albert.[1] Some of the unwelcome visitors, the report added, were cutting firewood and fence rails. Later, the *Saskatchewan Herald* reported that the highly respected Thomas MacKay and the highly controversial Charles Mair — both commissioned magistrates at Prince Albert — traveled to Battleford to interview the Lieutenant-Governor in the hope of finding some means of moving the unwanted Indians or furnishing armed protection against this "disagreeable company."[2]

Inspector James Walker of the Mounted Police was sent to investigate the alleged cattle killings and counted eighty-eight of the Sitting Bull Sioux at Prince Albert, twelve at St. Laurent and eight at Duck Lake. At Prince Albert, they had chosen to camp in the woods on the other side of the river but the outcasts were not staying there and police and churchmen were perplexed at their frightening appearances in strange places.

It was at this point in the crisis that the little lady teacher offered a proposal. Why not attempt a friendly understanding. "Let's talk to them and see if we can help them." To Inspector Bowen Perry she made a request for a tent to be used as a school in the camp. It was a nice idea, she was told, but it wouldn't work and nothing was done about it until Miss Lucy resolved to act alone if nobody would help her.

Two initial obstacles were perfectly clear: the first was in crossing the river and the second would be in convinc-

---
[1]*Saskatchewan Herald,* Dec. 17, 1878
[2]*Saskatchewan Herald,* Nov. 3, 1879

ing the Sioux that she was not a spy aiming to collect ransom money on alleged Indian murderers. She lacked a boat or canoe and her friends in church or police work refused to be party to a wild scheme which would take a defenseless girl into a community of savages. It was equally evident that the "savages" did not want her. But Lucy Baker was not one to surrender readily. When she saw a Sioux Indian boy on the street trying to sell some leather goods, she followed him to his dugout canoe at the riverbank and when he jumped into the thing to push off, she jumped in too and waved to instruct him to paddle to the other side.

Her reception at the Sioux camp was cold. The native people did not hide their feeling of resentment at her presence there. It was hinted that her life would be in grave danger if she insisted upon staying. However, she was already learning the Sioux language and she explained her wish to be helpful, particularly to the mothers and children. She made it clear that she intended to set up her own tipi the very next time she came.

Admittedly, she knew nothing about handling a canoe but she possessed determination and having finally obtained the use of such a boat, she set out, alone, to paddle to the Sioux side. Anyone watching would have been puzzled to know the direction in which she wanted to go. The canoe pointed in all directions until the mariner seemed to gain control and finally landed on the opposite shore, far downstream. Thereafter, Lucy Baker went daily to the Sioux encampment and gradually won the confidence of the children, then the mothers and finally the fathers. To spectators it was unbelievable. Little Lucy, single-handed, it seemed, had captured an entire band of the much-feared Sioux.

Came 1885 and the rebellion trouble around Duck Lake. Major L. N. F. Crozier, at the head of a detachment of Mounted Police and Prince Albert volunteers, confronted Gabriel Dumont and his half-breed army on a country trail west of Duck Lake on March 26, 1885, and the tragic outcome was twelve dead and twenty-five wounded on Crozier's side alone. There was consternation at Prince Albert and all the way to Ottawa. Lucy Baker wanted to go to Duck Lake and try to cultivate peaceful understanding. It was too late for such measures, however, and as an alternative she turned her home into a hospital for wounded men, with herself as nurse. She was busier than ever and when the rebellion ended and most people who had served were lining up to receive payment or compensation, she was not among them. She wanted no pay for simply doing what she said any good citizen should be glad to do under the circumstances.

Her next project: building a new house for herself, big enough to accommodate girls needing rooms and boarding accommodation while attending school. In the new home she cooked for her guests, washed for them, cleaned early and late, carried a full teaching assignment at the Nisbet Academy and in her "spare time," continued to provide the help and school services she believed were needed in the Sioux community.

As time passed, the little lady gained a better command of the Sioux language and then embarked upon another mammoth project, that of translating parts of the Bible to Siouan. She couldn't be idle when there was so much to do. In the best sense of the word she was a teacher throughout her life.

Her teaching extending over many years, reached men, women, boys and girls, and teaching included more than reading and writing — by far. It embraced knitting, baking, sewing, housekeeping, health — and best of all, a philosophy of good will and brotherhood.

In 1907, after almost thirty years of service in the Prince Albert area and indications of failing health, she retired and two years later, died at Montreal. She died a winner, having won the admiration and affection of all who knew her, including the Indians. Some people believe the Sioux, who seemed to be spending much of their time retreating from massacres, were incapable of friendliness but that was before Lucy Baker went among them.

Agnes Laut, writing about the time of Lucy Baker's

death, told of calling at the cottage home in Prince Albert to talk with this woman who had come more than thirty years earlier, defying hardship and danger, and stayed. In the writer's words: "Clergymen came out at the same time on the same errand; but they did not stay. The post was perilous and lonely, six weeks from the nearest town by fastest travel; and one after another — there was a twenty-year procession of them — the white-shirted gentlemen chucked their commissions (got 'a call' elsewhere) and withdrew; but Miss Baker with blue blood in her veins and high living behind, stayed on."[1]

And among the finest tributes was the old Sioux chief's ultimate proposal to her. "Miss," he asked in his own faltering way, "when my people have to move, will you stay with us and move too? We want you to live with us."

---

[1] Laut, Agnes C., "The Borderland Woman," *Collier's Outdoor America*, April 17, 1909

Courtesy Florence Andrews

MARY ELLEN ANDREWS: CAUGHT MILKING THE WRONG COW

Saskatoon's Citizen Of The Year in 1955 when the province was celebrating its fiftieth anniversary, was ninety-year-old Mary Ellen Thomson Andrews who saw the district for the first time in Rebellion Year, 1885, and had been dispensing the frontier brand of hospitality and cheer ever since. The selection committee's choice from seventeen nominated candidates proved most popular and local people added another title: Sweetheart of the Century. And as noted in that anniversary year, there was scarcely any part of Saskatchewan history of which she and her late husband, Captain E. S. Andrews, did not have some personal knowledge.

Miss Mary Ellen Thomson and the man she married came to the infant Saskatoon community at about the same time but by quite different routes and quite different modes of travel. Reports of rebellion on the South Saskatchewan River, north of Saskatoon, should have discouraged her and caused her to return to Alliston, Ontario, where life was sleepier and safer, but she was pursuing her plan to accompany her sister, Mrs. Grace Fletcher, and help to care for the four Fletcher children.

She told her mother she would be back in two months. But Mary Ellen, with pretty face and trim figure, liked what she saw on the frontier and liked the people she met and did not return to Ontario for about forty years.

Captain Andrews, on the other hand, was a Maritimer, raised at St. Andrews-On-The-Sea, and strange as it might seem, came to Saskatoon by steamboat. As an adventuresome youth, he went to sea and with the intention of becoming a career seaman, attended Naval Academy at Belfast, Ireland. But an arthritic ailment induced him to forsake the sea and seek an occupation in a drier climate. In 1884 he accepted an offer from the Temperance Colonization Society — the founding body at Saskatoon — to take a steam-driven riverboat, the *May Queen,* from Medicine Hat to the colony and thereby deliver some heavy supplies and rafts of lumber for building. His reward would be $100 per month and expenses, and it would be another adventure.

Before it could be launched on the river at Medicine Hat, the ship, purchased at Selkirk, Manitoba, had to be dismantled and taken by rail to the point where the Canadian Pacific Railway intersected with the South Saskatchewan River. Some of the settlers destined for Saskatoon in that spring of 1884 sought to spare themselves the hardship of the long trail journey from Moose Jaw to the settlement by continuing by rail to Medicine Hat and there transferring to the *May Queen* for the easier but slower river trip. The thirty-five-foot boat, drawing four feet of water when empty and five feet when loaded, had no chance of escaping troubles in a channel which averaged little more than five feet in depth. Gravelbars, submerged rocks, a crooked streambed — just about every navigational hazard except icebergs — coupled with the necessity of periodic stops to gather wood for fuel, accounted for numerous delays. But with patience and a friendly push from the river current, the noble ship which departed Medicine Hat on May 7, reached its destination without serious mishap two weeks later.

By this time, it was fairly obvious that the ship could

not make a return journey against the current and both the boat and the Captain faced the necessity of being stranded, temporarily at least, at Saskatoon. During the Northwest Rebellion in the following year, the *May Queen,* with Captain Andrews in control, was briefly back in service, this time to move wounded men from the scenes of fighting to improvised hospital facilities at Saskatoon. But settlers saw their hope for a reliable river service being dashed and the trail ruts to Moose Jaw growing deeper. In time the *May Queen's* engine was removed for installation in another ship at Prince Albert and the hulk remained a riverside derelict until carried away by floodwater a few years later. And the Captain, while waiting to collect this wages from the Colonization Society, was becoming fascinated by these settlers who seemed to be enjoying their big geographic separation from booze in any of its forms. He decided to stay and to confirm the complete change in his life — from sailor to landlubber — he was filing on a homestead on section 30, township 36, range 5, and getting ready to build a house just a short distance south of the spot on which St. Paul's Hospital stood later. The importance to the community of his decision to stay became quickly apparent; when the Rebellion trouble broke at Duck Lake, the Captain became the Man of the Hour as he assumed the command of the Home Guard.

Mary Ellen Thomson who came to help her sister in moving and getting settled, and intended to return to Ontario within a few weeks, was beginning to see reasons why she should not go back. From the moment of her arrival on June 10, when General Middleton was still in pursuit of Big Bear, the Ontario girl was feeling a strange enchantment. Perhaps the sex ratio of three males to one female had something to do with it. Anyway, forces which might have seemed trivial were changing the direction of her life.

It happened on a certain evening as the girl was trying to help her sister by performing some of the evening chores; she seized a pail and stool and set out to milk the

Fletchers' family cow. As she was settling down to the task and realizing that milking techniques in these remote parts of the Northwest Territories were really no different than in old Ontario, she was startled by a masculine voice remonstrating, "Lady, that's not your cow."

Looking up apologetically because of her error, she saw a man with a "longhorn" mustache and a dashing manner, and wanted to escape. But he wasn't really angry and did not hide his desire to engage her in conversation. Although flustered by her innocent mistake, she allowed herself to be detained. As the cow wandered away to graze and the pretty milkmaid stood with her back to the sunset, holding a stool in one hand and an almost empty pail in the other, the young man informed her that his name was Andrews — "Shelton Andrews from New Brunswick" — and instead of being put out by her intrusion upon his bovine property, he expressed the hope that she would again make the mistake of milking his cow.

A few days later there was a social gathering in the settlement and Mary Ellen again saw the man the local people called "The Captain," and coyly accepted his interest in her. She admitted knowing even less about boats than about the ownership of local cows but was interested and encouraged him to talk about the *May Queen,* for which he still had a feeling of affection.

The romance flourished and before the end of Mary Ellen's first year in the West, she and the Captain were driving away by horse and cutter on the winter trail to Prince Albert, to be married. There was no Protestant minister any closer and a 200-mile round trip didn't worry the young lovers in the least. They stopped at Caswell's at Clark's Crossing for the first night of the outward journey, at McIntosh's near the Fish Creek battlefield the second night, at St. Laurent the third night, and they were at Prince Albert at the end of the fourth day. "It was 60 below zero the day we arrived at Prince Albert," the Captain wrote, but it was not enough to chill youthful enthusiasm and the marriage was performed on March 2 by Rev. Williams of the Presbyterian Church. The minister was rewarded with a crisp ten-dollar bill although the Captain confessed later that he had been recklessly carried away at that moment. The wedding ring had been made in the settlement from a ten-dollar goldpiece.

The newlyweds started back over the wintry trail the next morning, to end their 100-mile honeymoon four days later. Now they seemed permanently welded to the colony which was to have been called Minnetonka until the leader, John Lake, was so inspired by ripe berries presented to him by an Indian that he renamed the place at once, Saskatoon.

The Captain had his homestead about which to think and his wife had the opportunity of helping her sister, Grace Fletcher, also a maker of history. It was in her honor that Saskatoon's Grace Church was named, and as the operator of one of the first general stores, she was to gain distinction for the volume of trade she conducted in buffalo bones. After the destruction of the great wild herd, the Prairies were littered with bones, giving the appearance of "a stony Ontario field." As railroads penetrated onto the plains, these bones were marketable at six dollars per ton delivered at a loading point. The gathering and shipping became big business, providing many homesteaders with grocery money and many of the Métis people with an occupation. At Saskatoon, the leading dealers were the three merchants, James Leslie, R. W. Dulmage and Grace Fletcher who together were believed to have shipped more than 3,000 carloads of bones to the United States to be used in making fertilizer and in refining sugar. Mary Ellen Andrews got to know the Métis who were fanning out with Red River carts and returning with half-ton loads of bones to be weighed and traded for groceries and staples. The Fletcher store was a popular meeting place for these people and the sisters could recall Edouard Dumont, brother of the celebrated Gabriel Dumont and a leader among the bone gatherers, coming to the store at the end of the season and admitting a debt because his purchases exceeded the value of the bones he delivered. But he was honest and cheerful and would say:

"Madam, I owe you eighty dollars; I will send you cattle." And true to his word, a couple of cattle would be delivered.

The Andrews family moved to live at the West Coast for a short time, then returned to build the big red brick house on a commanding site overlooking the river, at the end of Melrose Avenue. There the home stood as a landmark and social center in the community for sixty years. There Mrs. Andrews dispensed pioneer hospitality, offering the spacious floor when there was reason for a dance. There she could be formal and be "at home" twice a month, and there she could be just as informal and provided tea and homemade bread to everybody who knocked at the back door.

Captain Andrews died in 1935. Mrs. Andrews lived for many more rich and active years, symbolizing the spirit of the frontier, friendly and compassionate. The influence of her motherly dignity touched many lives and was then publicly recognized when at ninety years of age she was Saskatoon's Citizen of the Year. The recognition banquet was at the Bessborough Hotel and the guest of honor was presented with the B'nai B'rith scroll in recognition of "a lifetime of useful work in the community." It was a tribute to a lady who, in the words of Harry S. Hay, chairman of the event, "was unfailingly a friend when a friend was needed. . . . Her door was always open to the traveller. . . . The community was better because she passed this way."

Mrs. Andrews died a year after her city paid her its highest honor. She was ninety-one years old and it could not be overlooked that she had been a vigorous part of the community from its very infancy. Friends read again the citation presented to her when she was proclaimed Citizen of the Year: "She established a home which brings pleasant memories to so many. In that home was real western hospitality and kindness. . . . She was there to help friends and neighbors."

She achieved greatness, not in terms of dollars or bushels or barrels but in pioneer fortitude and simple dedication to neighborliness and quiet service. Happily, it did not go unnoticed.

Archives of Saskatchewan

ELIZABETH SCOTT MATHESON: A LADY DOCTOR ON THE FRONTIER

It was unusual enough to find a medical doctor practicing at any country point in the West in 1898. When the doctor was a lady and the area of service was as remote as Onion Lake, the circumstances seemed to border on fantasy. Even editors did not hide their surprise at learning of Dr. Elizabeth Scott Matheson — a real and qualified practitioner — returning to bring the benefit of her training to the predominantly Indian community, about 200 miles northwest of Saskatoon.

Nor was it to be overlooked that this woman's medical duties only added to an already long list of useful services. Elizabeth Matheson, possessing medium height, trim figure, beautifully chiseled features and penetrating brown eyes, was always quick to recognize tasks needing benevolent attention and wanted to undertake all. At one time or another she was a teacher, a missionary in foreign service, a homemaker, the matron of an Indian school, a medical doctor, a medical inspector of schools and the mother of nine children. Facetiously, a student of the western scene asked: "What else did she do?"

If the question demanded an answer, it could have

been told that she worked for and gained Indian respect and friendship, sufficient to be long remembered by the Cree and others over a big part of the country north of Lloydminster.

At the time of her graduation in medicine and return to the Northwest Territories where her husband, Rev. John R. Matheson, was in charge of the Onion Lake Anglican Mission, she was thirty-two years old, the mother of three children, and very conscious of the risks and dangers she had incurred by leaving her family to complete studies needed to become a practicing doctor. She was entitled to some personal misgivings about being absent from family and home to gain the goal of a doctor's degree, but her husband, well aware of the need for somebody trained in medicine, counseled that an increased capacity for frontier service would more than outweigh the sacrifices all members of the family would have to make during the time she would be away. She knew that her husband, eighteen years her senior, a man of dedicated principles, was right. She yielded to the call of conscience and returned to complete the requirements for graduation from the Women's Medical College in Toronto. The degree was from Trinity College.

Perhaps nobody was more surprised than herself at the turn of events. Only a few years previously, she was on a mission field in India, vaguely considering the idea of preparing herself for medical service there. But if she was surprised, she should have paused to realize that her whole life had followed an unusual and unpredictable course.

She was born at Campbellford, Province of Canada, January 6, 1866, while the principle of confederation of the British American provinces was still being debated bitterly. Her father, James Scott, knew all about the hardships in chopping Upper Canada trees and stumps to make a farm and was attracted by reports of better opportunities in Manitoba. In 1878, he moved his family to settle at Morris, south of Winnipeg. Daughter Elizabeth, age twelve at the time of the move, completed her primary schooling there and then went to Winnipeg for high school grades and teacher training. She taught school in Manitoba for a few years and it was at that period, when attending a Red River Valley picnic, that she met John R. Matheson, member of an old Red River family, presently engaged in construction in British Columbia.

He had been a trader and freighter and then a construction contractor. He was big and commanding and practical, and looked like a candidate for fortune. He was also completely captivated by Miss Elizabeth and probably would have married her at once. But restrained by the difference in their ages and their ideals, she could not agree.

A short time later, giving expression to an urge to perform humanitarian service, she volunteered to help at an Ontario home for orphan children. This led to a year's attendance at the Womens' Medical College and an invitation to teach at a Presbyterian Mission School in India. She accepted, undertaking to remain for seven years but an attack of malaria greatly shortened her tour of service and she returned home to Manitoba to recuperate.[1]

It was now six years since Miss Elizabeth had seen John Matheson although there were exchanges of letters. Her attitude was unchanged; as soon as good health could be recovered, she would resume medical studies and go again to the foreign field. But during 1891, according to her daughter, Ruth Matheson Buck, who became her mother's biographer, Elizabeth Scott visited Vancouver to stay for a spell with her sister and when there, John Matheson not only showered her with attention but convinced her that he was a changed man. Yes, he had attended the Crossley and Hunter revival meetings and was among the converted. Now he was prepared to devote the remainder of his life to some high moral cause. Elizabeth Scott was impressed and they were married before the end of the year.

---

[1] Buck, Ruth Matheson, "The Mathesons of Saskatchewan Diocese," *Saskatchewan History*, Winter, 1960

He was ready to embark upon missionary work with either the Methodist or Presbyterian church but the influence of friends and relations with stronger denominational bonds brought him to theological studies with the Anglicans and a posting to the Onion Lake mission, good for a stipend of $300 per year. But he was not complaining and said, according to his daughter: "I earned a good living serving the devil; I can earn a better one serving the Lord."

Moving to Onion Lake was not difficult but living there presented its own problems. In addition to administration, John Matheson would be expected to conduct church services at Onion Lake, Moose Lake, Long Lake, Frog Lake, Island Lake and Egg Lake.[1] Certainly he would not be idle, especially on Sundays. And periodically — at least twice a year — he would journey to Fort Edmonton, build a big raft on the North Saskatchewan River and after piling a great stock of supplies for the mission on it, push off and float for days to the closest river point to Onion Lake, there to pole his way to the shore and tie to a tree for the unloading.

The *Edmonton Bulletin* could report that, "Rev. J. R. Matheson came in from Onion Lake on Tuesday evening accompanied by the Bishop of Saskatchewan. The trip of over 200 miles was made in four days by the trail north of the river . . . Mr. Matheson makes one or two trips to town each year, taking down supplies for the school in scows." The editor then added: "Mrs. Matheson who acts as principal and matron, attended Trinity College, Toronto, and graduated in Medicine."[2]

Elizabeth Matheson grew to love the north country with all its hardships and dangers. The unspoiled natural beauty was one of its charms and even holiday trips to other parts lost much of their attraction. It was fortunate, because leaving Onion Lake was always complicated and difficult. Some observers might have said she was

[1] *Edmonton Bulletin*, Nov. 1, 1901
[2] Ibid.

"stuck" there. Anyway, a year after returning, the lady who had been trained amid the best facilities known to medical science, gave birth to her fourth child in her own bedroom, attended only by an elderly Indian woman of the community.

Being the only doctor on a broad frontier straining to reach the unexplored North could be a test of resourcefulness and fiber. At first, many of the native people chose to continue their reliance upon witch doctors and herbal remedies prescribed by the women of the tribe; but as months passed, more of them were rejecting the traditional treatments and turning to the sympathetic white woman whose successes were embarrassing the medicine men. The calls came from ever greater distances.

Happily, many of those horse-and-buggy adventures in attempting to relieve pain and sickness were captured and related with a daughter's understanding by Ruth Matheson Buck. One of those experiences occurred when the mission farm worker, Bangs, accompanied by his wife and son, drove sixty mission cattle to winter about seventy-five miles north of Onion Lake. At the most inconveneint place and distance the boy fell and suffered a seriously broken leg and was in too much pain to be moved. Winter was setting in but there was still insufficient snow for sleighing. The lad's condition was calling loudly for attention and the distraught father tramped as far as the Edmonton Trail and from there dispatched a message to the doctor, asking her pleadingly to come at once to do something for his son.

At the mission, the news brought expressions of anxiety and sympathy; but people living in the wilderness had to be practical and they asked what, if anything, could be done. The general conclusion was that in view of distance and the uncertainty of weather, it would be a mistake for Dr. Matheson to try to make the trip, especially when there was the Matheson's breast-fed baby to consider. "With all those miles of rough roads," friends agreed, "it would be ridiculous to take the risks in driving." It was easy to rationalize that the incidence of pain and sickness in the area would simply soar if anything happened to the doctor.

But Elizabeth Matheson, without arguing about the probable state of the roads or the practical considerations, replied firmly: "I am the doctor. I must go. I'll have to take the baby with me."

Her husband, proud of her heroic decision, said: "You're right but you'll have to take a team and wagon. Fraser is our best horseman and he can drive you, but remember, it will take you almost three days to get there. You'd better start at once and try to get as far as Frog Lake tonight."

Preparation was hastened and the three people, including the baby, started over the Carlton Trail, westward, with the lady wrapped in a buffalo robe and perched high on the exposed wagon seat, carefully holding the moss-bag of best Indian design which contained her baby. And Fraser, the ablest of the farm workers, gripped the reins with added firmness to show his understanding of the responsibility he was assuming. It would be a tedious trip but Mrs. Matheson knew that Fraser would get through if anybody could.

At the end of the first day, the little party camped at an abandoned Indian shack and throughout the second day the path twisted constantly as the driver tried to escape the treacherous ice on sloughs and lakes. The jolting of the wagon was beginning to have its effect upon Elizabeth's slender body, and her muscles ached. But there was no complaint and she knew the wagon was drawing ever nearer to the boy whose need was both great and grave. And then, at the end of that second day, they encountered the boy's anxious father, traveling by horse and saddle to meet the wagon and guide it over the remaining miles.

Just as John Matheson had anticipated, Fraser brought the team and wagon to the cabin sheltering the injured boy on the evening of the third day of travel and the lady doctor rushed inside to make an immediate appraisal of the situation. The boy was pale and obviously in pain. While finding a secure place for her baby, she talked to dispel the lad's fears, then turned to make an examination of the injury, a fractured femur. Without pausing to remove her coat, she was scurrying about with bottles and bandages, and ordering the two men, the boy's father and Fraser, to help her, the father to cut wood splints of stated size and Fraser to be ready to administer the chloroform she brought, precisely according to her instructions. But the young teamster who might be the best horseman in the Northwest Territories, revolted at the prospect of this job and the smell of chloroform made him sick. He had to be excused and the responsibility of handling the chloroform bottle was passed to a native woman who happened to be there; it would be her task to allow the anesthetic to fall one drop at a time, on the cotton mask placed over the boy's frightened face. But the Indian woman failed also, reacting to the boy's feeling of alarm by running away screaming that he was dying. When Bangs returned with the splints, he was ordered to administer the chloroform and although protesting that it was too much for him, actually carried out the chore exactly as the doctor instructed. Minutes later the fractured limb was set and bound and the doctor was satisfied.

Early the next morning, with more winter chill in the air, the wagon began rolling toward Onion Lake and home, the faithful big horses showing their enthusiasm to be going toward their own stable. Nightfall brought the travelers to a half-breed home where the kitchen floor carried a perpetual invitation to travelers who might wish to sleep on it. Next morning, the occupants of that floor were found to total eighteen, including several children, two priests and a few Indians.

The next day brought snow, so much that Fraser thought it necessary to borrow a sleigh and leave the wagon until the trails were again suitable for wheels. And then, after more hours and more miles, the doctor was at home, tired but happy in the thought of having responded to the call for help and happy because she had demonstrated to herself that she could rise to meet these back-country demands. It was the sort of call Elizabeth Matheson was to hear again and again; and always her answer was the same.

The Onion Lake enterprise grew and the Mathesons were kept busy. School attendance fluctuated with the weather and the moods of local youngsters, but Indian children, half-breeds, Caucasians, Protestants, Roman Catholics, all were welcome and some of the most needy were taken right into the Matheson home. At the same time, farm work expanded, partly to furnish food needed for the local population, partly for revenue because the mission had to be largely self-sustaining. When expenditures exceeded appropriations and revenues — as they generally did — the reconciliation had to be by private means but the Mathesons were resourceful and had their private enterprises like freighting, a trading business and a ranch with a hundred cattle and a few sheep near Fort Pitt. One way or another, the deficits were made to vanish.

Dr. Elizabeth returned to the Manitoba Medical College for a refresher program and bettered her professional standing by graduating again in 1904. She was now being invited to practice in growing towns and cities across the West where opportunities were most attractive but her choice was to stay at Onion Lake where her husband built her a small hospital and where hundreds of native and other people had come to rely upon her.

Rev. John Matheson died in 1916 and his wife continued her great work for another couple of years, bringing her Onion Lake record in medicine to twenty years. The native people did not fail to acknowledge their gratitude. One of those who later paid loud tribute was Rev. Edward Ahenakew who was ordained by Rev. John Matheson and whose first church assignment was as an assistant at Onion Lake. The power of example being what it is, this Cree gentleman aspired to become a medical doctor "like Elizabeth Matheson." With that laudable objective he enrolled at the University of Alberta but then found himself with a health problem and was prevented from finishing. He turned back to the Anglican ministry. If he could not emulate Dr. Elizabeth Matheson, he would try again to be like Rev. John Matheson.

Leaving Onion Lake, Elizabeth Matheson moved to Winnipeg where she was appointed to the position of assistant medical inspector for the public school system, an office she retained until 1941 when at seventy-five years of age, she grudgingly accepted the idea of taking a rest. But she had health and spirit and children to visit and she continued to live richly until January, 1958, when she died at the age of ninety-two full and wonderful years.

Manitoba Archives

CORA HIND: VOICE OF THE AGRICULTURAL WEST

"If members of my sex appear at times to be inadequate, it must be because a wise God created them to match the men," said Cora Hind when working with Nellie McClung to gain voting rights for women. Her efforts at that time helped to explain why Manitoba was the first province in Canada to grant equal voting privileges. But her public interests extended far beyond women's rights and there was a time when the surest way of settling a farm argument was to be in a position to proclaim: "Cora Hind said so."

There was distinction in nearly everything she did. Who should be remembered as the first typist and stenographer in all of Western Canada? Who was the first western woman to succeed in journalism? Who started farm market reports in the West? Who pioneered in the preparation of crop reports? Who was the early secretary of the Manitoba Dairy Association? Who was the first woman to ride a boatload of wheat from Manitoba's Port of Churchill? The answer to each question would be the same: E. Cora Hind of Winnipeg. What the members of the Western Live Stock Union said to her when in 1916 they presented her with a purse of $1,300 was repeated in essence many times by agricultural organizations wishing to express appreciation: "Among those whose names will for all time be most closely associated with the advancement of agriculture in the Western Provinces, you will occupy an honored place."

This writer's first meeting with her was at Brandon in 1913. She was there to attend a Dressed Poultry Show and be helpful. She made a speech and was busy with records and people but had time to explain the awards to an eleven-year-old boy who happened to be keeping a few chickens in a piano-box henhouse in his family's McTavish Avenue backyard in Brandon. With patience too rarely encountered among busy people, she explained about proper dressing of poultry and talked about crooked breastbones. As always, anything that would lead to agricultural betterment was a passion with her. It was small wonder that for many years no dean of agriculture or professor of animal husbandry spoke with more authority.

And the last time the boy of 1913 saw her was at the Saskatchewan Stock Growers' Convention in Shaunavon, Saskatchewan, June, 1942, only a few months before her death. She was an old lady with frail body. She accepted his offer to carry her up the stairs to her hotel room and later to carry her through street mud to a car waiting for her. She seemed like a weight of seventy pounds. The body was frail but the mind and determination were those of the Cora Hind her friends had known through the years. At breakfast each morning in the hotel coffee shop, she did most of the talking, which was all right because her breakfast companion was making notes.

Obviously, she should not have been attending a convention in southwestern Saskatchewan at that time, but nobody could have convinced her. Actually, the eighty-one-year-old lady went to Shaunavon twice for that convention; she was confused about the convention dates and arrived at Shaunavon one week too early. But, even at her age, she could not waste time by waiting there for seven days so returned to Winnipeg and came again a week later to keep in touch with rangeland progress and report the convention.

Cora Hind was in all respects the pioneer. She arrived in the West in 1882, when Winnipeg had a population of 7,000 and a water distributing system which was still on Red River cart wheels. She was born in Toronto in 1861 and her mother died when the baby was two years old. Wee Cora was taken by her Aunt Alice Hind to Grandfather Hind's farm in Grey County. Her father was a stone mason, known widely for his artistic designs in rock. He, too, died when the girl was quite young. But Aunt Alice gave care and affection unstintingly, and in after years, Cora repaid with love and attention of a similar kind until the aunt's death in 1908.

Nephews went to Fort Calgary in 1879 and sent glowing reports about the new West. Aunt Alice and Cora resolved to go west. They arrived at Winnipeg on August 7, 1882. The Gateway City was just getting over a huge binge in the form of a real estate boom and there were some "hangover headaches." Aunt Alice would do dressmaking and if Cora were to carry out the initial plan, she would obtain a permit to teach and apply for a school. But Miss Cora formed some new ideas. She had completed her high school grades in Ontario except for one condition in mathematics and secretly she hoped her poor algebra would prove to be an obstacle to teaching.

She hesitated to mention it, even to her esteemed aunt, but Cora Hind entertained a hope of getting into newspaper work and obtained a letter of introduction to W. F. Luxton, editor of the *Manitoba Free Press*. He received the girl courteously but refused to consider hiring a member of her sex for newspaper work. To quote Miriam Green Ellis, "The editor was not interested in skirts." His answer was: "Never."

"Thank you, Mr. Editor," she answered. "But things will change, and I'll be back."

It came to her attention that no business firm in all of Winnipeg—or probably in all the West—had a typewriter. It brought an idea. She would rent a typewriter in the

East and learn to operate it. No sooner had she mastered the noisy thing than the firm of Macdonald and Tupper bought a machine, reckless though the action might seem, and Cora Hind was hired to operate it at a wage of one dollar per working day. Sir Hugh John Macdonald could say in later years that his secretary was the first typist in Manitoba.

From the time of her arrival in Winnipeg, Cora Hind was active in just about every worthy movement. She worked faithfully with the Women's Christian Temperance Union and then with those who were campaigning for voting rights for women. In 1914 she stood with representative women of Manitoba when they presented their request for the franchise to the Premier of the province. Days later she participated in the famous Mock Parliament in which a House composed entirely of women debated and then defeated a motion to permit men to vote. Before very long, Miss Hind and her campaigning colleagues saw a change of government in Manitoba and then legislation which brought them the voting rights they sought.

Gradually, Cora Hind's interests were being broadened. Along in 1893 she had resigned from the law firm and established herself as a public stenographer. The new work brought her into contact with people of many professions — landseekers, clergymen, politicians, prospectors and so on. She was interested in all. Then, as it happened, she bought a bicycle and it took her into the farming communities where she could watch crops and cattle.

Gradually she found herself preparing reports about agricultural conditions and farm markets. And in 1898 she made her first comprehensive crop report. Rumors about frost damage were demoralizing business right across Canada. Eastern businessmen wanted the facts. Miss Hind packed her valise and left for the western grain country. After many miles by rail, many more by horse livery and hundreds of stops to rub-out some of the ripening wheat, the report was made and business accepted it.

The crop report to bring her the most in fame was that of 1904. By that time she was working for the *Free Press*. According to reports coming from Chicago, the western Canadian wheat crop was largely a failure. Cora Hind did not think so. She conferred with *Free Press* Editor John Dafoe. Irresponsible speculation about the size of crops was bad for everybody. Crop-guessing by people in Chicago would have to be stopped. Again she packed her well-worn leather valise, saying only that she would not be back until she had obtained what she believed to be a proper cross-section of the crop.

The Chicago estimate of wheat in the Midwestern Provinces was 35,000,000 bushels. Cora Hind said 55,000,000 bushels. When the Chicago merchants learned that a woman was challenging their judgment and estimating their error at 20,000,000 bushels, they laughed heartily. But their entertainment was rudely halted when the official figure for the West's wheat crop of the year was 54,000,000 bushels. Her critics became admirers and year after year thereafter she estimated the Canadian crops with amazing accuracy. "No one else," said one of her friends, "has ever been able to estimate the wheat crop with such precision year after year like E. Cora."

Traders yearned to know in advance what Miss Hind's estimate would be but until it was formally released, it constituted a top secret, something to be guarded like the contents of a budget speech before its delivery. And when it was released, it was accepted with about the same degree of finality.

But how did she manage to get into journalism? In the years when she was a public typist, still denied entry to man's world of newspapers, she was writing articles on agriculture and other western subjects and seeing them printed in the *Free Press* and papers elsewhere. To be published under a woman's name, they had to be particularly good. The editor of an eastern publication had the audacity to change the name of the author from "E. Cora Hind" to "E. C. Hind," presumably to hide the sex identity of the author but he was called at once to explain.

He confessed to an attempt to conceal something. The reply to the editor was blunt and unmistakable: The author was indeed a woman; the name E. Cora Hind; that name would be unaltered or there would be no more stories.

As a writer, Miss Hind was gaining recognition whether all male editors approved or not. In 1901, soon after John W. Dafoe became Editor of the *Winnipeg Free Press,* he invited her for an interview. He offered her a position and she accepted. Her department would be Agriculture and Markets. Already she was secretary of the Manitoba Dairy Association and a familiar figure at agricultural gatherings and conventions. She did not find it difficult to add agricultural fairs and exhibitions to her itinerary.

As the years passed, she continued her campaign for better farming. Rarely did she miss a farm convention. When a conference chairman at Edmonton was asked, on one occasion, when the meeting would begin, he replied very seriously: "When Cora Hind gets here."

She liked good clothes and, as noted by her fellow traveler, Miriam Green Ellis, "she was always proud of her neat ankles, just as the rest of us were proud of her head and talents." But being of a practical turn of mind, she dressed to suit occasions and made her appearance in showrings wearing breeches and high boots. It was unconventional and there were some unkind remarks, but everybody who saw her stepping into a judging ring wearing breeks, boots, Stetson hat and the beautifully beaded buckskin coat presented to her by the Calgary Exhibition officials, had to agree that the outfit was both attractive and sensible. And, after all, who had a better right to say what she should wear than the lady herself?

She lost none of her earlier interest in women's rights but was finding new and absorbing interest in cooperative marketing, in farm organization and a score of other subjects important to the West. When stem rust struck in 1911 and took a toll of $150,000,000 in 1916, she advocated public support for research which might lead to rust resistant varieties. She had faith in the Hudson's Bay Route as a short cut in shipping western grains to Europe and concluded that the only sure way of understanding the problems involved would be to travel over it.

The much-traveled bags were packed and Cora Hind went to Port Churchill in 1933, the second experimental year for the new route. Most of the captains of merchant boats refused to carry passengers, especially lady passengers, but, somehow Miss Hind, who could not speak Italian, convinced the skipper of an Italian freighter, who could not speak English, that he was taking her to England. There were still many doubts and fears about those northern waters. Less than one year earlier, the *Brightfan* struck an iceberg in Hudson Straits and sank but, nothing daunted, Cora Hind was outward bound on the *Juventus* with a quarter of a million bushels of western wheat. It was a fourteen-day trip and not a particularly comfortable one but the people of Western Canada learned much about the merits and demerits of the new route from her experiences and writings.

Numerous were the honors coming to her from groups recognizing her contributions to Canadian life. It was she who was invited to unveil a stone at the end of Lombard Street, beside the Red River, on June 15, 1932, commemorating the shipping of the first wheat from Western Canada in 1876. The Manitoba Sheep Breeders, wishing to express their gratitude, presented her with a flock of sheep, twenty-six head. From that time in 1920 she was an active sheep breeder and devoted more than ever of her spare time to knitting woolen socks. Friends said she drove many a convention lecturer to near distraction by sitting at a press table immediately in front of the speaker's platform and knitting furiously while other reporters were writing. In wartime, her output of woolen socks was one of the highest.

Bringing her unusual happiness was that honorary LL.D. degree received from the University of Manitoba in May, 1935. It was Chancellor John Dafoe's first convocation and although he had no part in nominating Miss

Hind for the high honor, it brought special satisfaction to him as well as to the recipient. Then, as a crowning tribute, in recognition of long and faithful service, the *Free Press* offered her a world tour. On her seventy-fifth birthday, she was flying over wheat fields in Australia. When she returned about the midpoint of 1937, she could look back upon an absence of two years and exploratory adventures in no fewer than twenty-seven countries.

Death claimed her on October 6, 1942. She was eighty-one years old with more than forty years of newspaper service in the field of agriculture. Her passing made news in nearly every country of the world because the little lady with the great grasp of agriculture had become an international figure.

Outwardly, Cora Hind was an extremely practical person, but beneath the surface were sentiment and sympathy in large measure. In her early years she had romances like other girls but a big part of her life was reserved for and given to her aunt. In the year of the flu epidemic, she was one of the busiest people in Winnipeg, trying to keep in touch with all the sick ones of her acquaintance. Each morning she made a huge pot of soup and some part of the contents was taken to every sick person she knew.

She understood what it was to be poor and many were the needy people who received regular help from her. A cleaning woman had troubles, a combination of man and money troubles, and would have lost her home if Miss Hind had not come to her aid. And she liked animals, dogs, horses, all animals. Miriam Green Ellis, friend and fellow journalist, told of driving Miss Hind on a crop inspection tour which ended at Edmonton. The Ellis pup, a setter called Laddie, occupied the back seat with the luggage. When a peal of thunder sounded loud and frightening, the pup dived into the front of the car and buried his head in Miss Hind's dress. Nobody blamed the pup but later, while riding in the back, the same small dog took to chewing the leather handles on Miss Hind's luggage.

By the time the party reached Edmonton, no handle remained intact. Mrs. Ellis was annoyed at the behavior of her pup and was about to punish the little animal but Miss Hind came to the dog's defense. Notwithstanding the difficulty of trying to carry three grips without handles, Miss Hind insisted that pups were supposed to chew things. Moreover, Laddie was her friend and it was his car in which she was riding. There was no punishment.

The name of E. Cora Hind was not to be forgotten. Following her death, the United Grain Growers provided the Cora Hind Fellowship for research in agriculture at the University of Manitoba, and the *Winnipeg Free Press* provided the Cora Hind Scholarship in Home Economics at the same university. The first Cora Hind Scholar in Home Economics, Miss Kristine Anderson, brought added honor to the award by winning the University Gold Medal in her faculty in her graduating year, 1947.

This lady, who must be seen as one of the most influential Canadians of her time, left much that would endure, a tradition for accurate reporting and fine journalism, an unselfish record of service and a new dignity for agriculture. And not the least of her bequests were gems of sentiment like "The Valor of Wheat," appearing first as an editorial and then as a message on her Christmas card. It conveyed much of Cora Hind:

> *Springtime, but the ground was cold and dry and the wheat grains lay waiting for warmth and moisture to aid them in beginning the growth essential to their task of providing the world with bread.*
>
> *Days passed and still no warmth or moisture came to them. Growing could no longer be delayed and the tiny rootlets were thrust downward into the hard ground in the hope of finding moisture, and slowly, very slowly, green blades forced their way upward to light and air, led in the struggle by the mother stem, only to be met by nipping frosts that killed outright many of the more fragile children and well nigh killed many of the mother stems. Those that survived persisted in replacing*

the losses; for had not the Great Master promised the world that 'seed time and harvest should not fail?' Theirs the gigantic task of implementing that promise.

The season advanced with scarcely any rain and with frequent and prolonged periods of burning heat alternating with cold nights and brief showers that too often brought hail in their train; so that many a mother stem was beaten into the ground never to rise again. The survivors of those terrible onslaughts murmured 'Noblesse Oblige' and struggled on, while the peasantry of the cereal world, the oat and barley, almost, if not quite, gave up the fight.

Slowly, very slowly, the wheat gained headway, but the struggle was not ended. As harvest approached, disease and insects added to the heavy burdens of the already hard-pressed plants, but they never faltered at their task. 'Only one head of wheat where there should be five or six,' moaned the farmers, without a thought of the valiant fight the plants had made to produce that one head.

Finally, as August burned its fiery way to a close, the wheat ripened; and there was a different tone in the long sibilant whisper that ran from east to west through the wheat fields. What was the whisper? Was it not 'victory'? Yes, 'victory' purchased at high cost, but victory. The valor of the wheat had conquered, and because of that valiant fight against adverse conditions, the world is once more partaking of the wheaten loaf, unconscious and uncaring that in so doing it is partaking of a sacrament.

The Public Archives of Canada

MARTHA LOUISE BLACK: WEDDED TO "MY BELOVED YUKON"

"We went in over the trail [of '98] on foot. We climbed those mountains and came down the waters of the lakes and rivers. . . . We became self-reliant. We knew what it was to get along without the amenities of so-called civilized life."

The words were those of the Honorable Member of Parliament for the Yukon, Mrs. Martha Louise Black, and were spoken in the House of Commons on May 20, 1938. Agnes Macphail, representing an Ontario constituency, was the first woman in Canada to be elevated to the House of Commons; Mrs. Black, elected in 1935 at the age of seventy years was the second. She denied that she was searching for another career but the pioneer who had tasted both luxury and poverty, who remembered the Chicago Fire and the intense madness of the Klondike Gold Rush, and who knew exactly what it was like to be lonely and cold and hungry in the North, hoped she would never be too old to enjoy a new adventure.

Without unusual curiosity and courage she would never have seen the Canadian North. Most people accepted the proposition that the cruel and forbidding Chilkoot Pass was no place for a woman — "bad enough for a man, unthinkable for a woman." Perhaps they were right. There were times when this lady would have agreed, because she faced not only the anticipated difficulties and trials in negotiating the near-500-mile trip from Skagway to Dawson City but had a few extra worries which were peculiarly her own. There were moments in that first year in the North, before her baby was born, when by her own admission, she wished for death. But Martha Louise persevered and won the distinction and honor and happiness the North held for her. She enjoyed Ottawa and liked an occasional outing to Vancouver and Seattle, but her deep and abiding affection was for "my beloved Yukon."

Born in Chicago, February 24, 1866, she was christened Martha Louise Munger. Her mother, daughter of a well-to-do Kentucky and Ohio family, was a cultured and gentle person, reflecting the influence of schools in Europe to which she was sent. Her father was the practical type who had no qualms about the laundry business if it promised profit. He was an eighth generation American after the first Munger came to Connecticut in 1645. Martha Louise was five years old when, according to story, Mrs. O'Leary's cow, stabled close to the Munger home, kicked over a lantern and started the awful conflagration which destroyed much of Chicago and left thousands of residents homeless. The Mungers were among those forced to flee before the flames to seek cold refuge at the lake shore. Having lost everything, their next residence for a period of rehabilitation was on what was known as Poverty Flats.

But George Munger was enterprising and fortunes improved quickly. Martha was sent to St. Mary's School, Notre Dame, Indiana. It was a little unusual for a Protestant girl to be attending a Roman Catholic school but her years there proved to be a good and happy experience. And then this plump and vicacious girl with skills in needlework, music and athletics — and a great fondness for the woods and meadows — met a handsome young man, Will Purdy, whose father was the president of the Chicago,

Rock Island Railway. Marriage followed in 1887. As a young wife, Martha enjoyed social life but was at heart a homemaker and she loved children. Two sons, Warren and Donald, were born.. The Purdys moved among people of prominence and wealth. Andrew Onderdonk, who was directing the building of the westward part of the CPR, was among family friends.

For Martha Purdy, the 90's were really gay. There were parties and plays and stylish clothes, and she and Will rode a bicycle "built for two," with the lady in the pair dressed appropriately in bloomers and cloth cap. There was the World's Fair at Chicago and life was exciting more than satisfying.

Then in 1897 came news of gold discovery on Bonanza Creek, deep in the Canadian North. The topic entered every conversation and people talked about going. Will Purdy announced that he was going; so did Martha's brother, George, and a cousin. Caught up in the enthusiasm, Martha resolved that if they were going, she was going too. At this point, an acquaintance of Martha's father-in-law came to report that an uncle had died at Dawson City, leaving a million-dollar fortune in gold dust and claims to him. As the beneficiary, this person would surrender half of the wealth to anyone who succeeded in identifying and securing the assets at Dawson. The elder Purdy thought this to be a challenging personal assignment for Martha if she were going, obviously enjoying the thought of his daughter-in-law becoming half a million dollars richer. Sure, she would take it on. Her sons could live with her parents during her absence and it would be a great adventure.

Just when all arrangements had been made for sailing from Seattle for Skagway, Martha's husband changed his mind. Contending that the north trip was attended by too many dangers, he favored a venture in Hawaii and inquired if she would accompany him to that place. She was shocked and angry. All plans had been made for the trip to the North and she held the passenger's ticket in her hand. She would abide by earlier promises; her answer to the question was "No." Moreover, she had been growing increasingly unhappy about a man upon whom she could not depend, and about her marriage. Martha and Will parted and never saw each other again. The separation led to divorce.

Traveling with her brother, George, and the cousin, Martha left Seattle early in June. The ship was crowded with people from every walk of life and the voyage was rough. At the Skagway end, baggage and supplies were thrown to the shore and a motley group of men met the boat to gaze at the new arrivals. Among those present was the notorious Soapy Smith, hotel operator, gambler and undisputed King of the Skagway Underworld, who had managed to fleece most people coming to that place with money. It was just a few days later, however, that Frank Reid, leader of a new vigilante group hoping to put an end to the Soapy Smith brands of crime, met the man face to face. Both drew their revolvers and shot simultaneously and both men died in consequence.

As everybody knew, the real test of muscle and spirit only began at Skagway. There were two possible routes across the nearby mountains, Chilkoot Pass and Chilcat or White Pass — about equally difficult. The decision was to go via Chilkoot. Leaving Dyea, there was the crowded walk to Sheep Camp at the foot of the Pass, then the extremely dangerous climb to the summit, marked by ice-encrusted rocks, bodies of dead horses and yawning precipices. The descent to Lake Lindeman and on to the village of Bennett was almost as difficult but at the latter point the wayfarers had forty-two miles of travel by foot behind them. Some of the fellow travelers had horses, oxen and dogs, all bearing burdens on their backs. Animals fell and fractured legs and were abandoned or shot. Men fell, cursed, wiped blood from scratches and cuts, and the lady in the party of six wanted to cry but managed to restrain.

At Bennett, members of the little group began the construction of a boat and waited three weeks for its completion. Floating and paddling from there, they cleared the Mounted Police checkpoint at the foot of Lake Tagish where their boat was reported to have been the 14,405th to pass in the year. They ran the boiling rapids in Miles Canyon and finally triumphed by arrival at fearful and wonderful Dawson City.

There at journey's end, the little party acquired a lot on "the other side of the river" where prices were less exorbitant, and built a cabin. With the least possible delay, Martha and her friends turned their attention to the "million dollar legacy" which was supposed to be awaiting a claimant. But it did not take long to see that the story was either a fabrication or a gross exaggeration and they began to look for more promising avenues to fortune. Each of them staked claims on his own or her own account.

As winter was tightening its icy grip upon the North, most men were leaving for homes in far parts. Martha, however, knew by this time that she could not leave. Her recent suspicions were confirmed; she was going to have a baby. What was she to do? She knew she could not make the long trip out and to remain at Dawson seemed like certain death. But there wasn't much choice; she simply had to stay. Her cousin left for home, convinced he would never see her again. Brother George would remain with her.

The weeks passed slowly and Martha felt a despondency she had never known before. People wintering at Dawson could not hide their belief that she would die in her ordeal. She shared the fear and wished at times it would happen quickly. The northern winter would have been depressing enough but to be in it as an expectant mother with less than good health and nobody to whom she could turn for medical advice, left her in despair. But Martha had what the frontiersmen called grit and instead of dying, she gave birth to a healthy nine-pound boy on the last day of January, when alone in the cabin. The feeling of depression vanished.

If she thought she was alone before the baby's birth, she had no reason to think so thereafter. The great rough miners, who felt shy about helping a pregnant woman, had no hesitation in accepting a mother and baby. They adopted the two and showered them with attention. For the rest of the winter, Martha lacked nothing her neighbors could supply, food, fuel, bedding, clothing, even gifts of gold dust.

There were other fears and worries in that memorable winter. Typhoid fever struck in epidemic proportions, then a fire that consumed a big part of Dawson. And as if that was not enough, the fire was followed by a mountain rockslide pointed right at the cabin housing mother and baby. But the slide was deflected by forces unexplained and the pair escaped.

With spring came a new wave of prospectors and to Martha's surprise, one of the incoming parties included her father, coming to take his daughter and grandchild home. By now she wasn't sure she wanted to leave but her brother was staying and would look after her claims. And so she would go, but not necessarily to stay away.

The homecoming was sweet but she was no sooner back in the south than she was feeling lonely for the Yukon. When her brother wrote early in 1900, reporting favorably about the claims, she was determined to go again and did.

On her return this time, she entered into a partnership for the development of her staked property and worked hard. Recalling that experience in the course of a speech in the House of Commons, she told of the respect she formed for those "working men and women of the country," and of her happy associations with them, of cooking for sixteen men and baking bread for as many more," with only the assistance of her twelve-year-old son. "I know what work is," she added.

Life seemed to assume a new dimension for this lady in 1902 when she had occasion to consult a lawyer and met George Black, a Maritimer, an Anglican and a Conservative, who came in one of the early waves of goldseekers and lingered to practice law. Two years later, August 1, 1904, Martha and George Black were married and began what was to be a long and happy partnership. She could not claim to be a daughter of New Brunswick but she could and did accept her husband's church and politics and brought to them the enthusiasm which marked everything she undertook in her life.

Matrimony did not restrict Martha Black's interests in any way. She found broader opportunities for service and time for communion with nature. She loved the great outdoors and tramped the countryside until she was recognized as an authority on wild flowers and all vegetation of the North. Although not Canadian-born, she gave leadership in organizing a local chapter of the Imperial Order of Daughters of the Empire and was honored with a national Life Membership.

George Black, in 1912, was appointed to the highest office in the territory, that of Commissioner of the Yukon. He was the seventh person to be so appointed to the post, which might be seen as the rough equivalent of lieutenant-governor in a province. The Blacks moved to occupy Government House, of which Martha Black was the presiding First Lady for the next four years. But at the outbreak of war, George Black heard the call of another service and left the government post to organize a Yukon Company and take it to England.

After the war, Black was again in the public eye, this time in active politics. Between 1921 and 1935 he ran and won in successive federal elections, representing his Yukon constituency, and in the 1930 to 1935 period when R. B. Bennett was Prime Minister, George Black was Speaker of the House of Commons. But in the latter year, poor health forced him to step aside. It was then that friends demanded that Mrs. Black be the Conservative candidate in the Yukon. She laughed about the proposal that she should be embarking upon a new career at the age of seventy years. But she accepted the nomination just as she had accepted a score of frontier challenges in other years, then campaigned with vigor that led to her election.

During the next four difficult years, the Canadian House of Commons benefited by her earthy views on many subjects and members listened with interest and respect. She spoke with courage and compassion. Although she sat with the Conservatives in Opposition, she supported whichever party or individual she believed to be in the right. "I shall be berated by many for saying this," she told the House, "but personally it is a matter of absolute indifference to me which party is in power. I want good government."[1]

The lady member for Yukon begged for protective measures in public health services to ensure strong bodies for young Canadians, "not because we are going to send them to war but because they will be the backbone of this country."[2] She asked for expanded cadet training, saying that she could speak from experience, having seen what it did for her own three sons who "have taken their places in the world as good, decent, law-abiding, middle-class citizens, the best class we have."[3]

She pleaded for pensions for the blind, regretting that "if you really want to be assisted, you have almost to conduct a crime. If you do murder, if you commit a theft, you are taken care of; you are fed and clothed and kept warm; but if Nature commits a crime against you, it is sometimes quite difficult to get help and so in all sincerity I ask the Government what they can possibly do for these poor people.[4]

She spoke for one Canadian language, blaming Europe's "multiplicity of languages, a modern Tower of Babel," for that continent's current troubles.[5]

On the proposal to build an Alaska Highway across Canada, she said she could "give this House a hundred reasons why it should be built and possibly I could give as many why it should not." But if the United States wants the road, she added emphatically, the Government of Canada should give approval on three conditions, that

[1] House of Commons Debates, April 18, 1939
[2] House of Commons Debates, May 27, 1938
[3] House of Commons Debates, May 19, 1936
[4] House of Commons Debates, March 9, 1936
[5] House of Commons Debates, Jan. 17, 1939

"the United States pay every cent of the cost of building through Canadian territory, employ only Canadian labor, and give Canada a free port of entry at Skagway."[1]

And in keeping with her fondness for the great Community of Nature, she urged closer observance of the terms of the Migratory Birds Treaty. What, she asked, could be more depressing than travel through country "denuded of its forests and its game . . . I well remember my grandfather telling stories about the clouds of passenger pigeons which flew through the air in his day, and about the horrible murder — it could not be described otherwise — of the pigeons which were netted, shot, packed in barrels and sent to the large cities in the United States and Canada. . . . Ducks and geese were slaughtered by thousands. . . . There was the general idea that from the breeding grounds there would always be millions of birds to fly south, but there came a time when the birds were scarce. It was only the Treaty which saved the trumpeter swan, the whooping crane, the eider duck and the wood duck. . . . we need our bird life."[2]

But the theme which Martha Black talked about most incessantly was the unique "Spirit of my Beloved Yukon." The country could produce gold and other metals, big fish and tall tales, but it was in optimism, comradeship and generosity of its people that Martha Black's Yukon was "unequalled anywhere else in the wide world." She clung proudly to that opinion.

---

[1] House of Commons Debates, Jan. 17, 1939
[2] House of Commons Debates, April 9, 1937

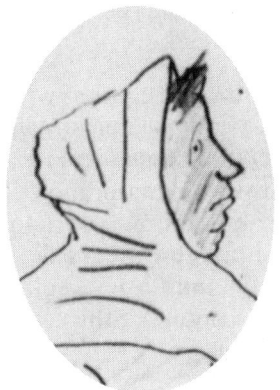

Glenbow-Alberta Institute, Calgary, Alberta*

CAROLINE "MOTHER" FULHAM: THE LADY KEPT PIGS

When Mrs. Caroline Fulham — better known as Mother Fulham — left Calgary in 1904, members of the police department breathed sighs of relief and prepared to celebrate the great day. Most other citizens were secretly sorry to see her go because she was, in those years before radio, television and movies, the best source of local amusement. As the leading entertainer on Stephen Avenue, she needed no make-up, required no rehearsal and followed no script. Her charm was in being herself, rough as it might be.

With a sharp Irish tongue and a loud voice, she had the last word in almost every argument and when more was needed, she could draw upon the persuasivness of two ready fists. Plump and powerful, she was a fair match for the best policeman on the beat. For one reason or another, the police officers saw much of her and knew that to escort her to a cell was normally a task requiring the chief and two constables — the entire Calgary force for some years.

*Only known likeness of Caroline Fulham

The lady could neither read nor write but such circumstances were not to restrict her in gaining publicity. Between visits to the police court and her daily appearances guiding her horse-drawn democrat on Calgary streets, she became one of the best-known personalities in the community. And while police officers did their best to spare her from trouble, men and boys seeking fun delighted to tease and annoy her, knowing they would get instant and often exciting reaction.

Nor were those fellows above playing tricks on her, as on that day when she left her horse and democrat in the lane while she visited the long bar of the Alberta Hotel. In her absence, the pranksters unhitched the horse from the vehicle and then, after drawing the democrat shafts through the woven wire fence containing the railway right of way, rehitched with horse on one side of the fence and democrat on the other. In due course, the lady emerged from the hotel, feeling good enough to forgive all her enemies or make some new ones. Unsteadily, she walked to her democrat, mounted and clucked to her horse to move on before realizing that something was wrong and progress would be impossible. Sensing mischief, she seized her buggy whip and dismounted to search for the miscreants, all the while muttering threats of violence.

For most of her years in Calgary, Mother Fulham lived on 6th Avenue, just a short distance west of the site on which Knox United Church was built. Her occupation was that of keeping pigs. With no bylaws restricting livestock within the town, her pig feeding operations were entirely legal, even though they drew criticism from neighbors. To feed the swine, she gathered kitchen waste from Calgary's best hotels and restaurants. Here was good and economical raw material for pork production and she chose to believe that she had a monopoly on the contents of all garbage containers behind the Alberta, Queen's, Royal and Windsor hotels, and Criterion and New Brunswick restaurants. When other feeders of pigs threatened to encroach upon her garbage preserves, she was prepared to protect her interests with force if necessary.

With regularity befitting a town's bell-ringer, she made the rounds to gather the precious pig feed. Sitting squarely in the middle of the democrat seat, with barrel in the back for the transfer of the pig feed, she employed a willow switch to urge her aging horse to something faster than a walk and slower than a trot, muttering uncomplimentary epithets in reply to rude remarks from the sidewalk spectators. When somebody would shout "Hurray for Ireland," the speaker could expect to hear the rejoinder, "Sure, you'd like to be Irish too, ye pur fool."

Sometimes the mischief-makers visited her premises at night to carry out some nefarious trick. On a certain St. Patrick's night when the lady was celebrating, visitors painted her pigs a brilliant green, and on another occasion, according to the *Calgary Herald* (September 1, 1903): "Mrs. Fulham last night was awakened by hearing some men around her yard and saw them running away. This morning she got in her buckboard and the wheels came off after the horse had gone a few yards, so she knew the men had taken the nuts. She thinks she knows who the men were."

She kept her most outlandish green clothing for St. Patrick's day and began celebrating early. Her pigs might be neglected but a thoughtful neighbor was likely to give them feed and water. On that Day of Days, she took special license to sing Irish songs from her throne on the democrat and, perchance, reach a state of intoxication long before it was time to attend the annual Firemen's Ball on that date.

Although uneducated, her wit was keen, as Dr. H. G. Mackid could testify. Meeting her on Stephen Avenue and seeing her walking with lameness, he inquired sympathetically if he could do anything for her. She replied that an ankle had been giving her trouble, to which the kindly doctor invited her to step inside Templeton's Drug Store where he could examine it. The doctor was, no doubt, aware that cleanliness was not one of the lady's obvious characteristics, but when she peeled down a stocking to expose the sore ankle, the doctor reeled at the sight of the unwashed limb and exclaimed impulsively, "By George, I'd bet a dollar there's not another leg in Calgary as dirty as that one."

Quick as a flash, the woman shouted back: "Put up your money, Doctor. I'm betting ye a dollar there is another and here's my money."

Before there was time for a retraction, Mother Fulham dropped her other stocking, thereby exposing another leg, just as dirty as the first one, and held out her hand to collect the doctor's dollar. (As told to the author by Dr. Mackid, May 3, 1956.)

They were altercations with police and neighbors that brought her name into the newspaper columns most often. And when she came to court, she would have nobody but the great Irish lawyer and personality, Paddy Nolan, to plead her case. Nolan may have enjoyed the assignments, even though he was never paid, because he was fascinated by the woman with the sharp tongue and was always assured of a big courtroom audience. When it was known on the streets that Mother Fulham and Paddy Nolan would appear together, everybody in the community wanted to be present. Sometimes the woman would be evicted from the court for reasons of undisciplined remarks and sometimes spectators had reason to wonder if the police were prosecuting the Fulham woman or if she was prosecuting the police.

Generally she was the defendant but in at least two instances she was the plaintiff. In April, 1890,[1] she was charging a Chinese employee of the Alberta Hotel with assault. As Paddy Nolan explained the circumstances, Mrs. Fulham caught the man bent over a garbage barrel at the rear of the hotel and administered a good Irish rebuke, either verbal or physical, and he struck her. But the evidence was confusing and there was reason to believe that the accused, instead of stealing garbage as

[1] *Calgary Tribune,* April 9, 1890

alleged, was simply trying to recover a dressed chicken he had earlier stolen from the hotel kitchen and hidden temporarily in the barrel. The case was dismissed.

On the other occasion when Mrs. Fulham was charging rather than defending, she accused her neighbor, the Reverend Jacques, of insulting her with improper language. J. A. Lougheed acted for the reverend gentleman and Paddy Nolan, as usual, was on Mother Fulham's side. The evidence indicated that the woman had threatened to slaughter the minister's hens if they continued to wander onto her property and he replied by calling her a "blackguard." She admitted that she did not know what the word meant but was sure it was not a compliment. Paddy Nolan tried to take the argument from there, saying that his client was too often the object of barbs and insults. It was time the authorities took a stand against what looked like "a Fulham Extermination Society." The lawyer for the defense replied that Mrs. Fulham was "a notorious nuisance" in Calgary.[1] Because of her presence and occupation, property in the neighborhood had fallen in value. To this the lady replied with some well-chosen abuse for the lawyer and was promptly ordered removed from the court. The defendant was fined one dollar and everybody present agreed that it was worth at least that much to be in attendance for the amusement.

For the next decade, she was one of the most frequent visitors at the police court, generally facing charges of disorderly conduct and generally ready to settle differences of opinion out of court by the expedient of a fight with the police. Editors knew that her story was always acceptable news and on October 21, 1901, she was reported as entering the *Herald* office and greeting the first man to face her with: "Good morning to you young man. An' it's an ill-used woman I am this day." While thus introducing the reason for her complaint, she placed a parcel on the desk, removed the wrappings and displayed a pile of dark-gray hair. Then, removing the ancient hat

[1] *Calgary Tribune,* December 2, 1891

from her head and pointing to her uncombed locks, said, "The bastes of policemen tore that from me head."

Her complaint did not end there. A few days later, when city council met in regular session, the Fulham lady, carrying the same parcel of hair, made her way to the mayor's chair and insisted upon having the full attention of the City Fathers. Yes, she had a grievance. She'd been sitting peacefully in the kitchen of the New Brunswick Restaurant on a recent night when, according to her story, Constables Fraser and Walden entered, seized her by the hair and dragged or forced her into the police wagon and lodged her at the jail where she spent the night. In the morning she was brought to court, charged and fined the "usual fee for being arrested." She had had enough of this, especially when the police took to pulling hair. She wanted the aldermen to fire all the city cops.

The mayor promised to look into the complaint but the lady wanted immediate action and was still talking loudly when the aldermen were considering the next item of business. "Sure an' isn't mesiff that knows the wickedness of thim both. Those policemen are bad men. Sure gintlemen, this is my hair them bastes pulled out."

But the mayor, when he investigated, heard the other side of the story. The lady had been celebrating as she did rather often and when the police were called to the restaurant, she was in a fine fighting mood. As for the hair, it was found to match the mane and tail of the lady's horse and there was reason to believe it did not come from a human head.

Then there were the memorable negotiations about the Fulham cow, Nellie, which lost its life when hit by a CPR train. The owner made complaint, saying compensation would have to be high because Nellie was a very superior bovine. A hearing was convened and the railroad officials pointed out that "No Trespassing" signs were posted prominently and neither cow nor person had any right to be on the railroad track.

But the cow's owner proceeded to nullify that point of argument, saying, "Ye pur fools, what makes ye think my pur old Nellie could read yer signs?" But failing to gain satisfaction from the company's minor officials, the lady wrote to Sir William Van Horne, president, and when he happened to be in Calgary, she forced her way into his private car and proceeded to hold him responsible for her loss. The president, with some feeling of sympathy, offered to find a replacement for the cow but that did not satisfy the woman because there was no other cow quite like Nellie. She contended it would take two cows to replace Nellie, but was obliged in the end to settle for one.

In any case, she exercised power and influence which might have brought envy to other citizens. And indirectly, she was the means of bringing a code of building restrictions to the city. Senator Lougheed, addressing the aldermen, said the time had come to bring in and enforce building regulations. "I for instance, have a number of lots in the vicinity of Mrs. Fulham's place and certainly no one would buy them when her pig ranch is taken into consideration. . . . Indeed, I had a sale balked just on that account."[1]

Calgary obtained its building restrictions at about the time the city's celebrated lady specialist in pigs was departing. The *Calgary Herald* carried the disappointing news: "Mrs. Fulham, who has been a noted character in Calgary for many years, has sold out her business and property and gone to Vancouver to live."[2]

The last news item to be found touching upon the lady was in the same paper about six months later: "Mrs. Fulham, who was without doubt the best known woman in Calgary, passed through the city on Monday night. She informed some of those at the station that she was coming back to live here in six weeks. This news will be received with mingled feelings."

Sure, she was often in trouble but deep in Calgary hearts was affection for Mother Fulham. Her spontaneity and unvarnished personality were refreshing, even on a

[1] *Calgary Herald,* October 12, 1901
[2] *Calgary Herald,* September 12, 1904

frontier. Calgarians would have been disappointed if she did not mark St. Patrick's Day by dressing in defiant green, or the twelfth of July by hurling shouts of derision at parading Orangemen.

But only those who watched her closely knew the generosity of her Irish heart. They alone knew the families she helped regularly with gifts of needed money, and the settler, Charlie Hawkes, who lost his three horses from glanders and had no money for replacements. The Sons of England presented him with twenty-five dollars but it was not enough. He met Mother Fulham on the street and told her of his predicament. Without comment, she pulled up her dress, exposing one of the perpetually dirty knees, took a roll of bills from a stocking and pressed forty dollars into the man's hand. "That'll help ye buy a horse," she said.

In spite of the remark made on the station platform, she did not return to take up residence in Calgary, but the memory of that great, roughcast keeper of pigs on Calgary's 6th Avenue lived on. If Calgarians did not actually love the Queen of Garbage Row, at least they missed her very much when she left.

Glenbow-Alberta Institute, Calgary, Alberta

EMILY MURPHY: CAPTAIN OF THE FAMOUS FIVE

Every successful team must have a captain or leader. In the case of Alberta's Famous Five fighters for the rights of women, as "persons," to sit in the Canadian Senate, the distinction of leadership belonged, unquestionably, to Mrs. Emily Ferguson Murphy — almost as well known by her pen-name, "Janey Canuck." Her four associates — Nellie McClung, Henrietta Edwards, Louise McKinney and Irene Parlby — would have brought power and prestige to any petition but these ladies admitted readily that the main credit for the Women's Rights victory of 1929 belonged to their esteemed friend, Emily Murphy.

It was but one of many triumphs in a lifetime of achievement. Edmonton friends never ceased to marvel at this woman who could be a magistrate, an author of note, lecturer, organizer, crusader and still have time to be a good mother, good housekeeper and good neighbor. Miriam Green Ellis, in speaking to the Canadian Women's Press Club meeting in Edmonton in 1956, said: "I have a snapshot of her in the front yard with a tiny bird on her finger. She was that kind of woman, firm and kind, gay and heartwarming. It was a nice place to drop in. You could always be sure of an invitation to stay for lunch, with good cheese as a finale."

She was short and plump and dark and jolly. She loved people and loved conversation. She was always good company. "Conversation," she said, "is the cheapest and best of all pleasures; it is life's finest pastime." She was the sort who could organize a national convention or box social and have everything so completely in hand that she would be ready to relax and enjoy the show with others attending. And here was the living proof that charm reaches its zenith when a person is natural. Sometimes gay, sometimes serious, Emily Murphy was ever herself and reserved the right to weep or laugh loudly as the spirit moved her.

Her laugh was contagious. "If we laughed more, there would be less need for medicine." Again drawing upon memory, Miriam Green Ellis recalled that evening when Emily Murphy, Nellie McClung and Irene Parlby were relaxing in Mrs. Parlby's room at the Macdonald Hotel. "As they came down on the elevator and into the rotunda they were laughing and talking like a group of teenagers. Mrs. Murphy did not giggle; she laughed, and so did the other Irish woman, Nellie McClung. Next day it was all over town that these three women came rolling out of the Macdonald drunk as lords which, of course, was funny to those who knew they were all teetotalers."

Born at Cookstown, Ontario, March 14, 1868, Emily Jemima, daughter of Isaac and Emily Jemima Ferguson, was given her mother's names. The babe was the third of six children and the family home in the Ontario village was a happy place. The little one grew to love games, horses, and even school, where she was commonly at the top of her classes. The father, with interest in land and a nigh-religious regard for education, was determined that his children would have every practical opportunity for schooling. With a special preoccupation about penmanship, he brought in special tutoring for his children. Three of Emily's brothers chose the profession of law and became distinguished King's Counsels, one of them being elevated to a judgeship in the Supreme Court of Ontario.

Miss Emily, gay and vivacious and known affectionately around Cookstown as "Sunshine," was sent at age fourteen years to attend Bishop Strachan School in Toronto and it was while there that she met a tall and blonde student of divinity who was attending Wycliffe College. He was Arthur Murphy and between the two there was love at first meeting. He urged her to hurry and grow up so they could get married. She cooperated as well as possible and on August 23, 1887, they were married. She was nineteen years old and he, a student parson with a charge at Forest, Ontario, was only a few years older.

What a difficult position for a fun-loving nineteen-year-old, to be under the gaze of adult eyes and expected to act and to lead as a parson's wife! The naturally lively and blithe girl was supposed to be dignified and circumspect. She made some mistakes, said the wrong things and laughed at the wrong time, and knew she was in disgrace. It was a trying period but the older people of the church learned to understand this vibrant girl and learned to love her. She became more and more involved with social work in her husband's congregation without surrendering her own personality. She was determined to be herself, believing she had to prescribe her own religion and let others prescribe theirs.

The Murphys' first baby was born at Forest and the second at Chatham. There were moves to still other church assignments, including a couple of years in England. The Murphys had been busy, happy people but their luck seemed to be running out. They lost their third child and then their fourth — both girls. Arthur Murphy's health began to fail. Church work was becoming too much for his nerves and he was advised to seek a change. Doctors recommended an outdoor livelihood, which meant that for the present at least he would be obliged to leave the ministry. While he was contemplating his next move, his wife was making time for writing; someone had to be a breadwinner.

Arthur Murphy resolved upon a bold move. He would try lumbering in Manitoba. He knew very little about forestry and even less about Manitoba but information coming to him hinted at opportunities in an area far northwest of Winnipeg. Late in 1903, the four members of the family were making a new home in the frontier village of Swan River beyond which the husband and father hoped to find fortune in the forests. Life there was not all good and not all bad. Absent were many of the comforts the Murphys had known in Ontario, but there were new freedoms. Mother Murphy could write more, ride horses to the limit of her desires, and shape her own life. She began a new book, *Janey Canuck In The West,* one which came to print in 1910.

For Arthur Murphy, forestry brought more of disappointment than success, but his business contacts revealed opportunities in land speculation westward as far as Tisdale and Melfort on the new railroad leading to Prince Albert. The resulting dealings in farm lands, especially in the black loam of the Carrot River Valley, proved profitable and the Murphys were back "on their feet." Business involvement suited Arthur very well and his health improved. Then, having caught the spirit of business, he had to be reaching out for fresh opportunities. He wanted to test out the business climate still farther west, and in 1907, Edmonton became the Murphy home. The Alberta city of that time, with eighty real estate firms looking for trade and twelve livery stables operating to capacity, had a human population of roughly 15,000. It had just been confirmed as the capital of the new province and everybody was busy and optimistic.

Edmonton and Emily Murphy accepted each other at once. She was fascinated by the old Hudson's Bay Fort still standing on a promontory beside the river, fascinated by Jasper Avenue with its people of many nationalities and many moods. She saw work to be done in social service, especially where women and children needed help. She got to know some Indian families, some immigrants who could not speak English, some women whose husbands were in jail, and she had counsel for all. Meanwhile, Arthur, seized by the Edmonton brand of free enterprise, was trying to develop coal mines on property situated beside the river on the east side of the city. He was constantly on the threshold of fortune but always it eluded him. Just as one of his promising coal mines was ready for production, the shaft was suddenly flooded, and after a week of pumping in the hope of rehabilitating it, he was forced to conclude that the water was being conducted by an underground vein from the river and his chance of emptying the shaft was just as good as his chance of pumping the river dry.

From coal mining, he turned to speculation in real estate. In the fierce excitement of Edmonton expansion, there were booms and busts but Arthur Murphy remained hopeful and cheerful and his wife remained busy. Between her writing and social work and the appearance of the Murphy mother and girls riding their horses on Jasper Avenue, they were soon the best-known citizens in the young city.

Emily Murphy was seeing more and more about which she wanted to write and books appeared at an accelerated rate. *Janey Canuck Abroad* was her first book, published before she left the East. Then came *Janey Canuck In The West*, published in 1910, *Open Trails, Seeds of Pine, The Black Candle, Our Little Canadian Cousins Of The North West,* and *Bishop Bompas,* the last named being published in 1929. At the same time, her articles were appearing in papers and magazines across the country.

She would have been a commanding personality in any community, being intelligent, articulate and personable. Her appointment to the office of Magistrate of the Juvenile Court in Edmonton in 1916 did not pass without surprise. That surprise, however, was occasioned by the fact that the new officer was a woman rather than by any doubt of the lady's ability to fill the position. It was an office in which no woman had ever presided and many men did not approve of the departure from precedent. Inasmuch as she was the first woman in the British Empire to be so appointed, the government action made history.

It happened this way: Ten or more girls caught in a police dragnet were being charged as vagrants and prostitutes. Several Edmonton women, who wished to see how female prisoners were handled, were asked to leave the courtroom because the evidence would be unfit for the ears of respectable women. The visitors, protesting mildly, departed. They talked to Emily Murphy and all agreed that if the evidence concerning women in the dock was unfit for female ears, it was certainly no better for male ears. It would be better if such cases were tried before a lady judge, with men barred from the court. They presented their view to Hon. C. W. Cross, Attorney General, and to their astonishment, he agreed. He even volunteered to seek government approval for the immediate appointment of a lady magistrate. Quite naturally, his thoughts turned to the lady who seemed to be so eminently suited for the post, Mrs. Emily Murphy.

She was surprised and mildly shocked by the invitation to take the position, but members of her family encouraged her and she accepted and became Magistrate of the newly created Women's Court. Messages of congratulations poured in, some of them from her lawyer brothers, who confessed their hope of some day receiving appointments as judges.

From her first day on the magistrate's bench she brought justice tempered with mercy. "Magistrates should not be there to blister people but to help them," she said. She demonstrated her sincerity. It was not uncommon for a wayward girl appearing before her to be invited to sit beside the magistrate and have a motherly arm placed around her waist while a very private conversation took place. Just as often a girl or woman in the prisoner's box was invited to the Murphy home for supper to allow for a quiet chat about morals and plans for the future.

Women were generally elated at her appointment and her performance. It was the second triumph for crusading women in that year, 1916. Earlier in the season, the legislatures of the three Midwestern Provinces had extended to women the right to vote in provincial elections. Women were on the march although some males in the community continued to nurse resentment at the idea of a woman filling an office like that of magistrate. It was not long after her appointment that the male prejudice surfaced and precipitated the long legal proceedings which finally confirmed an equality of the sexes and added to Emily Murphy's fame.

Before her was a lady charged with drunkenness and her counsel lodged an immediate objection to the case being heard by this woman because, under the terms of the British North America Act, she, as a woman, was not to be regarded as a "person" and could not, therefore, hold jurisdiction in the court. Something was quoted from English common law to the effect that "women are persons in matters of pain and penalties but not persons in the matter of rights and privileges." Apparently, the young lawyer had a point which could not be ignored. The objection from this lawyer of considerable standing must have worried the new lady magistrate very much. But she graciously acknowledged his right to make an objection, saying she would make a note of his remarks, and then went on with the case. To make matters worse, the same lawyer appeared before her from time to time, always repeating his objection. The undercurrent of resentment persisted among men who objected to a woman invading a field which had been exclusively theirs, but Emily Murphy smiled and tried to ignore it.

The matter of women's status as "persons" would have to be resolved and the question reached the Supreme Court of Alberta in 1921 when it was ruled that there was no legal reason for disqualification from public office because of any distinction of sex. That should have settled the matter but it did not. There was still the question to be ruled upon at national level. The Federation of Women's Institutes — of which Mrs. Murphy was the president at the time, 1921 — petitioned the Prime Minister to appoint a woman to the Canadian Senate. Certain other organizations were more pointed in their requests and asked bluntly that Emily Murphy be appointed to the Senate. With changes in the prime ministership, the requests were repeated but nothing beyond courteous acknowledgments came from the government. Sometimes there was reference to Section 24 of the BNA Act which allowed the Governor General, in the Queen's Name, to "summon qualified 'persons' to the Senate." Again, the old question of "persons" was showing its ugly head. Could a woman be regarded as a "person" in the light of the law?

Indignation was growing. The idea of excluding women from the Senate or anywhere else on such a pretext was clearly ridiculous. Something had to be done about it and the loudest demand for change was coming from organized women in Alberta. There, members of the Women's Christian Temperance Union, Imperial Order Daughters of the Empire, Canadian Women's Press Club, Women's Institutes and other groups were growing impatient and angry. They began looking to Emily Murphy for leadership and she was ready to lead. One of her lawyer brothers drew attention to a section of the BNA Act which permitted appeals to the Supreme Court of Canada for rulings on interpretations. If considered of sufficient importance, the Government of Canada would bear the cost. Five names were required on the petition.

It was agreed that Henrietta Edwards, Nellie McClung, Louise McKinney, Emily Murphy and Irene Parlby would be the petitioners and late in 1927 they met at Mrs. Murphy's home in Edmonton to prepare the petition. The Government of Alberta offered active support for the petition although this was largely nullified by the province of Quebec being opposed. The case was heard on March 14, 1928, Emily Murphy's sixtieth birthday. The petition was presented. The opposing counsel argued that no woman had ever been appointed to the British House of Lords and in the writing of the BNA Act, masculine pronouns alone were used. The eminent judges weighed the submissions carefully and concluded that the word "person" in the BNA Act did not include female persons.

The decision was received with deep disappointment but Emily Murphy was not one to quit in the middle of a fight. There was still the Privy Council in England. She discussed the matter with Alberta's Attorney General, Hon. J. F. Lymburn, and he promised the Provincial Government's continued support in taking the question to London. The presentation was entrusted to a Toronto lawyer, N. W. Rowell.

With Lord Sankey presiding, the distinguished jurists listened and on October 18, 1929, Lord Sankey delivered the decision: Their Lordships had concluded that the word "persons" included members of the male and female sex, that women were, indeed, eligible to be summoned to sit in the Senate of Canada.

The good news brought rejoicing in all parts of Canada, particularly in Alberta where Emily Murphy and her friends had persevered and finally won. Now, who would be the first woman to be appointed to the Canadian Senate?

There was no reason to think that Mrs. Murphy was at any time trying to promote her own chance of being elevated to a senatorship. Nothing was more evident than the unselfishness which characterized the work of a lifetime. But her friends hoped and expected that she would be the first woman senator just as she had been the first woman to become a magistrate. In this, however, they were to be disappointed. For reasons many people found hard to understand, no member of Alberta's Famous Five was ever summoned to sit in the Upper House. Only a plaque recognizing the contribution by the stalwart group reached the Senate lobby, to be unveiled on June 11, 1938.

But Mrs. Murphy was still sitting as a magistrate and her interests were still broad and varied like the landscape in her adopted province. She had been decorated by King George V to become a Lady of Grace of the Order of St. John of Jerusalem. She served as the first president of the Federated Women's Institutes of Canada, vice-president of the National Council of Women of Canada, president of the Canadian Women's Press Club, director of the Canadian Council of Child Welfare, vice-president of the Canadian Association of Child Protection, first president of the Women's Canadian Club of Edmonton, vice-president of the Social Service Council of Canada, and an officer of one grade or another in each of dozens more of Canadian organizations. In addition, she worked to organize many movements, including a campaign to prevent the importation of narcotics to Canada, about which she had the strongest feelings.

Sitting as a judge, she was surprised and shocked at the extent to which alcohol and drugs were responsible for crime and misery. All her life she had been active in support of temperance and after sitting on the bench, she became more and more involved in the fight against narcotics. In this, she worked closely with the National Council of Women. The control of opium entering Canada had been a matter of grave concern to members of that council from 1895. Mrs. Murphy remained one of the most energetic campaigners, declaring against the evils of drugs from the public platform and in her book *The Black Candle*, published in 1922. In 1924 she was the Canadian Government's representative to a League of Nations conference on narcotics in Geneva, an appointment heartily approved by National Council and everybody who knew her convictions.

The lady who was appointed to be a magistrate in 1916, remained in office for fifteen years and then resigned to devote herself more completely to her home, her family, her business interests and her writing. The two years following were relaxed and happy for her but they were short enough. She died suddenly at her home in Edmonton on October 26, 1933. Earlier in the day, she appeared to be in her usual good health, visited the city library, paid a periodic call at the police court and waited for the noon hour to greet working associates of earlier years, and did some shopping. She appeared all right at bedtime but death overtook her before midnight.

People everywhere read the news with sorrow and recognized her death as the passing of a truly great Canadian. The tributes — hundreds of them — came from all parts of the country. Mrs. W. J. Ross, president of the Local Council of Women, said what most people were thinking: "I believe the women of Canada have lost their most wonderful advocate of women's rights." And Nellie McClung, pained by the loss of a close personal friend, added: "Her work will live on . . . her memory will remain green."

In Edmonton, a popular riverside park was named in her honor and there for present-day visitors to see are two bronze plaques as permanent reminders of her useful life. One of these, provided by the Government of Canada, through the National Historic Sites and Monuments Board, carries these words: "Emily Ferguson Murphy, 'Janey Canuck,' a crusader for social reform and for equal status for women, she devoted herself to these causes with unremitting energy. Originator and leader of the movement for the admission of women to membership in the Senate of Canada, she became the first woman magistrate in the British Commonwealth, Judge of the Edmonton Juvenile Court. Her literary works include *Seeds of Pine* and the *Black Candle*. Born in Cookstown, Ontario, 14th March, 1868. Died in Edmonton, 27th October, 1933."

The other plaque, dated August 27, 1960, was "erected by the City of Edmonton Archives and Landmarks Committee, women's organizations and many friends." The message: "This memorial in honour of Emily Ferguson Murphy. Well known for her warm humanity and for her public service which brought her recognition throughout Canada."

Glenbow-Alberta Institute, Calgary, Alberta

LOUISE CRUMMY McKINNEY: DEATH ON BOOZE

Louise Crummy McKinney, a woman of many sterling parts, is remembered mainly as one of Alberta's "Famous Five" who signed the appeal to the Privy Council in 1929, seeking for her sex the right to be named to the Canadian Senate. The granting of the appeal represented one of the greatest political triumphs for Canadian women and members of the Famous Five were at once assured of bronze plaques bearing their names and other monumental expressions of honor in the history of women's suffrage.

Earlier — in 1917 — this prairie farm woman gained international distinction by being one of the first two females to be elected to a legislature in the British Empire, and the first actually to take her seat in the chamber. But notwithstanding these imprints upon the pages of political history, it was her long and unrelenting fight for temperance that constituted the principal battle in her career. In that lifelong struggle conducted in Ontario and then North Dakota and Western Canada, and finally on the world stage, she neither relaxed nor compromised.

Other members of that celebrated little Group of Five

became better known but the full extent of the McKinney influence was never adequately measured. To assess it properly, the assessor would have to weigh the effect of a close relationship which developed between the temperance and feminist movements. As one of the founders of the Women's Christian Temperance Union in Alberta and the West, she brought to it the concept that its influence should extend far beyond the problems of alcohol alone; the organization should concern itself with all matters of public morals. Such a philosophy brought social reform in widely different shades clearly into the orbit of the WCTU. In a sense, therefore, Mrs. McKinney's adventure in politics was the outcome of her involvement with temperance. Having been a leader in the hectic prohibition campaign preceding the Plebiscite of 1915 and then having seen the granting of voting rights to women in the next year, she had witnessed the clearest demonstrations of the power at the command of her sex and it was not surprising that she was ready to be a candidate for election to the legislature in 1917.

Louise was the sixth in a family of ten children, the second of three daughters. She was born at Frankville, Ontario, on September 22, 1868. Parents, Richard Crummy and Esther Empey, were Irish, the father having come from County Cavan to settle in the Upper Canada bush in 1842. Then, to a farm in Leeds County he brought his bride in 1857 — the year in which John Palliser was starting on his famous western expedition — and built a happy home on a foundation of the strictest Methodist precepts.

Louise was a bright girl, fun loving and popular. With a good Irish sense of humor and unusual talent in debate, qualities of leadership showed clearly. She graduated from Athens High School, nursing the hope of entering medical college, but it wasn't easy for girls to gain acceptance to medicine and she resented the discriminating handicap imposed simply because she was a girl. Instead of studying to become a doctor, she attended Normal at Ottawa and then taught public school in Ontario communities for four years. She enjoyed teaching but young people had the will to roam in those years as in later ones and she decided to visit her married sister living in North Dakota. Many Ontario people following land lures had located in the Western States and when in Dakota, Louise accepted another teaching assignment and prepared to stay.

This conscientious girl was becoming more and more exercised about the evils of alcohol and the necessity of adopting temperance or prohibition measures. So strongly did she feel about it even then that she would have committed the remainder of her life to the cause. After three years teaching, she took a position as a Women's Christian Temperance Union organizer there in the Dakotas. At this time James McKinney came into her life. He was a former Ontario boy, one who shared her interests in people, church and prohibition, and in 1896 they made a trip back to her home community in the East to be married.

Returning to what would be the home farm in North Dakota, Louise Crummy McKinney did not end her work for the cause of temperance, although it was now limited to volunteer service. The challenge was in no way lessened and in 1898 she became the district president and prepared to represent her area at the Silver Jubilee National Convention at Seattle in the next year.

From the time of their marriage, neither Louise nor Jim McKinney gave up the idea of returning ultimately to live in Canada and with the turn of the century there was a big movement of settlers from the Western States to the new farming country both north and south of Calgary, Northwest Territories. The McKinneys decided to sell out and move to find homestead land on the Canadian side where many millions of acres remained for the choosing. They came in 1903 and found a homestead quarter section to suit them near Claresholm, south of Calgary, almost in the shadow of the Rockies. The homestead on section 17 was two miles east and one mile south of the village.

Two topics dominated Claresholm conversation at the

time. One was the awful tragedy of the Frank Slide which on the morning of April 29, just a few weeks before the McKinneys arrived, saw a ninety-million ton portion of Turtle Mountain cascade down upon homes and the entrance to the coal mine and account for the deaths of no fewer than seventy-six men, women and children. The other topic inviting conversation concerned the political fortunes and misfortunes of the Northwest Territories, over which Frederick Haultain presided as premier. The time had come, most people agreed, for the area to be granted provincial status but Haultain's blueprint for the change was not acceptable to the Dominion Government and another two years had to pass before Saskatchewan and Alberta would be created.

In coming to the Territories at that time, the McKinneys were part of the biggest wave of settlers to cross the border northward. Among those coming were many of the West's most distinguished pioneers and leaders, men like Henry Wise Wood who settled at Carstairs and Charles S. Noble who became a McKinney neighbor for a short time. Noble not only came in the same year but he came from the same state as the McKinneys, North Dakota, and his homestead about three miles north of Claresholm, was six miles from James McKinney's land. Neighbors watched with fascination as homesteader Noble expanded dramatically from the stage of quarter-section farmer plodding patiently behind a pair of oxen and walking plow in his bare feet, to become, in less than twenty years, the biggest wheat producer in the British Empire — perhaps in the world.

The McKinneys came to farm but they had no sooner arrived than they were immersed in other activities. It was their influence mainly that resulted in the building of the first Methodist church at Claresholm and Mrs. McKinney was only in the district a few weeks when she was promoting a WCTU local. The Temperance branch was formed and Mrs. McKinney was its first president. One year later — still a year before the two provinces were formed — she was in Calgary to meet with women of similar convictions from Regina, Saskatoon, Edmonton and Medicine Hat to form the WCTU of the Northwest Territories. To the new organization embracing twenty locals, Mrs. Craig, of Olds, was named to be president.

After the two provinces were formed in 1905, the Territorial Temperance body divided accordingly and Mrs. Craig continued as the Alberta president until succeeded in that office by Mrs. McKinney in 1908. The Alberta organization continued to grow and flourish and Mrs. McKinney continued to guide it. Even in her most active political years, the temperance work had first call upon her time and energy. Having undertaken to study systematically the effect of alcohol upon drinkers and the nondrinking members of their families, she knew very well the hardship and suffering experienced. Such an enemy as drink should be destroyed; she was filled with zeal to outlaw liquor.

What a record she made! After forming the Claresholm local of the WCTU in 1903, she became the first president and, until 1930, the only one. In the Territorial and provincial fields she was president for twenty-three years. And that was not all; in the Dominion body of the WCTU, she was vice-president or acting president from 1908 for more than twenty-two years and in 1931, a short time before her death, she became president of the Canadian Union and vice-president of the World's WCTU.

During her years in office, every westerner became aware of the organization of women workers. In her presidential capacity she traveled extensively to keep speaking engagements, winter and summer. She personally directed most of the work of organizing and it reached the point where the mere mention of the name of Louise McKinney suggested WCTU, and vice versa. In many ways she was the Frances Willard of Western Canada. Miss Willard, the force behind the United States Temperance movement, resigned from the position of dean of women at Northwestern University in 1874 to become the full-time secretary of the new Women's Christian Temperance Union and then its president. She founded the World's WCTU in 1883 and became its president five years later. Louise McKinney met Frances Willard many times at international meetings and admired her greatly. The Claresholm lady attended the world meetings on various occasions, at Boston as early as 1907 and Lausanne as late as 1928.

Mrs. McKinney had her critics, of course. The liquor interests found her a formidable and persistent opponent and some of those who came under her attack said she was a fanatical old busybody. Her enemies spoke most boldly and loudly when she, in her eagerness to save Canadians from enslavement by alcohol and tobacco, suggested the exclusion of cigarettes from parcels going to soldiers in World War I. Had she been alive sixty years later when much more was known about the serious health dangers resulting from the use of cigarettes, she would have been calling for and demanding stronger measures to prevent advertising and reduce use. In the campaign preceding the plebiscite of 1915 in Alberta, she wished that tobacco as well as liquor could be controlled and outlawed by legislation.

With so much involvement in public service, it was to be expected that she would find common purpose with Nellie McClung and Emily Murphy and Irene Parlby and Henrietta Edwards. The organized temperance and prohibition workers in both Canada and the United States were naturally drawn into other social and moral issues, equal franchise for women, accommodation for immigrants, financial aid for widows and orphans and so on. Like every public spirited woman, Louise McKinney was interested in politics but upon her discovery that the old parties were drawing campaign contributions from liquor companies, she was disgusted and vowed that if she ever became a candidate in an election, it would be as an independent. So it was in 1917 when she agreed to be a candidate for election to the Alberta Legislature, standing in the Claresholm constituency. She was nominated and it was soon apparent that she was running essentially on a prohibition ticket. As a campaigner she was fluent and dignified and tireless, and she won the election. It was just a year after women obtained the right to vote in Alberta, Saskatchewan and Manitoba, and Mrs. McKinney and Miss Roberta McAdams, who was elected by the armed forces overseas, were the first two women to gain this provincial success in the British Empire. And because Miss McAdams was not present when the legislature opened at Edmonton, Mrs. McKinney qualified for the distinction of being the first woman in the British Empire to actually take her legislative seat.

Mrs. McKinney remained as an active member of the legislature for the next four years and failed by forty-six votes to be returned in the upset election of 1921 which saw the United Farmers of Alberta swept to power with thirty-nine out of sixty-one seats in the province.

During her term in the House, Louise McKinney became known as a member who could be aggressive without being offensive. One of the best debaters on either side of the Chamber, she had lots of moral courage and became recognized as an authority on parliamentary procedure. She supported all reasonable measures for social welfare and health, and introduced bills intended to make prohibition more effective, improve the lot of immigrants and bring better security to widows and deserted wives. One of her most important legislative contributions was the introduction of a motion which led to the Dower Act, ensuring a certain proportion of a deceased husband's property for his widow.

But defeat in her second campaign for the seat in the legislature did not worry her. She saw plenty to keep her busy and did not relax in the least. She became more deeply involved in church matters and was named to be a Commissioner for the first General Council of the United Church of Canada and was the only woman to sign the Basis of Union.

In her home community she organized a poetry and reading club, made herself available for counseling and consistently collected food and clothing for needy families. And constantly, of course, there was Temperance Education, the biggest challenge of her life, backed by the conviction that alcoholic beverages had no justifiable place in human lives.

The World Meetings of the WCTU in Toronto in 1931, at which she presided, were very much the climax in her life. Perhaps it was the way she would have ordered it. She became ill during the meetings and died soon after returning home. And her husband, James McKinney, another highly respected pioneer, died in the next year.

Coming so soon after the World Meetings, her death was treated as international news and expressions of admiration for her unselfish crusades came from near and far. As expressed by her only son, Willard — named in honor of Miss Frances Willard, "she loved her work and valued her life as God's gift. She was content to accept the events of life as they came but at the same time did her utmost to make 'all things work together for good. . . .' "[1]

---

[1] McKinney, Willard, *Louis McKinney,* undated, Dominion Literature Depository, London, Canada

Glenbow-Alberta Institute, Calgary, Alberta

IRENE PARLBY:
THE VOICE OF FARM WOMEN

An English girl raised with the proverbial "silver spoon in her mouth" and all the comforts of an upper-class home, should have been, by all the accepted rules, totally unsuited to life on the Canadian frontier. But for Irene Parlby of Alberta, it did not work that way. Nothing in her sheltered youth lessened the fondness she found for agriculture and her loyalty to it. Here, surely, was the setting for storybook romance: a beautiful girl, born in London, educated in some of England's best schools and under the strict eyes of governesses, raised in an atmosphere of Old World culture, and then transplanted by force of circumstances to the new Northwest of Canada where most homes were of log or sod construction and many with dirt floors. The girl who came for a brief holiday visit in that homestead country remained for the rest of her long life and became a distinguished leader.

Irene Parlby is remembered most clearly as one of Alberta's Famous Five who carried the fight for the recognition of Canadian women as "persons" eligible to be appointed to the Canadian Senate. With Henrietta Edwards, Nellie McClung, Emily Murphy and Louise

McKinney, she saw that long-protracted controversy end satisfactorily when the Privy Council sitting in faraway London rendered its decision in 1929; women were indeed persons and women could be senators.

But Irene Parlby's achievements and contributions extended far beyond matters pertaining to women's rights. In being given a cabinet post in the United Farmer's Government of Alberta in 1921, she was the second woman in Canada to hold ministerial rank. Her career in politics was a long one but it may have been in the farm movement that she found her biggest inspirations and her richest experiences. She was to the farm women's organizations of Alberta what Henry Wise Wood was to the men's.

Before her marriage, she was Mary Irene Marryat, born in London, January 9, 1868. Thus, she was sixty-five days older than her great fellow-worker in various social movements, Emily Murphy. Her father, a colonel in the Imperial Army Engineers, was stationed in India and home only temporarily at the time of baby Irene's birth. For two periods in her life the family home was in India but when she was sixteen years old, her father accepted retirement and the family returned to live in Surrey. The young lady received the broadest possible education. She studied music and elocution and might have pursued a career in the theater but members of her family thought it inappropriate for a girl of her rank. She spent some time at school in Germany, some time recovering from an illness in Switzerland, and some time visiting her mother's old home in Ireland. All the Marryats were cosmopolitan in their tastes and travels.

Early in 1896, the family home had as a guest a lady the Marryats knew as a girl in India and who, at the time of the visit, was Mrs. Alix Westhead, home from Canada where she and her husband had settled on a homestead ranch in the far Northwest. She told stirring tales about life in a frontier district where she was the first white woman to become a homemaker. The Marryats were fascinated and before the end of her visit, she startled all of them by inviting Irene to return with her for a holiday in her Buffalo Lake section of the Northwest Territories, about 700 miles beyond Winnipeg. Irene wanted to accept and, to her surprise, her parents gave consent. It was settled; she was going to Canada, even though most acquaintances were sure she would hate it in that lonely part of the world and make a quick return.

It was a long and weary journey, first a slow voyage by sea, then a slow train trip from Montreal to Calgary, a still slower one on the relatively new railroad north to Lacombe, at which point Charles Westhead met his wife and her guest to drive them by team and democrat over the remaining thirty miles of wet trails to the Westhead ranch. The summer had been particularly wet and bridges had been washed out in many places. But the Westhead horses were accustomed to fording streams and succeeded in pulling the democrat to safety on the opposite side of each creek or slough on the trail.

"My first drive from Lacombe, which was the nearest station, 30 miles away," she said later, "was a thing of vivid memories—tumbling out of one mud hole into another, doubling up teams to get through, dropping into a creek and praying the bridge of poles was somewhere under the water and we might be lucky enough to hit the middle of it in the waning light of a summer evening, arriving at the ranch about 11:30 p.m., tired out but thrilled with a feeling of adventure, to find a roaring fire of logs in the living room to welcome us."[1]

In spite of thrills at arrival, the English girl, completely strange to frontier hardships and hazards, did not escape misgivings about this wild land to which she was now committed for a holiday. It would not be surprising if she had prayed that the days would pass quickly to allow a safe return to her native land.

But she was quick to catch the charm of the countryside. The parklike valley stretching to a far horizon was beautiful. Her curiosity was awakened and she found

[1]*The Grain Growers' Guide*, September 25, 1918

much to study and enjoy in the Westhead horses and cattle, the native vegetation, the Canadian birds and then the neighbors living far apart. Most of those people living east of Lacombe and west of Buffalo Lake were interested in ranching more than in grain growing. Hence, settlement was extremely sparse. And almost all the men in the district were unmarried, a point which could never go unnoticed by single ladies like Irene Marryat.

Even though the ranchers and homesteaders lived far from each other, they came together for fun and conversation quite often. A building bee, a pig killing, a coyote hunt or a baseball game was enough to bring them out, and just days after arrival, Miss Irene met the Parlby brothers, Edward and Walter, from Devonshire. Edward, the younger, was the first to come to Canada, Walter having remained in England to complete his formal education at Oxford. They were fun-loving fellows who were ranching a short distance away in the general direction of Lacombe.

Naturally, all the bachelor settlers for miles around were interested in hearing of the lady guest at the Westhead place and even more when they saw this charming young woman with delicate features and refined manner. Every male among them had visions of capturing her affections and installing her as the Queen of his shanty or log shack. But in dispensing encouragement, she had more for the older Parlby man than for any other and he was at once finding excuses for driving to the Westhead home during evenings. He would be looking for a stray steer or coming to borrow a can of axle grease or present a bag of wild mushrooms.

On one of those lovely autumn days, Irene and Walter Parlby drove away toward Lacombe to attend a homesteader's party and the very next day, she was writing to members of her family in England, informing them of the enjoyment she was finding in the holiday and her decision to prolong it. Before the onset of winter, Irene told her friend Alix Westhead of her decision to remain in Canada; she and Walter Parlby would be married in the spring.

Bishop Pinkham came from Calgary to perform the marriage ceremony, which was to be at the little local church. He completed the trip as far as the Westhead home but a spring blizzard blew in and blocked the roads, leaving little chance of the wedding principals getting to the church. Consequently, the ceremony was performed at the house and the honeymoon consisted of a chilly drive through an abating storm to Walter Parlby's Dartmoor Ranch cabin, overlooking what came to be known as "Parlby Lake." Nothing looked very inviting when covered with deep drifts of snow but when the weather cleared and the trees dressed themselves in fresh leaves, Irene Parlby was sure the setting of her new home was one of the loveliest in the world. Life was rich; the countryside became more enticing every day; the tasks of making a garden and making a home were so satisfying.

"Everything was fresh," she said, "and the world seemed so young and interesting. Seeing a country in the making is an interest not given to everyone."

She was busy. There was so much to do, in the house and outside where horses and crops and gardens invited her. And with neighbors who were predominantly bachelors, she found herself cooking and mending for them. She longed to see parents and brothers and sisters again but she knew this was now her home and any absence from it would be only temporary. Two more years passed before she saw England and members of her family again. In 1899, anticipating the arrival of their first baby, Walter and Irene Parlby decided to take a holiday and time their stay in England to coincide with those hours when a young wife needs her mother most.

The holiday was good and then the baby son, Humphrey, arrived to capture the attention of admiring relatives on both sides of his family. Whether it was this new grandson or the stories related by his son-in-law, Colonel Marryat knew he had to see the Canadian Northwest. His visit followed shortly after Irene's return to Canada, and after a few more years, he and most members of his family moved to the same Canadian area, to stay.

The Marryats' arrival with all their belongings and acquisition of land not far from the Parlby place coincided roughly with the birth of the new provinces of Alberta and Saskatchewan. Inauguration day for Alberta, September 1, 1905, remained green in Irene Parlby's memory because she was among those present to see and hear the Governor General and Prime Minister of Canada as they officiated at a decorated stand on the north side of the river at Edmonton. It was not that she was among the invited dignitaries; rather, she was present because Walter Parlby was a member of the Alix polo team invited to participate in the program of events following the official ceremonies.

Rather suddenly, the frontier character was disappearing, like snow under an April sun. A railroad line was being built eastward from Lacombe and the nearest station was called Alix, in honor of Irene Parlby's friend, Alix Westhead. "We just hated seeing the railway coming and the mushroom shacks springing up and the fences shutting in all the nicest bits of range," Irene wrote. "But it had to come." Homesteaders, many from the United States, were flocking into the area and filing on the quarters of even-numbered sections. The newcomers, with the intention of growing wheat and oats, fenced their land, and those who, like the Parlbys, had settled with the idea of ranching more than farming knew they had to change their plans. But they accepted the necessity and were in a position to guide and help the newcomers and win support for community involvement, be it in school matters, sport or cooperative programs.

The growing population and changing scenes seemed to create more problems than they solved. Distance from big consumer markets, high freight rates, federal tariff policy making for higher prices on farm machinery, inadequate school and hospital facilities, and mistrust of the Winnipeg Grain Exchange were the subjects of common complaints and farmers knew they needed the political strength they could only gain by organization. Several groups or societies were appealing for farm support, including the Territorial Grain Growers' Association which had its birth at a protest meeting in Indian Head in 1901, and the Society of Equity with roots in the United States. In 1909, they were joined to give birth to the United Farmers of Alberta and among the new organization's best supporters were the Marryats and Parlbys. Walter Parlby was the first president of the Alix local.

Meanwhile, the women of the area, not to be left out of organization, met and formed the Alix Country Women's Club, with Irene Parlby as secretary. The club was active; a library for the village was one of its achievements and when the United Farm Women of Alberta organized, the Alix Country Women's Club became the very first of the U.F.W.A. locals. Not only were these events important in the history of a developing farm movement but they marked the beginning of a long and useful career of public service for Mrs. Parlby. She insisted always that she had no desire for public life, but one of her conviction and talent could not and did not escape. Her public involvement accelerated.

Women were allowed to take memberships in the United Farmers of Alberta for the first time in 1913. Two years later, at the annual meeting, a Women's Auxiliary was formed. Then, in 1916, at the beginning of the auxiliary's second year, Irene Parlby was elected president. It was a good year and the membership climbed to 1,600. The women were ready to transform their auxiliary to become the United Farm Women of Alberta. Upon reorganization, Mrs. Parlby was re-elected, thus becoming the first president of the U.F.W.A.

It was now up to the president to determine how the organized farm women would use their opportunities. They could have relaxed to make the annual meetings pleasant and sociable occasions and leave the rural problems to the men, or they could embark upon an aggressive campaign for social reform. The great and philosophical Henry Wise Wood became president of the United Farmers of Alberta at the same time the U.F.W.A. had birth and his advice was good. "Be active and aggressive," he urged. "Agricultural people have suffered more than other classes. You women have a task to perform." It was exactly the policy Irene Parlby intended to follow anyway, and she set out to travel and use public platforms available to her.

The new role was not especially easy for her. She spoke forcefully and well but she was still the cultured lady rather than a flamboyant saleswoman. By nature, she was bashful and retiring. But knowing what should be said, she was determined to say it. She would proclaim the cause of cooperation among farming people and all people; she would challenge the Federal Government to follow the example of the three Midwestern Provinces in granting voting privileges to women; she would call for municipal hospitals which might make hospitalization costs a charge against municipalities; and she would demand more consideration for widows and orphans.

And while carrying out these missions, she was doing wartime work with the Red Cross, serving on the Board of Governors of the University of Alberta and serving in various other fields where the needs of women were clear to her. She was determined but not unreasonable and nobody could ever accuse her of being fanatical about the role of women. In her own words. "Western farm women want no women's party. We value our privilege of working on equal terms with the men of our organization. We have heard much of the horrors of a man-governed world and man-made legislation, but Heaven defend us from a world governed solely by women."[1]

She was precisely what the farm women of that day needed. Although an idealist — as every woman is entitled to be — she was practical too. In writing to the *Grain Growers' Guide,* she said: "The farm women are looking fearlessly into the future; they have been building castles in the air for many years, they begin to see that through their organization the building of some of those castles may soon be begun on earth. They look for-

[1] *Grain Growers' Guide,* December 4, 1918

ward to the day when no farm man, woman or child will call in vain for nursing or medical aid, when all farm boys and girls will continue their education until at least 16, with some possibility of continuing their studies after that, when every district will have its community hall and a possibility of good entertainments, music, lectures, plays. They look to the time when the tariff walls will cease to deprive them of so many things that would make life easier, when co-operation will bring them the just fruits of their toil. They have no desire to eat the bread of idleness or grasp what by right belongs to another, but as they see the law of mutual aid working in nature around them, so they ask that it should be allowed to work freely in the human world, no man living unto himself alone, be he manufacturer, laborer or farmer. . . ."[1]

The cruel bruises of war she felt very keenly. In reporting to the U.F.W.A. in January, 1918 (*Grain Growers' Guide,* January 30, 1918) she said with characteristic feeling: "With black clouds of war still darkening the horizon of the whole civilized world, many of our farm mothers have had their hearts pierced by fragments of those shells which are falling on so many battle fronts. . . . It takes all the optimism, all the faith that we can gather up to enable us to discern the silver lining behind the dark and ominous cloud and to determine that, come what may, though we bend like tempered steel to the furious blasts of fate, we will never ignobly break. . . . Nineteen hundred and eighteen is before us calling for yet greater service, yet greater sacrifice. Civilization, such as it is, is at the cross-roads; in every heart there is barely conscious feeling of expectancy; in the silence it seems to us as though great things are stirring in the womb of time, we almost seem to hear the rustle of great events rushing to us through space. What is this old world about to bring forth? What part shall we shortly be called upon to play in this unknown future which is even now about to be born?

"Since the Great War began we have been busy cheer-

[1] *Grain Growers' Guide,* December 4, 1918

ing one another with the thought that the world can never be the same when at last the struggle shall cease. Poor old platitude, how mighty hard it has been worked and even yet it is not dead. What are we doing, you and I, to ensure that this stale platitude shall become a living truth?

"Who are we to say that war shall cease, the world be cured by the quack medicine of a glorious internationalism? Today the world is bleeding to death in its efforts to conquer a false ideal of nationalism, but the only true nationalism, the only true internationalism, is a spirit of mutual sympathy and understanding among all the people — in other words, the spirit of unselfishness which is the essence of this thing we call co-operation. Until we can bring about the birth of that new spirit among the nations, until we can grow it in our homes, our own communities, our own Dominion, [we might] as well cry out to the tides to cease their flowing, as well try to stop the stars in their course as bid wars to cease. Here is work for every individual woman of us, every group of organized women, work in the doing of which you may feel you are being perhaps a little nearer that time when there shall be a new Heaven and a new earth."

It was grand sentiment, beautifully expressed, and the convention audience applauded enthusiastically. But convention enthusiasm, as others have discovered, is difficult to maintain and Mrs. Parlby, the idealist and dreamer, became impatient and discouraged. Physically tired, she wrote to the *Grain Growers' Guide* (May 8, 1918), confessing: "I am beginning to get a little sceptical over convention enthusiasm; it is so effervescent — you take the cork out at the conference, and in a short time everything is frothing up and bubbling over, and it looks as though the most wonderful things were going to happen, but by the time all the delegates get settled down again in their homes, so often nothing but a flat mawkish sediment remains."

The fact was that Irene Parlby was not well and in September of that year, 1918, she submitted her resignation as president of the U.F.W.A. The announcement came as a shock to thousands of members and friends across the prairie and park country.

Came 1921, a year of political upheaval. There had been political rumblings within the United Farmers organization for some time and then, with a postwar slump in farm prices and growing annoyance about tariffs and wheat marketing, the protests became louder. The U.F.A. membership had reached 33,000 and at the annual convention of 1920, a political platform was adopted, also a determination to contest every constituency in the province at the next election.

The election committee, in carrying out its determination to have a well-qualified candidate in every riding, approached Mrs. Parlby, requesting that she allow her name to stand for election. Her health had improved but her reaction was negative. She had no ambition to sit in the legislature. She would work to elect the others. "But," it was mentioned, "you urged farm women to accept every opportunity for public service. You must accept." She paused, then agreed; if the people in her area wanted her as their candidate, she would indeed do her part.

The election was called for July 17, 1921, and the Liberals who had been in power from the birth of the province expected to be returned again. But it was not to be. The election results brought surprise to most Albertans, not excluding the organized farmers who won thirty-nine seats out of a possible sixty-one. The Liberals elected fourteen members, Labor four, Independents three, and Conservatives one. Mrs. Parlby was a winner and among the Liberals winning was Nellie McClung, friend of Irene Parlby, and between them were some unauthorized and unrecorded caucuses.

Nine days after the election, the Farmer members met in Calgary and chose Herbert Greenfield to be their leader. In due course, the Premier-elect announced his new cabinet which included J. E. Brownlee as Attorney General, George Hoadley as Minister of Agriculture and Irene Parlby as Minister without Portfolio. In being so named, she was to be the second woman in Canada and second in the British Empire to gain ministerial rank, having been preceded only by Mary Ellen Smith of British Columbia.

For the next fourteen years or throughout the life of the U.F.A. Government, Irene Parlby represented the Lacombe constituency and held the same cabinet position. She never really developed a love for politics but she was conscientious and won the confidence and respect of colleagues and members of the Opposition alike. While in office, she sponsored or gave active support to numerous provincial acts affecting women and children. She encouraged cooperatives so much that she was dubbed "Minister of Cooperation." She toured the Scandinavian countries expressly to study cooperatives there and when she accepted Prime Minister R. B. Bennett's appointment to be a Canadian delegate to the League of Nations, her highest hope was to find evidence of cooperation at that level.

At the spring convocation in 1935, the University of Alberta honored this lady who had served her province so long and well with an honorary LL.D. degree. It was another "first," because no lady had ever before received such a degree from the University of Alberta.

She might have returned to live in England or gone to the West Coast but her choice for the years of retirement was to settle again in her farming community. Ultimately she was back at Dartmoor Ranch where her son, Humphrey, was in charge. It was good after all those years in public life to be back in the peaceful setting beside Parlby Lake, so rich in memories, and try to get caught up with gardening and writing and housekeeping and welcoming visitors.

On January 9, 1965, Irene Parlby celebrated her ninety-seventh birthday, received the usual spray of flowers and message of affection from the Farm Women's Union of Alberta and numerous letters and telegrams from old friends all over Canada. It was her last birthday, however; she died the following July and was buried at the

Alix cemetery, at the heart of the district which she, as a bride, had adopted sixty-nine years before.

Glenbow-Alberta Institute, Calgary, Alberta

NELLIE McCLUNG: "LOVED AND REMEMBERED"

Every time a woman casts a ballot, she should pause to breathe a prayer of gratitude for the pioneer efforts of Nellie McClung, the unrelenting western crusader for women's rights and a score of other worthy causes. Her zeal was the main reason for Manitoba women being the first in Canada to have the right to vote and the women of the three Midwestern Provinces being the first in the world to gain the same.

The lovable rebel, to whom Manitoba, Alberta and British Columbia had the strongest claims, was in the front line of battle for social reforms for about fifty years, never lacking a good cause. If it wasn't prohibition or votes for women, it could be better working conditions for girls, minimum wages for all workers, women's property rights, mothers' pensions, public health nursing services, free medical care for school children or something else of importance to Canadian homes and homemakers.

She saw so much to do, and with only one lifetime in which to do it, she knew she had to hurry. But with extraordinary energy and imagination, she succeeded in having a succession of careers; at one time or another she was a schoolteacher, homemaker, author, crusader, social worker and politician, all of which she did with distinction. How could one person accomplish so much? Determination and tirelessness explained it in large part. She demanded some useful accomplishment from every day. One of her friends said she wrote her books while waiting to have her babies, but there was a disparity of numbers requiring explanation because she had five babies and fifteen books. As a mother who loved her home and family, she once said it could have been better if she had reversed a few things in her life: instead of producing fifteen books and five babies, she might have had fifteen babies and five books.

As Nellie Mooney, the youngest of six children from an Irish-Canadian father and a Scottish-Canadian mother, she was born on a Grey County farm in Ontario, October 20, 1873. The first contingent of North West Mounted Police had just completed its arduous journey by way of the Dawson Route to Fort Garry and the new province of Manitoba was only three years old.

When the little girl reached the age of seven years, the family moved to a homestead community in the Souris Valley. Until ten years of age she had no opportunity to attend school but thereafter, she made good use of her time and at sixteen was enrolled at the Manitoba Normal School in Winnipeg, preparing for a teaching career. Then, having qualified for a teacher's certificate, Nellie Mooney obtained an appointment at a school near Manitou. More than anybody could have guessed, the years in the district proved important in shaping the girl's entire life. The strongest single influence was that of the local church minister's wife, a woman of fine character, an ardent supporter of the Women's Christian Temperance Union and an advocate of equal rights for women.

Miss Nellie admired the lady and grew to share her convictions. Admitting the attraction, the girl told friends that the minister's wife was the only woman she had known whom she believed she would like to have as a mother-in-law. Whether the comment was intended to be taken seriously or not, the indicated wish was one to be realized. When the lady's son, Robert Wesley McClung, returned home from college, the two young people stared at each other with a fascination neither had known before. He was a fun-loving youth with good features and a ready smile. She was a beautiful girl of medium height and with precision in her speech. They enjoyed being together and before long they were married and Nellie McClung got the mother-in-law of her choice.

She took to writing. It was a most unusual pastime on the western frontier but rather logical for a girl who was bursting with ideas she wanted to share. Her first book, *Sowing Seeds In Danny,* appeared in 1911, the refreshing story of a small-town family struggling to survive. Danny was the youngest of nine Watson children whose father worked as a section hand on the railroad and whose mother augmented her grocery money by washing clothes for the neighbors. The first Watson home was a Canadian Pacific Railway boxcar, but as children were born, the quarters had to be enlarged, one shanty-like addition after another until the home "looked like a section of a wrecked train."

Canadians were surprised to find an author living on the Western Prairies, of all places, and bought books to satisfy a curiosity and learn something about this Danny fellow. Sales soared and the publisher rejoiced at having a book of Western Canadian origin which had to be reprinted again and again. Nothing like that had happened before. With sales reaching close to 25,000 copies, the book was profitable to the author, and naturally, she wanted to continue with her writing.

Through her books and magazines articles, Nellie McClung was becoming known far beyond the Manitoba community. Thousands of people who never saw her came to know her as the woman with strong opinions about prohibition and social reform. "Sure," she was saying, "women belong in the home, but not for twenty-four hours a day. They should have exactly the same freedoms as their men."

With a family of four sons and one daughter, the McClungs, in 1911, moved to live in Winnipeg where the father had been appointed to a new position in insurance. For Mrs. McClung, the big city offered big opportunities for study and big challenges for service. Here was poverty more pronounced than anything she had seen in the farming districts and here were men and women working under conditions that shocked her.

Almost at once she was engrossed in social work and seizing public platforms to speak out against the injustices she saw. And coinciding precisely with her arrival was the rejuvenation of the earlier campaign to obtain voting rights for the women of Manitoba. As early as 1893, there had been an Equal Suffrage Society in Winnipeg, of which Dr. Amelia Yeomans was the prime mover, but with her departure and lack of continuing leadership, the movement failed and disappeared. The most effective continuing force was the Women's Christian Temperance Union, of which Nellie McClung's mother-in-law was for a long time provincial leader. In the year in which Wesley McClung brought his family to Winnipeg, however, the Political Equality League of Manitoba was formed, with Mrs. A. V. Thomas as the first president.

Members of the new organization were deadly serious and their program was carefully prepared. Among other things, a speakers' committee was formed to train and direct young people to take and address meetings in various parts of the province. Although those who volunteered were predominantly young women, some young men offered their services and were accepted. The Provincial Government was not sympathetic but support was coming from some unexpected places. The WCTU had the longest record of support but now the Grain Growers' Association was giving endorsation and scattered editors — including Bob Edwards of the *Calgary Eye Opener* — were doing the same.

With other members of the League, Nellie McClung was more convinced than ever that to be effective in correcting social injustices, women had to have the instrument of the franchise. At once she was a leader, the League's most popular public speaker.

Came 1914. Nowhere in Canada and nowhere in the world had women been granted full voting rights in provincial, state and national elections. British women were gaining notoriety for their belligerence in the struggle; Emmeline Pankhurst and her colleagues had effected considerable destructiveness. Mrs. McClung, with no less zeal, believed it was not necessary to go on window-breaking sprees in order to gain attention. Her oratory and logic were the best of all instruments and she and her friends resolved to carry their cause directly to the Premier of Manitoba with an orderly show of strength.

On the afternoon of January 27, 1914, several hundred women and a few men representing the Political Equality League of Manitoba, the WCTU, the pioneer Icelandic Women's Suffrage Association, the Women's Civic League, the Mothers' Association, the Manitoba Grain Growers' Association and the Trades and Labor Council streamed into the Legislative Building in Winnipeg. They filled the halls, filled the Chamber, filled the galleries, and confronted the uneasy Premier, Sir Rodmond Roblin, while Mrs. McClung, as leader and spokesman, skillfully delivered the main message: If democracy was to be more than a sham, women had to be permitted to share to the full and Manitoba should be the first place to provide the necessary legislation.[1]

"We are not here to ask for a reform or a gift or a favor, but for a right — not for mercy but for justice. Have we not the brains to think, the hands to work, hearts to feel, and lives to live? Do we not bear our part in citizenship? Do we not help to build the empire? And in addition to all this we pay the life tax on existence. No man can know as a woman does the cost of human life.

"Perhaps you will tell me that politics are too corrupt for women. I've never heard a satisfactory explanation of why politics should be corrupt. There is nothing inher-

[1] *The Grain Growers' Guide,* February 4, 1914

ently vicious about politics and the politician who says politics are corrupt is admitting one of two things — that he is party to that corruption or that he is unable to prevent it. In either case we take it that he is flying the white flag of distress and we are willing and ever anxious to come over to help him. . . . How would you, Sir Rodmond, like to be governed by a parliament of women?''

The Premier, who had been in power for almost fourteen years, listened attentively and a little nervously. He was polite but at the end of the submission, when he was expected to reply, he confessed that he was not convinced by the argument from the ladies. He conceded that "this is a large, respectable, very intellectual delegation," but he could not get away from the view that the extension of the franchise would be a backward step.

"There is the question of conditions in the Motherland," he said gravely. "There the women are appealing to the authorities for the suffrage. As you know, we all draw our inspiration in legislation, theology, art, science and other subjects from the Motherland. Now, that being a fact that none will dispute, can you, can anyone, in confidence say that the manifestations that have been made by the women there constitute a guarantee that if the franchise is extended, what we have today will be preserved and not destroyed."

It was a horrible thought but "if a few short days of disappointment as in England, caused such hysteria as to endanger human life and result in the destruction of millions of dollars worth of property, is that not cause for the authorities to hesitate in extending the suffrage to women?"

His convictions were clear. If it was not safe for the Mother of Parliaments to trust women with the vote, it would be a mistake for Manitoba to rush into such a program. He had "great respect for women" but he would have to vote against any measure for the extension of the franchise.

Perhaps Nellie McClung did not expect any more in encouragement at that stage in the campaign but her determination was unshaken and she had a final comment: "Sir Rodmond, we have come to the last ditch in our onward march towards freedom and usefulness and we are stretching out our hands to you to help us over. It is now your move."

The Winnipeg women were making history and this was one of Nellie McClung's finest hours.

Convinced that a subtle approach would be more effective than violence, the women rehearsed for the famous Mock Parliament which was held in Walker Theatre in Winnipeg on January 29, 1914, just two days after their appearance at the Legislative Building. Humor and laughter might win where anger would fail. The Mock Parliament, a clever satire on the Roblin Government, was an overwhelming success. Winnipeg people laughed heartily and told their friends to be sure to see the show on the second evening. The star performer was Nellie McClung who played the part of Premier as the women in power rejected the request for Votes For Men. Playing with her were some well-known Manitoba personalities: Mrs. Francis Graham as Speaker; Dr. Mary E. Crawford as Minister of Education; Miss Kenneth Haig as Attorney General; Mrs. Genevieve Lipsett Skinner as Minister of Agriculture; Miss Clendennan as Provincial Secretary; Miss Alma Graham as Clerk; Mrs. Crossley Greenwood as Seargeant-At-Arms; Misses Florence McClung and Ruth Walker as pages, and Mrs. A. A. Perry as Leader of the Opposition.

Three gentlemen in the cast, R. C. Skinner, A. V. Thomas and Percy Anderson, were there as a delegation requesting Votes For Men, and seeing their petition sadly rejected. Men, it was aruged, were not qualified. The Premier delivered the decision: men could not be trusted with the ballots. "Men's place is on the farm."

The audience howled with laughter and friends of the government were embarrassed. Requests to repeat the performance at outside points came quickly. Nellie McClung and her friends were capturing Manitoba imagination and doing further injury to the aging and scandal-ridden Roblin Government which was to lose seats later in 1914 and go down to defeat in 1915. The new Premier, Liberal T. C. Norris, came to power with a promise that Manitoba women would be given the vote. Good as his word, the necessary legislation was introduced at the first session and on January 27, 1916 — two years to the day after Nellie McClung and her orderly army of women marched upon the Capital — the desired amendment to the Manitoba Election Act was given third reading. At the instant the Bill passed that final stage, eager women and a few male supporters crowding the galleries, stood and sang "O Canada," then took up the strain of "For They Are Jolly Good Fellows." What under ordinary circumstances would have been regarded as a serious breach of parliamentary conduct seemed to disturb nobody and pandemonium reigned for some minutes. The Manitoba women were the first in Canada to gain voting privileges although similar legislation was passed in Saskatchewan and then in Alberta just days later. In the final legislative vote in Manitoba, there was only one dissenting voice, that of the member for Ste. Rose, but the women were in a forgiving mood and invited him to their victory banquet to propose a toast to their success and he accepted.

But by this time of triumph in Manitoba, the McClung home was in Edmonton; Wesley McClung had been transferred and his loving wife accompanied him, even though she was in the best possible position for a political career in the province where her campaigning had been so effective. The Manitoba women, however, did not overlook the unparalleled part rendered by Nellie McClung.

It did not matter, however, where the lady lived; she would see plenty to do wherever she was and in Alberta she was involved at once in prohibition work and the local battle to gain voting rights for members of her sex. She rejoiced to see two Alberta women, Mrs. Louise McKinney and Miss Roberta McAdams, elected in 1917 to the legislature. Miss McAdams was elected while serving overseas but when Mrs. McKinney took her seat in the

Alberta Legislature, she was the first woman in the British Empire to do so.

Nellie McClung was elected as a Liberal member of the legislature in 1921, the year in which the Farmers' party was swept into power in Alberta. Miriam Green Ellis said that men in the Press Gallery at Edmonton "adjudged her about the best student of legislation in the entire group." Of course, her quick wit stood her in good stead. Those in the Press Gallery remembered when a young member with a reputation for giving his opinion on every question, complained about missing a certain opportunity to speak. Nellie McClung followed, "regretting" that proceedings were moving too fast for him, causing him to break a record, for, as far as she could recall, "the honorable member has never had an unuttered thought in this House."

Ever a forceful personality with unyielding views of right and wrong, she was a good member of the legislature but not a good party woman. She favored free medical and dental treatment for school children, mother's allowances, better property rights for women and she was not opposed to divorce and birth control. Her opposition to liquor never changed but prohibition was losing its former strength as a popular cause, and in the provincial election of 1926, she suffered defeat. But she was as busy as ever. Joining forces with Emily Murphy, Canada's first woman magistrate, she helped in the fight for the female right to sit in the Senate, taking the matter through the Supreme Court to the Privy Council to establish the fact under the British North America Act that women are indeed "persons" and must be eligible to sit as Senators.

Mrs. McClung did not escape criticism from those people who chose to believe that women should stay at home and give full time to families. But nobody could ever say that her family had been neglected. One son was a Rhodes scholar, one became a deputy minister and all five children did well and were justifiably proud of their mother.

Again the McClungs moved, this time, in 1933, to

British Columbia, where the distinguished wife and mother died in 1951. Miriam Green Ellis reminded friends that "the last few years were not easy for Nellie M." She suffered a lot but never lost her sense of humor. "Toward the end she was lying very still. Wes wondered if she had gone. But with a little twitch she opened her eyes. 'Oh, I'm still here. I'll never believe I'm dead till I see it in the paper,' and she closed her eyes again."

Who among Canadian women had more to show for a lifetime of service? In addition to careers in writing, teaching, homemaking, politics and crusading, she served as the only woman on the Dominion War Council in 1918, the only member of her sex to represent Canada at the Ecumenical Council of the Methodist Church in 1921, first woman on the Canadian Broadcasting Corporation Board of Governors, Canada's only woman representative at the League of Nations in 1918. If Canada had a superwoman, she had to be Nellie McClung, for whose memory the Women's Institute of Grey County, Ontario, erected a beautiful cairn on the property on which she was born, unveiling it with proper dignity in 1957.

Her tombstone in a Victoria, British Columbia, cemetery displays the simple epitaph: "Loved and Remembered." Nobody can know the political and social history of Canada — Western Canada in particular — without some knowledge of the life and contributions of Nellie McClung, the idealist, the one who insisted that "Nothing is too good to be true."

MIRIAM GREEN ELLIS: THE LADY WITH THE NOTEBOOK

"You're Miriam Green Ellis," said a Saskatchewan farmer, stopping her on a Regina street. "I've never met you but I know you. Every Westerner who can read knows you."

It was the sort of greeting directed at her hundreds of times. Being a big lady with commanding presence, she was relatively easy to identify. And if more were needed, her blue eyes, breezy manner, heavy walking stick, utilitarian dress at a time when women had not adopted breeches and high boots, and black Scottie dog following dutifully at her heels would remove all doubt. If she did not have the most widely known name in all the West in those years when she was covering the agricultural scene, at least nobody had a better knowledge of the country. Between Winnipeg and the Pacific coast, she knew the highways, the railroad timetables, the hotels, and the farms on which the best livestock were kept. The observation that Miriam Green Ellis could call most purebred bulls in prairie herds by their first names was an exaggeration but it was not as far from the truth as many people would have imagined.

Familiarity with the farming communities came from a forty-year association with agricultural journalism and twenty-four years as Western Editor of the *Family Herald and Weekly Star*. Her unceasing efforts to understand the constantly changing problems facing agriculture and present the story accurately gave her writing the full weight of authority. Often she was the only female in an audience of males attending a sale or convention and there were times when men resented her presence, but nothing would dissuade her when she knew it was her right and duty to be there.

With her passing on November 19, 1964, at the age of eighty-three, the West lost one of its most knowledgeable and loyal voices, and the story of her life and service deserves to be engraved beside the records of Cora Hind, Emily Murphy and Nellie McClung, all of whom were her close friends.

A Western Canadian by adoption, Miriam Green Ellis was born in the United States. Her parents were Canadians living temporarily across the border and the baby's birthplace was Ogdenburg, New York. Before the girl was old enough for school, the family returned to Canada and lived at Brockville, Ontario. Frequently in those childhood years, she spent summer months with a grandmother on an Ontario farm. There her interest in the outdoors and wonders of nature was awakened and throughout her life she found the greatest of delight in roses and robins and farm animals. It was beyond her understanding that modern boys would be obsessed with machines when dogs and horses and squirrels were so much more wonderful.

Although her career was in journalism, her earliest ambition was to be a medical doctor; but medicine was not regarded as a proper profession for a girl and she was discouraged. She turned to music and did well in Toronto Conservatory examinations. After teaching music for a while, she knew it was not the field to which she wanted to devote her life. She confessed to a secret fascination for journalism, about which she knew nothing.

Living at Prince Albert, Saskatchewan, when the place was still frontier, she submitted a news story to the local paper and at once the editor offered her a job as a reporter. That was in 1914 and she was embarking upon a career. Two years later she was reporting for the *Regina Post* and after another year she accepted a similar assignment with Hon. Frank Oliver, founder and publisher of the *Edmonton Bulletin*. Oliver was the robust pioneer who had ox-carted a printing press over the thousand-mile trail from Winnipeg to Edmonton in 1880 to start the first newspaper to appear on Alberta soil. After many years in both politics and publishing, he was a leading figure.

The Frank Oliver training and discipline made a lasting impression upon the young reporter struggling to prove that a woman could fill the role fully as well as a man. She accepted all assignments given to her, covered the legislature, the police court and public meetings, but her greatest pleasure was in getting away to report a country fair or plowing match.

"She's the best damned man I've got," said Frank Oliver, and then agreed that an attempt should be made to interpret agriculture more completely than it had been done before. If she elected to spend more time in rural areas, he would have no objection. It was all the encouragement she needed.

What Cora Hind was demonstrating in Winnipeg, Miriam Green Ellis was confirming at Edmonton, that men had no monopolistic claim upon the profession of agricultural journalism. Cora Hind, with the *Winnipeg Free Press* and Miriam Green Ellis with the *Edmonton Bulletin* were the first representatives of their sex to venture successfully into this field which was long regarded as for men only. And, having entered farm journalism, both attained a prominence which made male workers look with both wonder and admiration.

While covering agriculture for the *Bulletin,* Miriam Green Ellis ventured farther and farther afield and in 1919, set out to capture, first-hand, the story of the faraway Peace River country. It was the freshest of all frontiers at that time and she traveled as far as Waterhole, later known as Fairview. Accommodation could be anything from a mat on a kitchen floor to a vermin-infested room over a restaurant. But her reports were timely and lively and Frank Oliver was pleased.

Catching the vision of the new North, she wanted to see more of it and in 1922, while still with the *Bulletin,* she made a riverboat trip down the Mackenzie to Aklavik and gathered material for stories and lectures. It was one of the great adventures of her life and she proved to be a most capable person in interpreting the North for the benefit of Canadians and Americans. Following her return, she gave a series of ten illustrated lectures in New York and then accepted a circuit of Canadian Club meetings in Canadian cities to relate what she saw of the wonders and charms of the North.

Newspapers and magazines in many parts of the continent asked for stories about the Canadian Arctic and this demand caused her to quit the daily paper and adopt freelance writing. She knew her resources for articles about the North would become exhausted but the farm scene would offer unlimited opportunities. From the time of her first adventure in free-lancing, the *Family Herald and Weekly Star,* published in Montreal, was one of her best customers and before long she was the paper's leading western contributor. Nobody was surprised when, in 1928, she accepted the appointment of Western Editor of the Montreal paper and moved to make headquarters at Winnipeg. At once she began systematic coverage of fairs and exhibitions, bull sales, seed fairs and farm conventions. It was a program destined to continue for almost the next quarter of a century. For most of those years, the agricultural fraternity knew no more familiar figure than the Western Editor of the *Family Herald,* dressed distinctively and accompanied by a Scotch terrier dog. Her adoption of breeches as showring attire was seen as a rather daring gesture, and it was something of a sensation when she and her colleague and friend, Cora Hind, appeared together in such dress at an eastern exhibition. A few women looked the other way and, as told by the western editor, "one Ontario farm wife looked at my clothes and didn't invite me in."

But those breeches were adopted because they were useful and had pockets. On one occasion, however, embarrassing trouble started in a hip pocket. It was in the showring at Edmonton and Charlie Yule had just won a championship with a young Shorthorn bull. Miriam Green Ellis approached for a closer inspection of the champion and was greeted by a kick from the ungrateful young critter. The blow struck on the pocket of the controversial breeches. Minutes later, somebody drew attention to the odor of burning cloth. Men felt in their pockets for burning pipes and Miriam discovered that in delivering the kick, the champion bull had caused a package of matches in her pocket to ignite. Before the fire was extinguished, her pocket was destroyed and some pain was experienced.

Miriam Green Ellis was more than a reporter. In writing an article, she wanted the story behind the story, and in conducting the customary inquiry, she studied human behavior and found significance in everyday experiences. The changing scenes accompanying western progress intrigued her and the decline in human resourcefulness and vigor bothered her. "What is happening to the self-reliance of the pioneers?" she asked. "The railways and planes seem to be crowded by people traveling to Ottawa with demands and requests. They could do more for themselves and they should not be so ready to ask the government for everything."

As might have been expected, she was one of the pioneers in the Canadian Women's Press Club and a most enthusiastic member. With an association covering fifty years, many of her dearest friends were in the organization. As a long-time honorary president of the Saskatchewan branch of the Canadian Women's Press club, and occasionally a member of the national executive, she was a popular speaker at meetings of locals where members liked nothing better than to get their friend Miriam to reminisce about great personalities in Canadian journalism, Emily Murphy, Genevieve Lipsett Skinner, Agnes Laut, Susanna Moodie, Lillian Thomas, Kennethe Haig and scores of others.

Retirement came in 1952 and there was a big dinner in Winnipeg in her honor. Scientists, writers, civil servants, politicians and farmers came from five provinces to pay their respects and recall their experiences with "Miriam." They told of her devotion and loyalty to western agriculture. They told of her patience in ensuring accuracy for her reports. They told of her impatience when she thought the men around her were at fault. They told of Miriam and her short-legged Scotty dog being in the showring at Calgary when Arthur Crawford-Frost was showing Herefords and the cattleman said: "Miriam, will you please take that low-set dog out of the ring; it makes my cattle look long-legged by contrast." And they repeated the lady's own story about a time when she was in Montreal with Genevieve Lipsett Skinner, formerly with the *Winnipeg Telegram* and heard her tell how some "easy money" could be made by purchasing a certain market stock. Reluctantly, Miriam did buy a small amount of the share stock and then regretted her action. Next day she decided to sell and discovered to her surprise that the shares had advanced slightly in value and she could make a modest profit. Back in Winnipeg, when the women at the Press Club wanted to know what she had done in Montreal, the lady, with a sly grin, replied: "Well, I made a hundred dollars in Simmons' beds." But the members of the Press Club knew Miriam Green Ellis and were not easily shocked.

Western Producer Photograph

VIOLET McNAUGHTON: THE MIGHTY MITE

Of the Women's Editor of *The Western Producer,* somebody said: "She's little but she's wise; she's a terror for her size."

Violet McNaughton would have had to stand on tiptoes to make five-feet-two and her lifelong friend and admirer, Miriam Green Ellis, in speaking of the little lady's appearance to receive an honorary degree, Doctor of Laws, from the University of Saskatchewan in 1951, said: "Her ladies-in-wating had a bad time turning up enough of her ceremonial robes so she could walk."

But it wasn't necessary to be big and muscular to be an effective fighter and crusader, and again and again this dedicated little woman, like a mounted knight pursuing dragons and tyrants, carried her campaigns on behalf of farm women out across the Prairies and beyond.

Most Western Canadians came to know her as the first editor of the women's section of *The Western Producer,* a role she filled for exactly a quarter of a century after accepting it in 1925. But by that date she was already a well-known figure to rural people, especially in reform circles.

Association with western farming began in 1909 when this petite English girl, then Violet Jackson, came to Saskatchewan to join her father and brother, "bringing with me my piano and rolling pin." Saskatchewan as a province was just four years old and Saskatoon, where the immigrant girl paused briefly, had a population of about 12,000 and was fixed upon earlier in the year to be the site of the University of Saskatchewan. Along the Goose Lake Line, westward, most men were homesteaders and bachelors with a pronounced interest in every unmarried girl venturing into the area. Romance followed almost immediately upon Miss Violet's arrival and before long she married homesteader John McNaughton of the Harris district and moved to take up housekeeping in his sod hut. Like his wife, John McNaughton was scholarly and thoughtful, and like her he was small in stature. Neighbors referred to them as "the pony pair."

Violet McNaughton had much to learn about the Canadian Prairies but she was no stranger to farming, having grown up on an English farm from which she had turned to accept a teaching career. As she cycled through the beautiful English countryside, going to and from her school, her attachment for the land and fondness for nature were solidly cemented. Someday, she knew, she would return to the soil. In the meantime she was becoming overwhelmed by the many social needs of her time, voting privileges for women among them. She became an active supporter of the suffragette group although she never confessed to participation with Emmeline Pankhurst in window-smashing sprees.

In Saskatchewan she felt the same restless urge to be active in improving conditions for women, especially farm women. John McNaughton was already an enthusiastic member of the Saskatchewan Grain Growers. Why, she asked firmly, shouldn't farm women be able to participate in such an organization along with their men? The answers did not satisfy her. She was unrelenting, and as a consequence, women were admitted to the pioneer agrarian organization in 1914 and Mrs. McNaughton became the first president of the women's section. That was just the beginning of her public service on the farm frontier.

She was not an office-seeker. More important than being in a position of leadership was the hope of obtaining better medical services for farm women — all women — and better home conditions. The establishment of municipal hospitals followed and she was encouraged.

Then there was the long struggle to obtain equal franchise for members of her sex. In demanding voting privileges for women, she had the support of the Grain Growers' Associations — or they had her support — and she was doing in Saskatchewan what Nellie McClung and Emily Murphy and Henrietta Edwards were doing in the neighboring provinces. As Miriam Green Ellis recalled: "She was the first president of the Saskatchewan Equal Franchise League; I know because I was secretary."

She had her own quiet and determined way of getting things done and when she knew she was in the right, she would not be deterred. Some of her friends could tell that while birth control information and aid were still contraband, she had underground channels, by means of which needy mothers could obtain assistance.

In the light of her campaigns and writings, it was not surprising that she was one to whom the governments looked for advice. In 1918, for example, in the last months of World War I, the federal government invited her to Ottawa to obtain her views about farm and resource problems. And private members, both federally and provincially, were frequently seeking her opinions. Moreover, with success in organizing farm women in Saskatchewan, it was to be expected that she would be asked to assist in similar undertakings in other provinces — including Ontario. And when the Canadian Council of Agriculture was organized, who was to become the first president of the womens' section? The answer: Violet McNaughton.

She loved the home farm west of Saskatoon, loved even the memories of the sod house used in the homestead years, the experiences with oxen and the necessity of hauling water by means of oxen and stoneboat, when after much loss from splashing on the rough trail to the homesite, the exasperating oxen were ready to consume all that remained. It was then necessary to go back for another load of water. She loved the realization of progress on the Harris farm and the tranquillity of the prairie scene. But it was too much to hope that anyone with Violet McNaughton's convictions and vitality and talent would be left to relax in the farm setting.

It was obvious that she could write with skill, but a career in journalism was something she had not considered — until that day in 1925 when Harris Turner, Editor of the infant *Western Producer* in Saskatoon, invited her to join his editorial staff and take charge of a women's section. Turner, left totally blind from World War I service, had varied experience in journalism. He and his friends took over a bankrupt paper and published *Turner's Weekly* in 1918. But it failed to survive beyond 1920, by which time he was a member of the Saskatchewan Legislature. Again he held the position of editor when another paper, the *Progressive,* appeared on August 27, 1923, just after the start of the campaign to launch the Saskatchewan Wheat Pool. Very soon, the *Progressive* was renamed, appearing on September 18, 1924, as *The Western Producer,* to be the official organ of the Saskatchewan Wheat Pool.

For the new position of women's editor, Harris Turner wanted someone who had the earthy feel of the farm, someone who could speak for as well as about rural women. He had watched Violet McNaughton and wanted her to join him. She not only accepted but remained for twenty-five years and continued to contribute her column, Jottings By The Way, for still more years.

In the second issue in which her section for women appeared, April 19, 1925, she issued A Call For Women Readers. Western women, she said in the Call, want to do more than make a living; they want to live a full life with better homes and more conveniences. "Will you cooperate with me in using this page for discussion of efforts that we can make to attack economic problems . . . and social ones too? Will you send in ideas and suggestions . . . comments on the Poultry Pool, our educational system, labor saving devices, how to make farm life more attractive, and on the hundred and one questions that please or vex you? The mail bag is fairly full now, but there is room for more letters from the women readers."

Farm women accepted the challenge and the McNaughton pages bristled with vitality. At first she conducted her editorial responsibilities from the farm home where there were only two incoming and two outgoing mails per week. "But rain or shine or 40 below, the mail always came through and my deadline was saved."

Being a well-known personality before assuming the new work of journalism, her columns were widely read and readers included men almost as much as women. Topics ranged over a broad field of human affairs, homemaking, farm economics, medical aid for prairie mothers, gardening, conservation of resources, international understanding, and certainly anything which might further the cause of peace.

Her citizenship had a global quality about it and differences in race and skin color had no place in it. Perhaps her attendance at London University where students from many parts of the world attended, stimulated her cosmopolitan interests. She was a most appropriate choice to represent Canada at the Women's International League For Peace and Freedom, held at Prague. Immigrants to Canada, especially women and children, were ever a concern to her and she labored to establish hostels for them in widely scattered parts of the country.

Any human need was enough to bring her to action, whether it was inadequacy in hospital facilities or an absence of library services, or any of a score of other matters touching Western women. Friends recalled the strong stand she took on behalf of better training for deaf children. Speaking on the occasion of the first Farm Women's Week at the University of Saskatchewan, she demanded: "Is there a woman here who could rest content if she knew that there were children in the province imprisoned, shut off from the world around them by lack of hearing?" Certainly she could not and would not rest content while people were neglected or suffering needlessly or being oppressed. It was in recognition of such record of service that Violet McNaughton, in 1934, was honored with Membership in the Officers' Division of the Order Of The British Empire, entitled thereafter to write O.B.E. after her name. And after 1951 when she was the recipient of an honorary degree from the University of Saskatchewan, she was Dr. Violet McNaughton.

Retirement from the position of editor of the women's section of *The Western Producer* came in 1950 but it was not complete retirement because she continued to write and continued to be busy with other things. Having been associated with the paper from its beginning, she was too much a part of it to accept complete separation. In a sense she had been part of it even before its beginning because she was a director of the Saskatchewan Grain Growers' Association when the organization recognized the need for a weekly paper. Looking back upon her work in journalism she insisted that it had been "a labor of love" and she would continue to contribute a column at least. "I'll rest when I die," she said.

Prairie people would not forget her, as she never forgot them. Her memory was almost proverbial. On this point Miriam Green Ellis wrote: "One day she borrowed a song from me and in due course it was returned; now who else but Violet would have remembered, twenty-five years after, from whom she had borrowed a song."

The image she left was that of a bright-eyed little lady, plainly dressed, often too busy to stop for dinner, making no effort to attract attention, but friendly and sympathetic and filled with that brand of determined resolve which kept Saskatchewan people on their homesteads through years of drought and adversity.

"A Bonny Fighter," was the way her coworker, Rose Jardine, described her.

Provincial Archives, Victoria, B.C.

EMILY CARR: ARTIST AHEAD OF HER TIME

It took Canadians a long time to discover Emily Carr. Even the leading art connoiseurs of the period overlooked her. It was another case of an artist being without honor in her own country. Had she practiced conventional painting, it might have been different. But as an exponent of creative art — bringing feeling such as the camera cannot catch — she was half a century ahead of her time. Most viewers simply did not understand and it bothered her. Rather than expose her pictures to public ridicule and invite a viewer to pronounce them "grotesque" and "hideous," she was inclined to keep them to herself. And when they failed to satisfy her fully, she chose to destroy them quickly. Nobody will every know how many of her paintings were consigned to the garbage can or the flames of the kitchen stove.

Her sisters, knowing she had the talent to be a most popular artist, pleaded with her to make the kind of pictures people wanted and forget about "this new way of seeing things"; better, they argued, to paint objects as they are. But Emily refused to change, even though change might have brought a promise of public acceptance and a guarantee of bigger monetary returns. Honesty demanded that she paint her objects as she saw them. The impressionist pictures from her brush were part of her, almost like children of her own creating, and if nobody was interested, she would paint them anyway.

People knowing Emily Carr would have been sure that she would paint and write and act by her own convictions. They could say she was eccentric but she would be herself. Neibhbors talking in whispers made rude remarks about that Carr woman living alone and painting funny pictures, calling her a crabby old maid. Some wished she would move away and take dogs, cats, monkey, and various other animal pets constituting her strange menagerie with her.

They knew her only as they saw her on the street, slightly forbidding in appearance, defiant in walk, chunky in build, drab in dress and never without at least one dog. That she loved children and animals was well known and that she was impatient with human adults was almost as well known. But the fact remained that citizens of Victoria did not really understand Emily Carr and Canadians elsewhere allowed her work to pass practically unnoticed.

Instead of making her living by the sale of paintings as even a mediocre artist would hope to do, she was obliged to run a boarding house and breed dogs and sell pottery to pay for her paints and her food. While some artists sold paintings to meet the cost of keeping dogs and horses, she sold dogs to support her unprofitable indulgence in art. It was easy for her to conclude that she was a failure. Only later in her rather tortured life was the excellence of Emily Carr's work recognized and the lady herself acclaimed as one of the great Canadian artists. By that time it was beyond her belief.

She was born in Victoria on December 13, 1871, the year in which British Columbia became the sixth Canadian province to enter Confederation. A severe snow storm gripped Vancouver Island on the night of the baby's birth, perhaps an omen of the gales which were to rage within her in later years. Her mother was a small, frail and gentle lady, her father a severe and uncompromising disciplinarian. He was an Englishmen who joined the gold rush to California and found the venture profitable. Returning to England, he married and took his bride back to California. After a few more years, he brought his young family to Victoria where he built a fine home a few blocks from the waterfront at Horseshoe Bay.

Emily was the youngest of four girls in the family and by most opinions, the problem child. The others were well mannered. Emily was unpredictable, her moods about as changeable as the Pacific breezes. Too often her antics were unbecoming in one of Victoria's "best families." She was an attractive child and fairly clever but nobody knew what she was likely to do next. She had an unsavory affinity for the barnyard; she was the one who tore her clothes, climbed trees, fell in the mud and wandered away and became lost in the forest and enjoyed it. If one of the girls was in trouble, it was sure to be Milly, as Emily was called most often.

From earliest years, she had a passionate fondness for animals and this appeared to inspire her art. Even before reaching school age, she was sketching her dog, observing the instructions she voiced in later years, to draw or paint from living subjects rather than copy. While still little more than an infant she was sketching a portrait of her father, sufficient to please him to the point of pressing a gold coin into her hand.

Miss Emily lost both parents before she was out of high school years, her mother first and her father two years later. She missed her mother particularly, the only member of the family who seemed to understand her peculiar tastes and dreamy ways. The father's estate was sufficient to provide further education and Emily chose to attend the Mark Hopkins School of Art at San Francisco. That school, at which she enrolled when almost eighteen years of age, proved to be a happy experience and she remained there for six years, studying the techniques of traditional art, still unconscious of the new idea of trying to capture her own feeling about a subject and recording it in paint.

Widespread economic recession in the 90's had its effect upon her father's estate and Emily was obliged to discontinue her studies, but back at Victoria she was asked to start an art class for children. With a natural fondness for little people, she agreed to the assignment and gladly converted the hayloft of the family barn to a studio and surrounded herself most happily with beginners.

At this time, too, a great and lasting interest in Indians and Indian ways was awakened in Emily's breast. Totem poles, dugout canoes, dogs, costumes, Indian villages and primitive countryside with big trees presented challenges she had not known before. The Indian people proved refreshing to know and her travels among them made her want to stay and write and paint. And the native people liked her, called her Klee Wyck, meaning "The Laughing One." It suggested that Miss Emily, who saw much to be criticized in Victoria society, found the Indian people more conducive to good laughter.

There were the usual number of love affairs in the girl's life, one of them more serious than the others. Sometimes her love was sought when it was not given, she admitted, and sometimes it was given when it was not wanted. No doubt anyone of her temperament would be fickle and none of the romances survived. This may have contributed to frustration and she remained throughout her life a rather lonely woman.

Having saved some money, she resolved to get away again, this time to study at the Westminster School of Art in England. But London was not such a good experience as she expected. Health failed and she was in hospital for a time. But she remained for five years, all the while longing for the totem poles and Douglas firs and the mountains.

Back in Victoria, she knew she had to make a living and although she wanted to paint Indian scenes, there was the pressing necessity of doing something more rewarding. She might be erratic and volatile but nobody could say she was not versatile; at this point she became a cartoonist for a newspaper and performed very well.

Like most people with artistic ways, the Carr girl fancied change and when an invitation came to teach art at a sophisticated club in Vancouver, she accepted and moved and found herself giving instruction to ladies and their children. When classes ended, she lost no time in traveling again to Indian country, this time to the far Yukon. And although her last return from overseas had been sweet, she was again attracted by the thought of more study in Europe and was shortly on her way to enroll at the Académie Colarossi in Paris. Sister Alice accompanied but again the big city brought disappointment. Emily was sick and lonely and missed British Columbia more than at any time in her life.

Happy to be home again, she undertook to do more teaching. She was coming to realize, however, that she was not cut out to be a teacher. She was an impatient person at the best of times, especially with adults, and maturity was making her worse. In addition, her new enthusiasm for modern art — that new way of seeing things — was making her less tolerant of the traditional form. Students who favored the photographic kind of art were told rather rudely to buy cameras. "It is for the artist to enrich the picture with his feeling," she insisted. But in Victoria and Vancouver she was not very convincing.

When discouraged, she would turn again to the Indian country — she and her big English sheepdog — and pull her canoe ashore beside some remote rivers. The Queen Charlotte Islands gave her a sense of peace such as she had not felt for years and she saw a thousand scenes she wanted to paint. The Indians accepted her and the idea of making her home in one of the coastal Indian villages with good totem pole scenes did not escape her. But she had to face reality and returned to Victoria to try again to settle down.

There was a local showing and Emily hung a few pictures inspired by the recent tours of the back country. Public reaction was no better and Emily's sister urged again that she dismiss the "new way of seeing" and concentrate on the simplicity which people understood and believed they liked. "Presented that way, your pictures would sell."

It didn't matter. Perhaps the photographic kinds would sell but Emily had no intention of painting contrary to her convictions. Before she would change to something in which she did not believe, she would give up painting for good. More than ever convinced that she had failed to impart a message to the British Columbia people, she was giving serious attention to other ways of making a living. When some of the family real estate was sold, she decided to build an apartment house and subsist by the collection of rent. That way she could have ample room for her animal friends, and if she ever wanted to paint again, she could make a studio in the attic.

Through the years of the First World War and for some time thereafter, Emily Carr was able to pay her way by renting suites and keeping boarders and breeding dogs and selling pottery of her own making. It wasn't very satisfactory, and she was crankier and more frustrated and sometimes sick. When she was obliged to enter a hospital for a spell, the care of her numerous animal friends fell in a most unwelcome manner to her sister and presented a minor crisis. With five dogs, a parrot, a monkey, canaries and various other small things like squirrels, chipmunks and white rats, poor Alice was bewildered and wished again her sister would reform.

Notwithstanding her resolution to quit painting, she returned to it now and again and worked furiously for days at a time, turning out canvas after canvas, consigning some of her productions to the refuse, some to storage in the attic. There was not more than slight demand from buyers and such painting as she was doing was appearing more and more as a fleeting pastime. Even her surplus dogs were finding a better market than her pictures and nobody was really upset about it.

But fortunes can change suddenly and did. Marius Barbeau of the National Museum in Ottawa visited her.

He had heard about the lady in a circuitous way from Indian agents and wished to see for himself. On the occasion of his first call, made without prior intimation, she was loathe to let him see her work. She knew nothing of him and nothing of the Ottawa Gallery. So many people had admitted indifference and even scorn for her distorted and vivid portrayals of scenes along the West Coast and in Indian villages that she suspected all strangers of seeking only entertainment. When Barbeau came about 1925, he wanted to select fifty of her pictures for a National Gallery display to feature West Coast art. Ever skeptical, she had to be coaxed but finally agreed and then accepted a personal invitation to attend the showing in Ottawa.

By this time, Emily Carr was fifty-six years old and much of her earlier enthusiasm had suffered from a form of malnutrition. But the reception at Ottawa surpassed anything she might have anticipated. Here she met members of Canada's Group of Seven and talked long with one of them, Lawren Harris. Members of the Group had no previous knowledge of her work but were ready to admit to both surprise and delight in seeing her canvases. The acknowledged Great of the East had discovered an unsuspected Great from the West and they showered her with praise.

Her entire being was now fired with enthusiasm. Harris and his friends had demonstrated that an artist does not have to paint simply to please the public in order to be successful. She was eager to get back to Victoria to renew her painting as she believed it should be done. She was not attracted by the abstract painting she saw on the trip but her belief in creative art was confirmed. It was like a rebirth for her and the next few years saw her painting prolifically and developing a clearer individual style. Some of those paintings were now being hung at showings in far parts of the hemisphere and to her utter astonishment she was offered a one-artist display at Victoria, the event being sponsored by the Women's Canadian Club. Adding to the significance of the moment, Emily Carr was the invited speaker at the club luncheon (March 4, 1930). She was probably the most surprised person at the meeting and in her own inimitable way, she convinced most of her listeners that they might have been too ready to condemn the form of art with which they were not familiar. She knew many of them hated modern art and she agreed that some kinds should be hated. But what is wrong, she asked, with trying to bring a scene to life and making it dance and vibrate with what the artist is able to see in it? She had waited long for this moment of apparent vindication and the realization was sweet.

In her exuberance, Emily Carr wanted to write as well as paint and with editorial help in correcting her atrociously bad spelling and other technical errors from a friend, Ira Dilworth, of the Canadian Broadcasting Corporation, success came quickly. When failing health prevented long canoe trips to her favorite haunts, she could give more time to writing and her first book, *Klee Wyck,* won the Governor General's Award for non-fiction in 1941. Five other books appeared under her name, three of them being published after her death. They were *The Book Of Small* published in 1942, *The House of All Sorts* in 1944, *Growing Pains* in 1946, and *The Heart Of A Peacock* and *Pause* in 1953.

It was not until almost the end of her life that the sale of her pictures reached its peak. It took Dr. Max Stern, a Montreal art dealer and great salesman for Canadiana, to do it. The Carr pictures had never been easy to sell, at least not until Stern came upon the scene. He traveled west in 1944, making a search for artists, and was elated at what he found in Emily Carr's stockpile, an accumulation of some 400 paintings stacked like war surplus. Overjoyed and ready to pronounce her Canada's only "authentic artistic genius," he offered her a feature showing but she did not share his optimism about sales and hesitated. Unenthusiastically, she allowed him to take sixty pictures and was pleasantly surprised to learn from the cheque Dr. Stern mailed to her a short time later that he had sold fifty-four of the paintings in two weeks. It was the best cheque she had ever received and with more bouts of illness, she needed the money.

She suffered from a stroke and was instructed to stop painting, stop all activity. The advise was ignored and she had a heart attack. When she should have been resting to recuperate, she was discovered in the forest, painting at a feverish rate, admitting that her time was running out and she wanted to spend as much of it as possible doing what she loved most to do, painting those outdoor scenes. She died on March 2, 1945, age seventy-four, leaving behind a magnificent monument of art, constructed with paintbrush and pen.

Courtesy Mr. V. Callihoo

VICTORIA CALLIHOO: GRANNY

She was Mrs. Victoria Callihoo, with good Indian and French blood in her veins and when she died on April 21, 1966, she was 104½ years old, the respected Granny of the Lac Ste. Anne settlement, northwest of Edmonton. She remembered tribal battles between Blackfoot and Cree, remembered the annual buffalo hunts on the plains, remembered when the family tipi was pitched on the spot where Edmonton's Macdonald Hotel was built, and remembered with affection her old friend, Father Lacombe. She saw the old and the new, witnessed the Wonder of the West as few people had seen it.

She admitted to having had many birthdays but she refused to grow old. She never gave up dancing and was partial to the Red River jig, that energy-consuming performance which originated in the Métis colonies around old Fort Garry. In 1935, when seventy-four years of age, she entered a Red River jig competition conducted by the Northern Alberta Pioneers and Old Timers Association in Edmonton — of which she was a life member — and won the contest and the tanned buffalo robe offered as first prize. Although the Red River jig was enough to tax the stamina of a young person, Victoria Callihoo again astonished her friends and relations attending a big gathering to mark her hundredth birthday by performing the jig, "the way it should be done." Nor was that the last time; when she was 103 years of age and attending a Native Society rally, Granny took to the floor and danced her favorite jig to the delight of spectators and with evident satisfaction to herself.

At the age of ninety she wanted to buy a horse for driving purposes and heard that her grandson, Pat Callihoo, had one for sale. She went to inspect the animal and asked, "How old is he?"

The reply was: "Seven years."

The elderly lady, bright and agile, wanted to be sure. She moved to the horse's head and with a professional touch, opened the animal's mouth and made an examination of the teeth. "Pat," she exclaimed in tones of confidence, "you can't fool your grandmother. That horse is twelve years old."

But she made the purchase at the price she considered right, hitched the horse to her buggy and drove for pleasure and convenience during the next few years.

She was born at Lac Ste. Anne on November 19, 1861, and was christened Victoria Belcourt, her given name being taken from that of the British Queen at the time. Her birth came just two years after Captain John Palliser completed his famous survey of the country and eight years before the Government of Canada contracted to buy Rupert's Land from the Hudson's Bay Company.

The father, like most men at Lac Ste. Anne, did some farming, some freighting, some hunting and trapping, and her Cree mother, recognized by her people as a Medicine Woman, was kept busy in helping to cure sick and injured friends. That mother knew exactly what native herbs to prescribe for blood poisoning, which ones for stomach disorders and which to appease rebellious intestines. When the family went on one of the annual buffalo hunts — always attended by dangers and injuries — she was so busy with sick and injured people that she rarely had time to help the other women at skinning the buffalo carcasses and drying the meat.

In an article printed in the *Alberta Historical Review* (Winter, 1960), Victoria Callihoo related the events in the first buffalo hunt she attended as a girl. She was thirteen years old and filled with anticipation when she climbed aboard a Red River cart to ride out with the great hunting party. The memory was vivid. It was the year the Mounted Police trekked westward from Fort Dufferin to build the remote post they called Fort Macleod, and the buffalo herds were still big and numerous. Leaving Lac Ste. Anne as soon as the leaves were out on the poplars, the cavalcade was enlarged by additional Métis folks joining at St. Albert and Fort Edmonton. Eventually there were about one hundred families in the gay party. Because of the constant danger of encountering hostile Blackfoot warriors, it was not considered safe for people from the northern communities to hunt alone. One year they went as far as Tail Creek town.

Fording the North Saskatchewan River was the first ordeal but the men had done it before and knew how to find the shallowest water and the best footing near where Edmonton's High Level Bridge was built later. Often, the river level was high in the spring and the crossing dangers were increased.

The hunters speculated about how far they would have to drive before sighting the big herds. They did not expect to encounter the best hunting opportunities in less than two or three days of driving and when they camped for their first night out, they completed plans for the climactic attack, whenever it could be made. The general organization for the hunt was approximately the same as at Red River although the annual outings from the area of the Selkirk Settlement were on a larger scale. When the Red River hunters went out on their summer hunt in 1840, the count showed 620 hunters, 650 women, 1,210 Red River carts, 655 horses, 586 oxen and 542 hungry dogs looking forward to the great engorgement of the canine year. Buffalo killed on that outing numbered 1,475 and pemmican made in the field was said to be close to a million pounds.

The Lac Ste. Anne and St. Albert hunting expedition might have been seen as a small replica of the corresponding event originating at Red River. A captain was selected and explicit hunting rules were adopted. Everybody knew what to expect in punishment if rules were broken, and good discipline generally prevailed. Scouts rode ahead in the hope of spotting a suitable herd, and when the hunting party drew near and prepared for the assault, excitement ran high. Men selected their fastest horses and armed themselves with flintlock guns and all the necessities in powderhorns and gunball bags. Experienced hunters could reload their guns while horses continued to dash after the retreating herd. A few of the native people continued to hunt with bows and arrows but they knew their technique was failing.

At the signal from the captain, the mounted men started, slowly and as quietly as possible, in the direction of the unsuspecting herd and increased their speed as they came closer. Their hope was to come as near as possible before frightening the animals into a stampede of escape. At last, as the hunters were within favorable range, they dashed forward at a mad gallop, shooting as they bore down upon the fleeing brutes.

Most hunters would kill at least one buffalo each. Experts would shoot several. Victoria Callihoo remembered Abraham Salois of St. Albert, later of Tail Creek, who was known to have killed thirty-seven animals — a record — on a single hunting run.

During the few minutes of shooting, all was noise and dust and confusion. At best, it could be expected that a few riders would be thrown, a few human bones would be broken and a few horses would be gored by attacking bulls. But when it was over and the dust had settled, the hunters retraced their steps to claim the animals they had shot, and meet the women coming from the camp by cart to skin the animals, cut up the meat and get it ready for drying and grinding, the preparatory steps in the making of pemmican. The younger girls like Miss Victoria were given the task of maintaining the fires to ensure that smoke was striking the drying meat hung on rails. Smoke would keep the flies away and also impart a desirable flavor to the meat. For fuel they used wood when available, otherwise buffalo chips.

"Ah, that pemmican," Mrs. Callihoo said wistfully. "We didn't go for calves because we did not like veal, but when that meat from grown animals was dried and pounded and mixed with fat and saskatoon berries, it was the best food anybody could have." And so, with carts piled high with pemmican packed in buffalo rumens or sewed in buffalo robes, members of the party felt rewarded and happy. There was no need to hurry and when they made night camps on the return journey, they relaxed, told stories and sang old hunting songs.

Life was not easy, but as Mrs. Callihoo declared, her girlhood years were pleasant memories. She attended school only briefly and mastered very little beyond reading, and writing her own name. She remembered when she first saw real money and wondered why it should be necessary. Her people had always been able to buy and sell on a barter basis and perhaps it was better that way because there was less incentive to hoard wealth. There had been some Hudson's Bay Company tokens in circulation but it was only when the Cree in her part received their first treaty payments that she and members of her family saw the real "cash money."

Home life was simple and good. Houses, as Mrs. Callihoo recalled in the *Alberta Historical Review* (November 1953), were constructed from spruce logs, with hewn logs for a floor. Lacking glass, her people stretched wet rawhide from a calf over the window openings and made it secure with slats and pegs. When the hide became dry, it was tight like a drumhead and would admit some light although it was not transparent. Blinds and curtains were totally unnecessary. Poles served as rafters and these were covered with big strips of spruce bark laid like shingles to turn the rain. Logs were chinked with mud, outside and inside, and then freshened on the inner surface with a whitemud wash.

Within the house there was neither table, chair nor bedstead. Members of the family squatted on the floor at mealtime and rolled their bedding on the floor at bedtime. And while there was no stove, there was an open fireplace — perhaps two at opposite ends of the house. Heavy copper pots for cooking purposes hung over the fireplaces, generally half full of meat. In her early childhood, Victoria Callihoo did not see either kerosene lamp or candle. Until the latter became available, there was no light at night except what was thrown by flames in the fireplace.

They made their own brooms by tying willow twigs together and gathered moss for a multitude of household purposes. "Moss was an essential," she said. "We even used it instead of diapers, stuffing it into the moss-bags in which the babies were laced up. And we used moss to wipe the floors after scrubbing."

Her childhood diet would seem restricted by modern standards, including very little except fresh buffalo meat, pemmican and fish. Her people had no flour but in time they grew barley and found ways of grinding it to a meal for soup and baking. Also, they roasted barley until it was black and used it for making a coffeelike beverage.

The Métis were friendly people and, simple though it was, social life was good. Many of those living in the Lac Ste. Anne and St. Albert districts were related and there was much visiting back and forth, frequently to feast and dance.

At the age of seventeen years, Victoria Belcourt married Louis Callihoo with French and Cree and Iroquois in his pedigree. The young couple farmed at Villeneuve, then at Ste. Anne. Louis Callihoo was an enterprising fellow and operated a sawmill for a time, then a hotel at Lac Ste. Anne, all the while maintaining his farming interests because his wife saw the farm as the best place to raise her expanding family. Altogether, she had twelve children, six boys and six girls, and she was busy. But she was robust, like most people of mixed races. She was slightly bigger than average, with black eyes, hair which was still dark when she was ninety, and a nicely chiseled face showing fine character. Proud to call herself a Métis, she was more at home with the Cree language than with English and she preferred moccasins for her feet and a shawl for her head. She was a good cook, especially in making bread and baking beans, the foods that really satisfy. She was an expert teamster, having actually participated in freighting for the Hudson's Bay Company between Edmonton and Athabasca Landing. At that time, both Victoria Callihoo and her husband were driving freight teams on the trail.

She was also handy with a gun but her performance was not perfect, as members of her family recalled with some amusement. They could tell of the day when Mother, walking in the woods, encountered a bear and instructed her son, who was accompanying her, to run home for her gun, while she kept watch on the animal. In a few minutes he was back with "mom's old muzzle-loader" and with the first shot she finished the bear, one weighing 500 pounds. But her children could tell, also, about that day when her aim was not good. A hungry hawk swooped into her yard and seized upon Mother Callihoo's rooster. While the predator was struggling to get its prize off the ground, the lady rushed to the house to get her gun. Aiming hurriedly, she fired but the wrong bird received the bullet; the frightened hawk flew away, unharmed, while the rooster lay dead from the blast.

Victoria Callihoo loved the old ways but it did not mean that she rejected the advantages coming with the white man's civilization. Although her husband had no formal education and she had only a trace of it, both were proud to see their children attending school, the boys at Dunbow Residential School southeast of Calgary and the girls at St. Albert Convent. In the next generation, there were university degrees with members of the clan moving into highly responsible positions in the public service. And, it should be noted, Mrs. Callihoo had the first player piano in her part of the country and the aging lady sat and furnished foot-power to give her the music she loved, for hours at a time.

She found pleasure in her radio but was not overwhelmed by all modern inventions, many of which were leading people from Nature's refreshing paths to the high-speed avenues of artificial living. She was just past the age of one hundred when she talked over a telephone for the first time. The conversation was with her daughter, Mrs. J. W. Laderoute, of Gunn. The pioneer lady was greatly impressed and pleased, especially when she discovered that this amazing invention would permit her to talk in either English or Cree.

After the death of her husband in 1926, Mrs. Callihoo lived alone in her home at Gunn. That was the way she wanted it until she was 101 years old. It was her community. One of her oft-repeated hopes was that nothing would ever take her far from Lac Ste. Anne with all its natural beauty and associations for her. But with numerous friends and relatives, she was rarely alone. She liked visitors and welcomed them at any time but the New Year's season was a time for special entertaining in her life. Even when she was a very old lady, she held Open House on New Year's Day. Members of the family wanted to be at Granny's house at some time on that day.

After attending a midnight frolic to see the New Year come in, she would repair to her own house to make ready for the day-long party at which she would preside with evident delight. At any time after four in the morning, her oldest son would arrive and all the other sons and daughters and grandchildren would follow in time for breakfast. That early morning gathering was for her immediate family; the rest of the day was for everybody who cared to drop in — and nearly everybody within driving distance came.

When her children, grandchildren and great-grandchildren visited her on the holiday in her hundredth year, they received her customary good wishes and heard her say when they were leaving: "Now Happy New Year and I hope you'll all be spared to be with me at this same time next year." It did not seem to occur to her that she might be the one to go before another year passed.

And in line with her optimism and faith, her own physical vigor seemed undiminished. She had her first medical examination at the age of ninety-nine and the doctor assured her of what she already knew, that she was in good health. She never indulged in smoking or drinking and was proud of her record of self-discipline. When asked for her formula for achieving long life, she replied, "Behave yourself and work hard."

It must have been something of a record when Mrs. Victoria Callihoo and seven of her sons and daughters were qualifying for the Old Age Pension at the same time.

Her notable record did not go unnoticed in more remote parts and she was the subject of many newspaper articles. Sometimes she was paid the public honor she deserved, as when she was invited in 1949 to unveil the Historic Sites and Monuments Board of Canada cairn at Elk Island Park commemorating the Canadian efforts to save the prairie buffalo from extinction, and to officially open the Historical Society Museum at Sangudo in 1959.

In her advanced years, Mrs. Callihoo spent much of her time at sewing and knitting. With 241 descendants at the last count before her death — 12 children, 57 grandchildren, 165 great-grandchildren and 8 great-great-grandchildren — there was plenty of needlework to keep Granny Callihoo occupied. Knitting afforded the best opportunities for reflection, thinking about other years, thinking about her expanding clan, thinking about many of the younger ones receiving university degrees and good employment. She had so much about which to think and so much to make her happy.

She died on April 21, 1966, in her 105th year and was buried at Villeneuve. As the great crowd gathered to pay respect to the departed lady, it did not go unnoticed that her life, in a most striking way, was like a bridge between buffalo days and modern society; between the travois as a means of transportation, which she knew when she lived for a time on the Michael Reservation, and the unbelievably fast travel she lived to see; between the times when Indians and Métis were numerous enough and strong enough to have annihilated members of the newcomer race and the later years when those native people represented a relatively weak minority. Victoria Callihoo witnessed one of the most spectacular area transformations seen in a single lifetime in world history.

Provincial Archives of Alberta Photograph Collection

DORA ALICE "MA" BRAINARD: HOUSE BY THE SIDE OF THE ROAD

"Even if you can't pay for your dinner, you don't need to let poverty hamper your appetite when you're in my house," Ma Brainard would say while stoking her old Majestic wood-burning range and carrying platters of steaming food to the long table. And after dispensing her unique brand of hospitality for many years, during which time nobody had ever been turned away, the aging lady became a North Country legend, like Twelve Foot Davis and Jim Cornwall and Baldy Red. Ask anybody from Grande Praire or Beaver Lodge or Dawson Creek.

Frontier life was always marked by "lights and shadows" but in the case of Dora Alice Brainard, the lights seemed especially bright and the shadows especially dark. The winter storms were more devastating and the results more heartbreaking; but the satisfaction of overcoming the reverses and rendering useful public service was all the reward she sought. Here was a lady, bright-eyed, busy and stooped, who knew exactly what it was to "live in my house by the side of the road, and be a friend of man."

In addition to all else, Ma Brainard was a character

with a fine sense of humor and a droll Southern way of expressing herself. "Where did I come from?" she repeated to a question. "Well, in the first place, it was North Carolina but, Lord, that's so long ago that even the climate has changed. You know, I've been in this country since the year after the province of Alberta was formed."

Born at Hendersonville, North Carolina, in 1879, Dora Alice grew up where farmers drove mules and grew cotton and tobacco. Then, marrying a chunky and muscular cowboy and rancher, Lee Brainard, she lived in Montana and became the stepmother to his young son, Albert, by his deceased first wife. Although new to ranch life, Montana style, she adapted readily and loved it all. Lee Brainard was an energetic fellow and his family was in a position to live comfortably, but in both husband and wife the spirit of adventure was strong enough to rule their lives largely. They were hearing glowing tales about ranching opportunities across the boundary, in Canada. There the grass was said to be nutritious and belly-deep, high enough for calves to get lost in it. Chinook winds, recurring with benevolent regularity throughout the winters, removed the costly necessity of cutting and stacking hay. Why remain longer in an area where winter feeding was inescapable? The decision to move was made in haste and led to one of the legendary winter tragedies on the Canadian range.

It was about midsummer, 1906, when Lee Brainard, along with his son and a cowboy helper, White by name, rounded up his 700 cattle and 100 horses and began the fateful northerly drive to Canadian grass. Mrs. Brainard would remain behind until the men found an acceptable location and a home was ready for her. In the meantime, the three men would live in a covered wagon fitted out for the journey.

Neither cattle nor horses were cooperative at first and additional help was needed to get them started. Then they accepted the necessity of moving to new ranges, for which Brainard had made no prior arrangement. Actually, he had very little idea of where he was going. He was not aware of any reason to hurry. It was better to travel slowly and avoid needless loss of condition on the animals.

Men, cattle and horses crossed the International Boundary at Wild Horse in Alberta's southeast and skirted the Cypress Hills. A halt was called at or near Medicine Hat where Lee Brainard visited the local land office to inquire about leases. But the government officers could give him no encouragement because no sizable areas remained for leasing — not unless he went much farther north where winter conditions would present added feeding problems.

Brainard gave the signal to press on. There was difficulty in crossing the South Saskatchewan River but with each succeeding day thereafter the herd was ten or twelve miles farther north. The boss was cheerful. Unfamiliar with the country and still preoccupied with confidence in open winters, he did not seem to realize that he was driving out of the chinook belt and into an area where an attempt to winter cattle without reserves of hay was sheer folly.

Men and animals forded the Red Deer River and continued northward. The country was showing signs of autumn and the nights were becoming cool. The herders were following Berry Creek and a few miles northeast of present-day Hanna, they encountered a broad grassy valley, apparently unoccupied by either homesteaders or ranchers. There, north of where Richdale was located later, Brainard decided to winter. The range seemed to fulfill a dream. While surveying this expanse of grassland, Lee Brainard met the Hunt brothers who were running cattle nearby and he was reminded that with 800 head of livestock and no feed in store for the winter, he could, indeed, be inviting trouble. But Brainard was a gambler and he was betting on the chinook winds sparing him from disaster. The Hunts offered to sell him hay for his young cattle, but ever the optimist, he refused to buy.

Sad to say, the newcomers were due for an awful shock. The winter of 1906-07 started early and continued late into the usual time for spring, to be remembered as one of the most severe in Western Canadian history. Before the end of October, Brainard's cattle were finding only the most meager grazing where grass protruded on the hillsides. As the days became colder, the cattle were losing weight. Late in December, Brainard knew he was facing an emergency; he had to move his cattle or let them perish.

His decision was to use the first mild spell to drive the herd in the direction of the neighboring ranch where he might still be able to buy hay. The mild spell came in January and cattle and horses and covered wagon were started in the direction of the Hunt ranch and possible relief. Confidence returned, but after one mild day, a storm blew in from the northwest. It struck without warning and without mercy. Temperatures plunged far below zero and driving snow all but blocked visibility. By no means could men on horses keep the cattle together. The weakened animals turned their rumps to the wind and drifted as if searching for shelter. Most of them never found it and most of them perished.

For the men, the prospects were little better than for the cattle. They used all the wood they had for fuel and realized that their clothing was far from adequate in such savage blasts from the northwest. There was no longer anything they could do to save the cattle which had vanished in the swirling blizzard and the men knew as they felt the sting of frostbite that they would have trouble enough saving themselves.

The first to collapse was the faithful cowboy helper and nothing Brainard and his son could do had any effect in reviving him. In a short time he was dead. After another hour or two, Brainard's son, Albert, was giving up and in desperation the father tried to carry the boy as he staggered forward, not knowing where he was going. The boy was gradually freezing to death, just like White. When all signs of life had departed, the stunned father laid the two bodies together in the snow and set out to try to save himself. Again and again he was about to quit the struggle, die in the snow, but just as often he found the strength to move his frozen feet a little further until, finally, he stumbled against a building which proved to be the Hunt ranchhouse.

Miraculously, Lee Brainard survived and late in the winter his wife had him back in Montana where she nursed him to recovery. He lost his frozen toes but managed to save his feet and late in the spring he was again in Alberta, scouring the countryside, looking for his cattle. Of the 700 he had driven from Montana, he located fewer than twenty-five head still alive. The survival rate among the horses was higher but the terrible experiences of that winter became memories with which Lee and Ma Brainard had to live for the rest of their lives.

Brainard, like other pioneers of his generation, was not one to surrender readily. Almost immediately, he brought more cattle to Alberta and his wife accompanied to make a home. Although convinced that such a winter would not be repeated for many years, he accepted the practical necessity of putting up hay for winter use and his cattle operations prospered. There were other reverses, of course, including prairie fires, but it was not until he saw the large influx of homesteaders to his area that he decided to move again. No cattleman of his generation could stand the thought of being encircled by settlers, and after conducting a rough reconnaissance of alternative areas, Lee and Ma Brainard loaded livestock and farm equipment and shipped to the Peace River area. From the railroad, they drove beyond the rim of settlement and, finally, beside Sinclair Lake, northwest of Beaverlodge, they stopped to homestead, build a long, low log cabin and continue their ranching operations.

The new home fronted on the old Pouce Coupe trail and it was not long before traveling people discovered it as an unfailing haven of hospitality. After their tragic experiences on the Prairies, both Lee and Ma Brainard vowed that never again would they permit blinds on their windows, never again would their window be without a light at night and never would their door be bolted.

When government officials had a request for a post

office in the district, they named it Brainard and asked Ma to keep it in her house, which she did for over forty years. It worked out to everybody's satisfaction and in later years, when someone wished to write a note of appreciation to the lady who ran the stopping place, and did not know her address, nothing more was needed than to mark the letter: "Ma Brainard, Alberta." The letter would be delivered.

Lee Brainard died in 1938, age seventy-nine years, while his wife remained to administer to the needs of wayfaring men and women for many more years, adding steadily to her reputation for hospitality and originality. People traveling between Beaverlodge and Dawson Creek remarked thousands of times: "Let's try to reach Ma Brainard's for dinner." There was no need to make reservations in advance; Ma could adapt to a small group or a big one and her fried chicken and apple pie were as delectable at one time as another. Her idea of preparedness when the traffic might be heavy was to have one chicken in the pan, one chicken ready for the pan and one or more in a coop beside the kitchen door, ready for the ax.

And Ma's comment was like a fringe benefit, an added feast of fun and entertainment. "We don't charge anything for the high-society style we put on here," she might tell her guests as they sat on benches in the log cabin, waiting for empty chairs at the table. "I've figured it takes a heap of polished silverware to do as much for a hungry man as a slice of homemade bread spread with fresh butter. And if I thought anybody was leaving my table hungry, I'd ram another slice right down his pink gullet, whether he liked it or not."

Among those who planned itineraries to be at Ma's place for southern fried chicken at a noon or evening were prime ministers, premiers, bank presidents, Hollywood personalities, professional hockey players and at least one Governor General, Lord Bessborough. The lady of the house found special pleasure in recalling the visit from Sir Henry Thornton and members of his party who were especially appreciative. For Sir Henry, it was "the best meal in my memory." That day stood out in Ma's memory, partly because of the expressions of gratitude, partly because of the enormous appetites displayed by the railroad men. Seventy-two people, all hungry, stopped at the log cabin for meals that day. But it did not really matter who they were; all received the same welcome and the same tasty fare.

Sometimes Ma Brainard had as many customers enjoying the shelter of her house and bunkhouse as she had at mealtimes. This was particulary true when much of the local freight was moved by horse-drawn wagons. As many as twenty teams might be tied in her stable or yard overnight while twenty men searched for bunks or places on the floor of her house where they could spread their blankets. "We can always find room for one more bedroll," she would say with a smile.

She rarely left home after the death of her husband, but until past the age of eighty years, she was still dispensing the kind of fine food which brought fame to herself and to her part of the Peace River country. She was still Ma Brainard and she liked the name. "If anybody shouted Mrs. Brainard," she quipped, "I guess I'd look around to see if there was another woman in my kitchen."

The lady who made simple hospitality a specialty was taken to Grande Praire hospital in January, 1967. It was her first such experience in a long lifetime. Even on one occasion when, while helping to repair the stable roof, she fell off and broke a leg, she did not stop for hospitalization. On that point, she could not understand why she did not break both legs, "unless one was stronger than the other." But she did not like being confined to hospital; even in those last weeks of her life, she wanted to get back to work. "I have to be working to be happy," she said again. "When I die, they can bury me with a broom and a dishpan and it will be all right with me."

There at the hospital, Ma Brainard died in February, 1967, age eighty-eight years. It was like the end of an era.

Courtesy Mrs. V. Hopkins

JULIA SCOTT LAWRENCE: GRANNY OF THE NORTH

For those in attendance, it had to be the "Birthday Party of the Year," making July 27, 1969, a date to be remembered. The farm lawn bordered with midsummer flowers provided the perfect setting and ripe raspberries fresh from the garden and buried in ice cream, provided the perfect climax for the banquet laid out on the shady side of the trees. And at the head of the long outdoor table sat the ninety-year-old guest of honor, Julia Scott Lawrence, slightly overwhelmed by all the attention but beaming delight at being surrounded by friends and relations who loved her.

It was a big gathering. Even without the guests who had no claim to family relationship with Mrs. Lawrence, there would have been a crowd. Granny Lawrence had fifteen children, eight daughters and seven sons, all except one born in her far northern community without benefit of doctor or hospital. Grandchildren at the time of the birthday numbered fifty-five and to a question about great-grandchildren, the pioneer lady replied: "Goodness gracious, I must make a new count, but let's say a hundred."

As her husband, Sheridan Lawrence, became known as "The Emperor of the Peace," so Mrs. Lawrence, whose birthday was being recognized, earned the title of endearment, "Granny of the North."

With members of her "clan" around her, the lady responded gleefully to questions and recounted pioneer experiences, mainly those of 1886 when she, as seven-year-old Julia Scott, was accompanying parents and younger brother, Osborne, on the two-month journey from Winnipeg to faraway Fort Vermilion, close to the northern border of present-day Alberta. From Calgary, the closest point on the railway of that time, it would be some 600 miles "as the crow flies" and at least 800 by cart trail and river route.

Julia's father, Rev. Malcolm Scott — later Archdeacon Scott — was going to Fort Vermilion as a missionary. Anglican Bishop Bompas was the author of the idea to establish a mission and farm in the remote North and E. J. Lawrence, who had been teaching school in the Province of Quebec, joined Rev. A. C. Garrioch to travel to the distant site in 1879, where they built a school and mission. Now, seven years later, more helpers were needed for the church project and the Scotts were responding to the call.

Leaving the railroad at Calgary, the Scotts loaded their possessions on a horsedrawn wagon — furniture, sewing machine, boxes of books, a crate of hens, two small pigs and two kittens. The pigs were the special responsibility of the blue-eyed little girl with reddish hair. Known as Jack and Jill, the small and saucy bottle-fed pigs were pets upon which she could lavish affection, just as with the kittens. But there was another reason for taking the porkers; one was a male and one a female and it was hoped that they would mature and provide the foundation for pig herds across the New North.

At Red Deer where all travelers faced the hazards of a river crossing without benefit of bridge, the Scotts overtook the Henry Lawrence outfit from Waterloo, Quebec, also going to Fort Vermilion for service in the church scheme. Members of the Lawrence family had intended going to the northern mission field in the previous year but the Northwest Rebellion trouble changed many plans and Henry Lawrence — brother of E. J. Lawrence — went alone, leaving his big family to join him at a later date. Sheridan, one of the six boys, was sixteen years old and big enough and strong enough to do a man's work and was doing it. There was plenty to do because the Lawrences were taking two extra wagons to accommodate extra equipment needed in the North. One of the ox-drawn wagons carried members of the family and supplies needed on the trail; one was loaded with mixed freight including a pair of stones for a gristmill and machinery for a sawmill; and the third bore the dead weight of a Waterous steam engine.

When the Scotts overtook the Lawrences at Red Deer Crossing, the wagon with the steam engine was stuck in the mud and it required extra teams and extra human hands to extricate it. Little Julia Scott could not be expected to do much in moving the stranded wagon but she had her own problem: The two small pigs were growing so fast that their crate was already too small and something had to be done about it. Perhaps Dan Cupid was at work even then because the Lawrence boy, Sheridan, who might have been fully occupied with the wagons, recognized the girl's need and turned aside to reconstruct the crate to Miss Julia's specifications. If Sheridan had any premonition that he was working for the girl who would one day be his wife, he kept the secret well to himself.

From Red Deer River the Scotts, with less freight, drove on ahead at the customary speed for wagons, two and one-half miles per hour. They knew, however, that they faced many more weeks of trail travel by day and hard roadside beds at night. They were pleased to find the road from Red Deer to the North Saskatchewan to be moderately level and moderately dry, and Edmonton offering the luxury of a river crossing by ferry. Then another hundred miles to Athabasca Landing where there was the frightening encounter with a forest fire, close enough to singe some hair and whiskers. But when the fire passed, the Scotts transferred their belongings to small riverboats to be propelled by Métis muscles all the way to the west end of Lesser Slave Lake. At that point they faced the necessity of another long haul or portage to Peace River Crossing, ninety miles and much of it through forests.

It was a relief to be at Peace River, even though there was still the dangerous river adventure. By this time, Julia and Osborne had whooping cough, making it more important to reach journey's end as quickly as possible. The pigs and kittens and hens were in good health but some of the hens would travel no farther because hungry Peace River dogs snapped off a few heads protruding from the hen crates and nothing could be done about it except to chase the dogs away and dress the hens for the stewpot.

As soon as enough logs were rolled into place and pegged to form a raft, the freight was placed thereon and the family moved under the shelter of a tarpaulin suspended over a portion of the heavy structure. "It was just like a playhouse," Mrs. Lawrence recalled, "and the big raft was our back yard."

Indians were employed as river guides and on July 7, the raft was poled from shore to be caught in the powerful current and whisked away for a 300-mile journey. The plan was to float day and night but on the first night the native guide supposed to be on duty fell asleep and the raft grounded on a gravel bar, necessitating an unpleasant midnight effort to get it back in the stream. Thereafter, Malcolm Scott remained constantly on lookout duty and after a total of only forty-eight hours of river travel, the raft was poled to the Fort Vermilion shoreline. Malcolm Scott and members of his family knelt to pray, then went ashore to announce their safe arrival and report to Henry Lawrence that his family was following with the steam engine and probably not far behind.

Fourteen years later, Sheridan Lawrence and Julia Scott met at Westbourne, near Portage la Prairie, August 21, 1900, and were married. Later on the same day, they turned their faces toward the far northern community which would continue to be their home. Since the first time they had gone north to Fort Vermilion, the means of travel had not changed much. By this time, however, Sheridan Lawrence was a man with varied business interests in the Peace River region, farming, ranching, trapping, trading, freighting and so on, and he could afford to have his own buggy at Edmonton waiting only for a borrowed horse to take the newlyweds away on the 100-mile road to Athabasca. From there they would travel by boat to the west end of Lesser Slave Lake, just as they had many years earlier, except that this time the stylish buggy was taken along on the boat for use on the long portage from Lesser Slave Lake to Peace River.

Then for the final portion of the honeymoon journey, from Peace River Town to Fort Vermilion, the moderately prosperous bride and groom could still find nothing better than a raft, but Sheridan Lawrence, with more and more experience born of necessity, knew exactly how to make one in a hurry. This time, however, recognizing the comfort a wedding trip is expected to command, a tent and stove were set up on the raft to serve for a leisurely ten-day voyage, floating short days and tying up early in the evening when and where an attractive riverside spot was sighted.

"For a honeymoon, I'd take a raft every time," said Mrs. Lawrence in 1969.

The first Lawrence baby was born in September, 1901, and babies seemed to come rather often thereafter, until the total number stood at fifteen. It was then that Mr. Lawrence was supposed to have declared: "I wouldn't take a million dollars for any one of my kids, and I wouldn't give two cents for another."

Sheridan Lawrence traveled much and might have been seen anywhere between Winnipeg and the Arctic Circle. Mrs. Lawrence was the homemaker and there was no situation with which this resourceful lady could not cope. When the upper millstone became loose, she leveled the bottom one, made it secure by flooding it and letting the water freeze, then she poured lead to hold the offending stone. It worked.

When the Lawrences needed a school, they built their own — Lawrence Point School with grades from one to nine — and boarded the teacher. And by winning the coveted Governor General's Gold Medal, Margaret Lawrence brought distinction and credit to both her family and her school.

Neither cultural nor spiritual matters would suffer in Mrs. Lawrence's community, even though some people said the region was far from so-called civilization. She ordered an organ — first of its kind so far north — and it was delivered from Peace River by sleigh in 1909. When a church was needed, the Lawrences again volunteered to build one. When asked if they would furnish a minister too, the reply was "No, but we'll supply a congregation."

It was always "open house" at Lawrences. If twenty people dropped in unexpectedly at mealtime, they could expect to hear Mrs. Lawrence say: "Dinner will be ready in a couple of minutes." If they happened to arrive at the moment of family prayers, each would be handed a Bible and instructed to join in the devotions. And if the nearest doctor was 300 miles away when the babies were born, he was still 300 miles away when sixteen of the seventeen people in the family were stricken with smallpox at one time. Mrs. Lawrence was the seventeenth member of the household, the only one on her feet, and all the sick people were nursed back to health.

At ninety years of age, Granny of the North was living alone in a Peace River apartment, preparing her own meals, doing her own housework and enjoying her independence and good health. She might travel south for a spell in the winter but she was generally ahead of the birds in returning to the North in the spring. Peace River remained her home until her death on April 6, 1974, just days before her ninety-fifth birthday.

At the memorable party marking her ninetieth birthday, a guest leaned toward her and asked: "How would you like to repeat that long journey from Calgary to Fort Vermilion the way you did it in 1886?"

A look of wonderment appeared. She paused as if in doubt about having heard the question correctly and then answered: "I suppose a woman of ninety would be foolish to try it." Then, after another pause for reconsideration, her eyes brightened and she added: "But if I were ten years younger, say only about eighty, I'd love to do it." It was the spirit of Granny Lawrence; it was the spirit that conquered the frontier.

Courtesy *Saskatoon Star-Phoenix*

MARGARET NEWTON: TRACKING DOWN THE STEM RUST

It must have been foreordained that a girl from Montreal would be the first to overcome the prevailing prejudice against women attending in regular classes at agricultural colleges, and then go on to become a world authority in her chosen field of plant pathology — and one of the leading strategists in winning Western Canada's war against the crop killer, stem rust in wheat.

The life history of the stem rust organisms on wheat at the time of Margaret Newton's entrance to university was still a mystery. The disease could, however, be devastating and costly, as in 1916 when the attack on western fields robbed wheat growers of an estimated 100 million dollars and left them with a feeling of helplessness, a fear that they might be forced to quit growing wheat for good. But as demonstrated many times in history, tragedy and adversity are progenitors of progress and the resulting assault upon the merciless plant disease not only achieved its purpose but qualified to be remembered as one of the classical triumphs for modern science.

The disease was not really new. Rust spores were probably floating in the air around the Mediterranean many centuries ago but until several years after the epidemic of 1916, practically nothing was known about control. In the absence of factual information, growers seized upon conjecture and superstition. A western outbreak in 1904, when Margaret Newton was still in her teens, brought advice to farmers to burn their stubble and butts of old strawpiles in order to destroy the sources of new rust infection. It was a technique which would have been quite useless, in the light of later discoveries about the complex and double-host character of rust propagation. The rust problem was crying for scientific attention. The Newtons were among the first to hear the cry.

Margaret Newton had to be a scientist or the conspicuous exception in a family of scientists. Not only were all members of the family engaged in scientific pursuits but all were distinguished in their respective fields. The father, John Newton, a chemist, inspired his children to a love for science and found the utmost reason for satisfaction in their performances. Of the five children — two girls and three boys — all graduated from Macdonald College and thereby received their bachelor's degrees from McGill University. And as if that were not a record in itself, all five went on to qualify for master's degrees and then doctor of philosophy degrees, all in one branch of science or another. One brother became president of the University of Alberta; one was professor of soil science at the University of Alberta; one was head of the Federal Research Laboratory at Saanichton, British Columbia, and the sister was a member of staff in botany at Macdonald College.

Brother Robert was the first to enroll at and graduate from Macdonald College. Margaret might have been first but her initial application was discouraged. An agricultural course was for males; the girls could take home economics, certainly not agriculture. But Miss Margaret knew what she wanted and tried again and, strange as it seemed at the time, was accepted; also accepted at that time was Pearl Stanforth who elected to specialize in horticulture. Together, these were Canada's first girl graduates from any agricultural college in the country. Not only did Margaret Newton graduate from a college in which she was initially unwelcome, but she graduated with the highest honors, Governor General's gold medal and scholarships which would allow her to continue her studies in pursuit of higher degrees.

Her chosen field was botany and while mastering at Macdonald, her work brought her into contact with that profoundly earnest botanist, Prof. W. P. Fraser, who was soon to move to Saskatchewan and through whom she was to come to the attention of Dr. W. P. Thompson, head of the biology department of the University of Saskatchewan.

Research in rust was about to receive fresh impetus. A special conference was called by Deputy Minister Grisdale of the Federal Department of Agriculture. It was the first declaration of public interest in the menace or the first that something might be done to counteract it. Much of the convention time was spent — and wasted — in discussions about cultural and field practices which some people saw as the only hope in checking the crop destroyer. It was then that Dr. W. P. Thompson, of Saskatchewan, made the bold and surprising proposal for an approach through plant genetics, one aimed at making or finding new varieties. To support his proposal, he noted that while common wheats like Red Fife and Marquis had surrendered helplessly to rust infection the year before, emmer wheats and certain others with inferior milling qualities, displayed natural resistance. What he was suggesting was a breeding program aimed at the production of a rust resistant variety or rust resistant varieties which would still possess the supreme bread-making qualities of Marquis. It sounded fantastic to those who saw the proposal as an attempt more or less to take selected old varieties apart, shuffle the pieces and put them together again in more advantageous combinations. It might mean crossing a high quality variety like Marquis with a kind having nothing else than rust resistance to offer and hope to incorporate the best of two races in one new strain.

"Perhaps it can be done," the plant breeders replied, then set about to do it. It was at this point that Margaret Newton, proceeding toward her doctor's degree at the University of Minnesota, became actively involved. In some ways, she was already a leader, showing that the problem was more complicated than even most biologists had supposed. Instead of one race of stem rust organisms, she found many. She was able to warn that a wheat variety having resistance to one race of stem rust, would not necessarily be able to stand up against another. She was able to isolate and identify fourteen races of stem rust and had reason to suspect that by mutation and hybridization, still more rust races might be created. It was the first intimation that even though the plant breeders were successful in developing varieties with resistance against the stem rust which struck in 1916, their work and the work of the plant pathologists would be unending.

The University of Saskatchewan studies were expanding and Dr. Thompson, knowing of Miss Newton's work and successes, made an arrangement with Dr. Stakman of the University of Minnesota to have her spend half of her time at Saskatoon, to pursue some puzzling questions presenting themselves. It was to her advantage, also, to benefit by the influence of another great professor of biology, and for a couple of her graduate years she commuted between St. Paul, Minnesota, and Saskatoon, Upon graduation from Minnesota, however, Dr. Thompson wanted her services full time and she accepted his offer of an assistant professorship in plant pathology. There she remained for three years or until moving on to the new Dominion Rust Research Laboratory at Winnipeg.

In the meantime, another rust studies conference was called by the Federal Department of Agriculture, the main purpose being to establish the research program on a proper cooperative basis, with the universities working in conjunction with the government. The Federal Department of Agriculture was now building special facilities for the rust studies at the University of Manitoba and when they were completed and ready for use in 1925, Margaret Newton left the University of Saskatchewan to devote herself completely to the program as laid out at Winnipeg. An Associate Committee on Cereal Rust was formed and at last the attack on stem rust promised to be big and comprehensive.

Inevitably it took a few years to produce positive results but in 1935 the first tangible dividends were announced in the form of two new wheat varieties with the desired resistance to stem rust and milling qualities similar to Marquis; one was Renown from the Dominion Rust Laboratory and the other was Apex from the University of Saskatchewan. After another four years the Dominion Laboratory released Regent and in 1946, Redman. During the same period, a Minnesota variety, Thatcher, was found to do well on the Canadian side and was accepted widely. Distribution of Selkirk, another creation from the Dominion Laboratory, began in 1953, and there were still more varieties to come if western growers were to stay ahead of their rust enemy.

For the plant pathologists and plant breeders, the task was without end, and there at the Dominion Rust Research Laboratory Dr. Margaret Newton remained for many years, becoming senior plant pathologist. Working with pathologist Dr. T. Johnson, she discovered some sixty-five new races of rust, thus providing a basis for the breeders to build upon.

Her work was of importance abroad as it was at home. As the author of forty-two scientific papers on stem rust she was emerging as a world authority on the subject, and her advice was sought by workers in many countries. Accepting an invitation from Russian counterparts, she visited the Plant Breeding Institute at Leningrad and had a chance to take an attractive Russian appointment to trace rust development in the area where it is thought to have originated, Turkestan. Of course there was a lure about such an adventure and if she had been considering herself alone, she would have accepted the offer. But she consulted her bother, Dr. Robert Newton who had been successively professor of field husbandry, professor of plant biochemistry, director of biological investigation for the National Research Council, dean of agriculture and president of the University of Alberta. His words were thoughtful: "The overseas assignment could be a rich experience but the work in rust research in Canada would suffer if you left. You should remain."

She did remain, but all the while those rust spores with which she had been working were undermining her own health, producing an asthmatic condition which became chronic and finally forced her retirement in 1945. She moved to live at Victoria where she could continue to enjoy the wonderful world of vegetation without the further aggravation from the spores of stem rust. But her contributions to improved crop returns across the country were not forgotten. She had been elected to become a Fellow of the Royal Society of Canada in 1942 and was the recipient of the Flavelle Gold Medal for outstanding work in science, in 1948, with the presentation being made by her respected mentor of early years, Dr. W. P. Thompson, the new president of the University of Saskatchewan. In 1956, the University of Minnesota presented the lady with an "Outstanding Achievement Award," and in 1969 she received an honorary doctorate degree from the University of Saskatchewan.

Dr. Margaret Newton died at Victoria on April 5, 1971, age eighty-four years. Friends tried to make an inventory of her contributions. It was not easy, but it was not overlooked that she would number among Canada's leaders in science, to be remembered as an international authority on physiological races of wheat stem rust and member of a notable team of workers which undertook to beat the stem rust demon and triumphed to the extent of greatly reducing crop risks across the West and enriching the country's agriculture by hundreds of millions of dollars.

Courtesy Edna Jaques

EDNA JAQUES: 3,000 POEMS LATER

Regardless of the circumstances which led her to live elsewhere, Saskatchewan people asserted a firm proprietary claim upon Edna Jaques, one of Canada's best-known writers of poetry. And conversely, she never ceased to declare her fondness and allegiance to the prairie region where she grew to maturity and won many of her earliest successes in writing. Being part of the community of Briercrest, southeast of Moose Jaw, where the family settled to homestead before there was either a Briercrest or a province of Saskatchewan, could adequately explain an attachment.

One of the clearest demonstrations of the writer's abiding loyalty to the Wheat Province was her decision to place her voluminous collection of manuscript materials — 3,000 poems in fifty-three scribblers, along with copies of thirteen books she had seen published — in the Provincial Archives in Saskatchewan, not far from the district in which the earliest of the poems were written. It was to be expected that eastern universities and archives would want these treasures and appeal to the author living in retirement at Willowdale, near Toronto; but it was to the archives at the University of Saskatchewan that the papers, packed carefully in a fireproof steamer trunk, were shipped by express.

Edna Jaques was born at Collingwood, Ontario, 1891. Her father, Charles Jaques, was a captain on a Great Lakes passenger ship plying between Collingwood and Fort William. Craving a change of occupation, he announced unceremoniously in 1902 that he was through with sailing and intended to join the landseekers moving west into homestead country. Edna was a girl of eleven tender years and was not expected to have an opinon but her mother, on hearing the father's decision, fainted promptly. According to the daugher, however, Mother "could faint the quickest of anyone I ever knew."

Anyway, the family was on its way to a prairie homestead and all the uncertainty and hardship normally entailed. The district to be marked by Briercrest was thirty miles from Moose Jaw and level enough that a coyote might be seen a mile away. The long train journey from Collingwood to Moose Jaw afforded no more luxury than a colonist car with hard slatted seats could provide. Father Jaques who had traveled ahead to make some preparation, was able to meet his wife and children at the Moose Jaw end and drive them to the homestead. He had purchased four bronco horses and a wagon and could report the erection of a stable on the new quarter. There was still no house but one double stall in the stable was being reserved to accommodate the family until better accommodation could be constructed. At this point, according to Miss Edna, the newcomers proceeded to farm, "making all the mistakes greenhorns ever made."

For the five children — two older and two younger than Edna — it was an exciting adventure with gophers, prairie flowers, country baseball, and attendance at a rural school. Also, it seemed to offer a favorable "climate" for a young person with talent for making poetry. In Edna's words, "They were good years, when the prairies gave forth their increase without much coaxing"

Girls in the homestead country had only the slightest

chance of escaping matrimony. Popular girls had no chance. Edna Jaques was popular and married a young neighbor, William Ernest Jamieson, and moved to a homestead in the Prince Albert district. A daughter was born but the glamour of log-cabin life faded and after four years, Edna Jaques Jamieson, taking the daughter with her, was striking out to make her own way. There was no hope of gaining a living from poetry alone and she took work of various kinds, secretarial, reporting for a newspaper, sewing and even that of stewardess on a steamship. The years of World War II found her in Ottawa, writing publicity for the Wartime Prices and Trade Board. Before returning to Briercrest, she worked for the *Vancouver Province*.

Through all those years and experiences, she lost none of her fondness for making poetry, and her reputation was growing. Although no author expected to make a living by writing at that time, her creative interests and efforts were a source of great joy and satisfaction.

When did this girl known as the Prairie Poetess or the Scrapbook Poetess of the West, begin her writing? The question is best answered by words from her own pen in 1974[1]: "It all began over 70 years ago. I began writing poetry as soon as I knew that cat rhymed with hat. The little lines would form in my mind, from God knows where, and I'd put them down on scraps of paper and hide them in the attic. One day I was reading them over, propped up against the haystack when my brother Clyde saw me and said: 'What are you reading?' and snatched the paper from me and ran. He came back and said: 'You didn't write that, you couldn't have, or did you?' I nodded 'yes' and he said: 'Why, they're lovely, just lovely,' and went away shaking his head."

A short time later, when it was Edna's turn to accompany the parents or an older brother driving by team and wagon to Moose Jaw, she was persuaded to take a couple

---

[1] Jaques, Edna, "The Way It Was," *Western Producer,* Jan. 30, 1975

of her poems, just in case there was an opportunity to show them. It was Brother Clyde's idea and he, at seventeen years of age and able to handle a team of horses, was to be the driver on this trip. The verses selected to be taken to Moose Jaw were carefully rewritten and the pages were rolled and tied with a hair ribbon. It was an outing the girl could not forget. The spring day was warm and the meadowlarks sang joyously. At mid-day, halfway to the city, Clyde and Edna stopped beside a creek and ate a picnic lunch while the horses were allowed time to take feed and water.

At Moose Jaw, Edna and her brother spent the night at the home of cousins and early on the next morning they set out to obtain the needed family supplies — the main reason for making the long journey by wagon — and pay a call at the office of Thomas Miller of the *Moose Jaw Times*. As they neared the editor's office, Edna began to lose her nerve. The great editor would have no interest in or time for her verses, she was sure, and was ready to run away. But Clyde, sensing her trepidation, assured her that she had nothing to fear. She had confidence in her big brother but made the mistake of thinking he would accompany her all the way to Mr. Miller's desk.

When they reached the editor's door and heard the invitation to "come in," Clyde opened the door and gently pushed the frightened girl inside and retired down the hall to wait for her. The girl from Briercrest was speechless until Mr. Miller asked her name and she managed to say it. When he inquired if she had something she wished to deliver to him, she tiptoed to his desk and placed the two pages of poetry tied with a ribbon in his hands and backed away shyly. He read each poem, smiled graciously and said: "You keep on writing and come again when you visit Moose Jaw."

It was told later that the editor, after Edna left his office, said to one of his assistants: "Did you see that little girl with the pigtails? Well, she is writing poetry and don't be surprised if she, some day, writes her name across Canada."

The poems delivered that day were the first the girl saw in print and the thirteen-year-old was moved with resolve. A year later she sent a poem to Evangelist Billie Sunday who not only acknowledged it but had it set to music and sang it at services.

Nobody would say she was an immediate success in her chosen field but encouragement came from many quarters. John Kerr, of the *Moose Jaw Herald,* would take a poem "and give me a couple of dollars to pave the way a bit," and Nellie McClung wrote to say: "You have the gift, Edna dear, to ring bells in the hearts of people." *The Saskatchewan Farmer* began carrying her poems and ran them for nearly twenty-five years, paying $1.50 for each one printed. And then Napier Moore, an eastern editor, wrote: "If you are the Edna Jaques whose poems are appearing in the *Saskatchewan Farmer, Maclean's Magazine* would appreciate if if you would send us some from time to time." Praise was coming from high and unexpected places and the poetess heard Prime Minister Mackenzie King confess shyly: "I've been your ardent fan for over 20 years."[1]

When asked about which poem brought the best response, her thoughts turned to 1918 when the war was drawing to an end and she was working as a seamstress at Holy Cross Hospital in Calgary. The poem, "In Flanders Fields" by John McCrae had appeared recently and Edna Jaques, continuing to use her maiden name in writing, was inspired to pen a reply to it. With nothing better at hand, she wrote on the bottom of a spoolbox, then sent the poem to the *Calgary Herald* where it was printed. As it appeared in print, it began:

> *We have kept faith, ye Flanders dead,*
> *Sleep well beneath those poppies red.*
> *The torch your dying hands did throw,*
> *We held it high before the foe,*
> *And answered bitter blow for blow,*
> *In Flanders Fields.*

[1] Jaques, Edna, *The Best of Edna Jaques,* Modern Press, 1966

The poem was picked up by Everywoman's Club, a wartime organization in the United States and printed along with the Belgian National Anthem to be sold for ten cents per copy to raise money for the restoration of the Louvain Library in Belgium, destroyed in the course of war. A total of more than a million dollars was raised The poem was then recited at the unveiling of the Tomb of the Unknown Soldier in Washington.

The lady from Briercrest wrote poetry under many and strange circumstances, even when flying in a plane high above Calgary. The *Calgary Herald* during exhibition week in 1919, invited her to make a flight with War Hero Freddie McCall, and write a poem about it. She agreed to being a passenger and McCall offered her a choice of three afternoons. She chose the middle day which, as things turned out, was a fortunate decision because a passenger was killed on the first day and the plane landed on the top of the merry-go-round at the midway on the third day. It surprised readers of 1919 that a woman in flight could be sufficiently relaxed to compose poetry. Perhaps some part of the creation was conceived before she went into the air but in any case she delivered the poem soon after tasting "the sky's vast depth" and being back on the ground.

> *There like a bubble of wanton joy,*
> *Skimming the breast of the sky,*
> *As under our feet like a painted toy,*
> *The little town goes by.*

She did not write for the scholarly few and made no attempt to be profound. Her verses were for the common people and they loved her work. By her own assessment, her poetry was "clad in homespun and the rough weave of common folks." Her verses were simple, clear and friendly, the expressions of a person who harbored no guile, no bitterness. But as a writer in *The Canadian Author and Bookman* (Helen Palmer) could say: "As an exponent and skilled practitioner of this type of verse, Edna Jaques has no peer in this country."

It could be added that she was one of the few authors who was able to come even close to making a living by writing poetry.

When they called her the Scrapbook Poet of the West it was because so much of her poetic work was clipped from the columns of papers and magazines to be accorded places of honor and permanence in family albums, old Bibles and files of very personal treasures.

It is not easy to select a typical Edna Jaques poem, especially when there are 3,000 from which to choose. Twenty judges might pick upon twenty different titles but for the present purpose let the selection be "A Happy Woman," published first in *The Hills Of Home* and then in *The Best of Edna Jaques*. In it the author reveals considerable about her own refreshing philosophy:

A HAPPY WOMAN

I met a happy woman
    Whose face was calm and sweet,
Who loved her home and all therein;
    The folks along her street,
She praised her children, told how nice
    They were to her and Dad,
And seemed to take a special joy
    In everything she had.

The morning glories climbing up
    Around her kitchen door,
She seemed to think she'd never grown
    Such lovely ones before,
Shop windows filled with glowing fruit—
    Spring flowers on display,
Set every fibre of her heart,
    To dancing for the day.

She didn't need a coach and four,
  To make her day complete,
She made her round of friendly calls,
  On her own sturdy feet,
Enjoying everyone she met
  And leaving in her wake,
A trail of happiness that spread,
  Like ripples on a lake.

I think the secret of her charm,
  Was just in being wise
Enough to see the simple things
  With clear contented eyes;
Holding aloft the precious flag,
  Of piety and grace
A happy woman growing old,
  With laughter on her face.

Edna Jaques moved to Toronto in 1939 and bought property at the lakefront near Oakville which proved worthwhile because land values went up and up. Finally she shared the home of son-in-law and daughter, Murray and Joyce Sugar at Willowdale, where she could indulge in gardening and continue to write.

Came her eightieth birthday in January, 1971, and there was a birthday party of the daughter's and son-in-law's planning. It was a happy affair, a time for recollections about homesteading in Saskatchewan, her first poems, her lecture tours, her nearly 200,000 books published, her good health, her way of living and the record of never having tasted liquor, her loyal friends and so on. One of those friends phoned to offer his best wishes while she was reminiscing; he was a sailor during the war, she explained, then confided proudly: "He sent me a nice fan letter many years ago and I mailed him a copy of my book, *Roses in December*. Now, today, he tells me he carried that book across the Atlantic 21 times, and around the world once."

And what now for the eighty-year-old poetess? It might be a proper time to end her writing and traveling but she had no intention of being idle. "I hope I will never be so old that I can't think of something useful to do." Her proposal to stop traveling was not to be taken seriously because in the next year she bought herself a new cowgirl outfit with white hat, fringed vest and skirt, and flew to visit the Calgary Stampede. And when she said she thought she would stop writing Edna Jaques poetry, her friends hoped she didn't mean that either.

Courtesy Mary Cody

MARY BARTER CODY: TO NURSE CODY "WITH LOVE"

It was Cereal's proudest day, Sunday, August 11, 1968, and hundreds of native sons and daughters were back in the home community of eastern Alberta to pay honor to a little lady who had been nurse in or matron of the village hospital for almost thirty years. Over the platform of the Community Hall where the big crowd gathered was a huge banner carrying the words: "TODAY'S QUEEN."

The Board of Trade sponsored the event but former residents from far and near responded with enthusiasm to the idea of returning to present the day to Mary Barter Cody, "With Love." All who actually participated in the platform program and, indeed, most of the visitors under the age of forty-nine years wore baby bonnets to identify themselves as babies born under Mrs. Cody's supervision in the little Cereal Hospital. They were there from many parts of Canada and a few parts of the United States, hundreds it seemed, and Mrs. Cody, beaming with pride and pleasure, said: "You are all my babies." Each of those "babies" brought a picture of himself or herself to be included in a big album presented at the end of the day to the happy guest of honor.

The program began with a special welcome from Mayor C. J. Peacock in which he recalled Mrs. Cody's unfailing devotion and the numerous acts of kindness and mercy which marked her years of service; it ended with a solo, "May The Good Lord Bless and Keep You." A lot of hearts beat a little faster and many eyes were moist enough to need wiping as the audience stood to pay the main tribute so splendidly earned by the lady described by one of the visitors as "The Florence Nightingale of the Prairies."

The determination to become a nurse came to her more than sixty years earlier when, as a teenager, Mary E. Barter was returning from Amherst, Nova Scotia, to her home in the Gaspé part of Quebec province. Her people were hard-working farmers at Grand Cascapedia, on the north shore of Baie Chaleur, where even primary school education was of necessity difficult to get. She was the fourth among six Barter children — three sisters older and two brothers younger — and schooling was cut short until a year when she found opportunity to make up part of the deficiency with a term at the Academy at Amherst. Now she was on her way home from that Nova Scotia city, eager to see members of her family again. But as the Intercolonial Railway train lurched and jerked through the sleepy villages along the shore, she became fascinated by a nurse who was traveling with a very sick patient, probably en route to hospital at Quebec City. The young lady in neat uniform looked lovely as she ministered tirelessly to make the sick person comfortable and the little girl was filled with admiration. Then and there she resolved to become a nurse.

But such a resolution was not easy to carry out; limited schooling made it difficult for a girl to gain acceptance to a training course. The eastern hospitals would not take her, but to her pleasant surprise, an application to Medicine Hat General Hospital brought the opportunity she so much desired. The only objection to it was in going so far from home. Medicine Hat seemed like the end of the earth. When she presented herself for registration late in

1912, she had the feeling of being in a foreign land. "The Hat" was still a cowboy community, distinctive only by its use of natural gas. Its hospital was a solidly constructed sandstone building with about sixty beds and a nursing staff consisting of Matron Victoria Winslow and ten graduate nurses. The round-faced girl of twenty years should have been homesick but she was soon engrossed with nursing tasks — twelve hours of duty per day, six and a half days per week — and she loved it. Her cash salary was six dollars per month but there were other rewards — like satisfaction.

The three training years passed quickly enough and graduation came on June 2, 1915. Seven girls — Edith Hunter, S. E. Kirkham, Margaret E. Learned, Mary E. Barter, Elsie Charles, Ethel McLuhan and Emma Read — had completed the course. Carrying flowers and wearing high, white, button boots and stiffly starched uniforms long enough to hide them, the girls stood to repeat the Florence Nightingale International Pledge: "In full knowledge of the obligations I am undertaking, I promise to care for the sick with all the skill and understanding I possess, without regard to race, creed, colour, politics or social status, sparing no effort to conserve life, to alleviate suffering and to promote health . . ."

Four special awards and prizes were available to members of the graduating class that day and when the winners were announced, Nurse Mary Barter had qualified for two of them, the thirty-five dollars in gold offered for the nurse standing second in general proficiency, and an award presented by Dr. F. W. Gershaw — later Senator Gershaw — for the best record in practical work throughout the course.

Mary Cody was now ready for work elsewhere. She was not required to write exams for the rank of Registered Nurse at that time. "I was given my title of R.N. in 1948," she wrote, "but didn't have to write the exams."

She accepted hospital work at Fernie, British Columbia, and there met a young fellow, Duncan Cody, who made her think of matrimony. They were married in

Lethbridge, in 1916, and it appeared that a career in nursing was being terminated. Fortunately, it wasn't. In June, 1918, the Codys went to Cereal by train and were met by Frank Kyle who took them to his hotel in the village. Then for a time they lived and worked on the farm of Staff Wilson, Mr. Cody's brother-in-law who lived about eighteen miles to the north. It was not an exciting life except for the weekly expedition to town on Saturday night. Everybody for twenty-five miles around went to Cereal at that time, whether supplies were needed or not. The Thomson Store was the principal hangout — "a great place to meet neighbors and pick up the community news and scandal" — and the store remained open for as long into the night as anybody wanted to stay.

Mrs. Cody was hearing a proposal to start a small hospital in the village. Naturally, she was interested but she was surprised when the doctor of the community suggested that she open and run the place when it became a reality. There was no question about the big prairie frontier needing the service but she did not think she was ready for such an assignment, and instead of waiting for the plan to mature, she went to Provost and worked in the hospital there from July to November.

In the meantime, Dr. Ernest Chandler, with the help of his wife, Mabel, succeeded in opening a small hospital in Cereal. The Prairie Circle of the Women's Institute provided the modest structure, previously a small private home of one-story construction, with glassed-in veranda, a few low-growing shrubs trying to survive in the dry soil, some ivy clinging to the low walls and a plank sidewalk in front. It was not imposing. And strangely enough, the lady who was to supervise the hospital for many years and give it a special character, was one of the first patients.

It was the year of the devastating epidemic of influenza and Mary Cody, returning to the Staff Wilson farm in November, promptly contracted it. Doctor Chandler drove out from Cereal to see her and ordered that she be taken at once to the new hospital. Perhaps he was still hoping to persuade her to accept a nursing position there.

Taking a patient from the Wilson farm to Cereal was not a small matter and there were complications. In the absence of an ambulance, Milt Dilks was directed to come with his McLaughlin touring car and a feather mattress used exclusively for sick people being conveyed to hospital. Weather was wintry but by placing a footwarmer containing hot coals or bricks under the mattress, a patient could get some localized protection against freezing. In this instance, the footwarmer proved defective; burning coals from the metal chamber escaped and, making contact with the mattress, threatened a conflagration. As Mrs. Cody recalled: "I felt myself getting hot but didn't say anything until the men smelled smoke." Sure enough, the mattress was burning and a halt had to be made for firefighting.

The flu epidemic grew worse. The little hospital was inadequate. The village hotel was converted to an emergency hospital and volunteer help was obtained to operate it. There were deaths and the community was paralyzed. Mrs. Cody recovered quickly and remained to nurse — never did get completely away for the next thirty-one years. The longer she remained, giving anesthetics, assisting in surgery, helping to bring babies into the world and making a little hospital serve a big need, the more essential her presence appeared. When Doctor Chandler was on a country call, which was often, she was expected to be both nurse and doctor.

Weeks after Doctor Chandler's death from a heart attack in 1923, Dr. John Esler came to Cereal and just as quickly won admiration. He was a dedicated fellow and he and Mrs. Cody formed a team of workers that was to become a medical legend in the area. Born at Blake, Ontario, he was now fifty years of age and not a total stranger in prairie Alberta. He was known as a good and conscientious practitioner but had the reputation, also, of a "rolling stone." After graduation in medicine, he practiced in Ontario, then in North Dakota, and in 1909, he located on land south of Hanna with the idea of combining homesteading and the practice of medicine. But it did not prove very satisfactory and he moved back to Ontario. Now, in 1923, he came again to the prairies and settled at Cereal. It was his last major move and Cereal was the Esler home until the doctor's death in 1938.

In 1932, Doctor Esler persuaded Mrs. Cody to take over as the matron of the shabby little nine-bed institution. Its accommodation at the time consisted of a six-bed ward for women, a two-bed ward for men and a so-called private ward for very sick people. The kitchen served as a nursery, with baby baskets resting on chairs until they had to be moved to escape drafts. The small dining nook served also as an X-ray room. The cupboard in the nurse's bedroom furnished storage space for sterile dressings and the closet in the same room doubled as a dark room for developing X-ray pictures. And what was called an office "had to be cleared out each time we had an operation or a maternity case."

In Doctor Chandler's time, sterilizing was done in a wash boiler. Dressings to be treated were wrapped and placed on a sling suspended from handle to handle, then "steamed for hours and dried in the oven." People had to be resourceful. It was the pre-antibiotic period and although some of the techniques were primitive, the hospital was clean, "shining like a new pin," and its medical record was good. All possible precautions were taken and Mrs. Cody could say that there had never been a serious bout with infection such as every hospital administrator feared. Structures and facilities might be lowly but the care and dedication were of a high order. The doctor and matron, devoting most of twenty-four hours per day to their patients, earned thanks and praise. Their combined efforts coincided with the most trying period in Western Canada's history, when their prairie area was ground down by drought and depression working together. In that big country from which their patients came — an area stretching from Empress to Veteran, from Hanna to the Saskatchewan boundary — there was practically no money with which to pay schoolteachers and no more for medical and hospital bills.

But members of the Esler-Cody team knew their hospital was needed and they would have to make do with limited facilities. Fortunately, both were resourceful. Doctor Esler was handy with hammer and nails and made many of the repairs at the hospital. Mrs. Cody actually took linen from her own home to augment the hospital's meager supply. "We tried to feed our patients well," she recalled, "but after they had their meal, the maid and I had very little for ourselves."

Doctor Esler was not in all respects a "horse-and-buggy doctor" because he varied his means of travel. During the depression years he traveled mainly by automobile, often by saddle horse or horse-drawn vehicle, sometimes on foot, occasionally by plane and rather often by freight train. He knew members of the freight crews and knew their running schedules. It happened rather often that a freight train would stop at a country crossroads to let the doctor transfer to a sleigh or wagon and just as often, he flagged down a freight train at an unscheduled and unmarked place between stations, "thumbing a ride back to Cereal," as it were.

Many times those country trips were exhausting. Sometimes he was racing with the stork as on that day when he went over a winter trail by homemade snowmobile and literally pushed the machine up every hill on the twenty-five-mile stretch to Youngstown. Arriving at the isolated farmhouse, he was greeted with a frantic call, "Hurry Doc," then led into a bedroom just in time to usher twins into the world and bring emergent care to the seriously weakened mother. It was a clear case of saving three lives.

On just such a country mission, the beloved doctor who tried to respond to every call, regardless of weather or distance, developed pneumonia and died in his little hospital a few days later. He was known to be sick when he started out to the distant farm, perhaps sicker than the patient he went to see. Death came on July 1, 1938, and people across the plains mourned.

The editor of the Cereal *Recorder* wrote for all who knew the doctor: "Dr. Esler is dead, a friend of humanity and a messenger of mercy to those who suffered from pain and disease, his loss will be mourned by this community and the surrounding districts for many years to come. In the discharge of his duties he never let personal consideration, weather or roads hinder him from reaching the bedside of any sufferer from disease or accident. . . . He is gone and the whole community mourns, but his memory will be enshrined in the hearts of those who knew him until time shall cease."

The Esler-Cody team was now broken but Mary Cody continued in service and Dr. Esler was followed by Dr. G. O. Patton, a young man under whose leadership the little hospital was enlarged. Negotiations were started for a Municipal Hospital. In 1945 the Women's Institute relinquished all claim to the original building and contents, turning everything over to the Municipal Hospital Board, without compensation. With the new status there would be government grants and better equipment.

The accommodation was extended and the equipment improved. And Mrs. Cody, still energetic, still dedicated, continued as matron until 1949 when with her husband, Dunc, and son, Donald — later Dr. Donald Cody with a big city practice — she left to make her home in Calgary. It was not easy to leave, and for the citizens of Cereal it was harder to see her leave, as the expressions of affection and the public gift of a purse of money showed. When she returned for the gay celebration in her honor in 1968 — then a widow — she confessed to having spent the busiest and happiest days of her life at Cereal Hospital, which was often referred to locally as "Mary Cody's Hospital."

But in going to Calgary, she was not retiring from useful service, not by any means. She was still a nurse and still very much in demand. Now and then she responded to an urgent call to come back to Cereal to relieve. Her dark hair had turned to gray but the big smile was unchanged and so was the spring in her step. She could still walk the three miles from her home to downtown Calgary when other means of transportation were not at hand and think nothing of it. And at the age of eighty she was still performing as a nurse, still walking to work at her son's medical clinic at six o'clock in the morning, not because she had to start so early but because she wanted it that way and it would leave her with more time for hobbies and other interests at the other end of the day.

One who knew her in those late years said of Nurse Mary Cody: "A grand neighbor, one with the dynamics of a firecracker and the ideals to make her a source of inspiration to all who knew her."

ELLEN FOSTER: FRIEND OF GOD'S WILD CHILDREN

She was a bashful little lady with a mild voice, a big heart and unrelenting dedication. With extraordinary artistic talents, she became a musician of note and might have gained similar distinction in painting and poetry. But overriding all else in her life was a love and compassion for animals. Even a brief visit at her home, a rather shabby house on Calgary's 17th Avenue, S.W., offered all the relevant evidence. Hanging on one wall of her living room was a beautiful oil painting bearing her name and showing West Highland cattle standing as monarchs in their Scottish glen; on another wall, among various certificates, was one denoting musical attainment in violin, the Licentiate of the Royal School of Music, London; on remaining walls were pictures of animals and throughout was the heavy odor of cats, betraying the presence of the nineteen felines sharing her house. All were cats which had been abandoned by previous owners and destined to starve or freeze until adopted by Miss Foster.

"These are my winter boarders," she said in gentle voice. "As long as I have something to eat, they'll eat too." Diets however, differed; the cats were still carnivorous while Miss Foster had not departed from her vow of fifty years earlier that she would never again be guilty before her Maker of eating His other animal creatures.

She liked people, but they had disappointed her so often, leaving her puzzled. Their utter callousness toward animals disturbed her. Even many professing Christian principles showed no concern. "What is wrong with churchmen who loudly proclaim doctrines and remain silent in the face of moral atrocities against animals?" she asked. "When are churchmen going to take a stand on practices like vivisection, the taking of wild furs by means of the awful steel traps, hunting when the hunters have no need for meat, and the abandonment of cats and other domestic animals to perish in Canadian winters?

"Oh, the arrogance of a race whose members try to convince themselves that they hold some special license from the Creator and can rightfully use or abuse all other living forms as they choose. For too long people have engaged in a form of warfare against Nature and Nature's children and then wondered why they have made no progress in the pursuit of a dream of 'Peace on Earth.' "

"Having spent my early years in the trapping region, north of Edmonton," she told in a letter to the press (*Albertan*, December 1, 1970), "I learned about the terrible suffering inflicted on our Canadian wild creatures on the trap lines, and how they would sometimes chew off a limb to escape the slow torture. Since that time, trapping and the memory of it have been like a horrible nightmare to me and for that reason I have refused to wear furs of any kind. While it is probably true that most women do not realize the hours of torture their furs represent, the fact remains that the fur industry flourishes mainly to satisfy the vanity of women, therefore, we of the feminine sex should do something about it. We have been asked to speak up loud and clear insisting that more humane, quick-killing traps be substituted for the leg-hold trap, which should be thrown on the scrap heap along with other instruments of torture."

The Fosters came from Preston, Lancashire, England, where Miss Foster was born in 1895. Coming to Canada in 1901, the father worked for a short time near Millet and then took a homestead at a place then known as Mellowvale, near the present village of Dapp. On the new farm, the Fosters were twelve miles from a store and there was no school within a day's drive in any direction. There was no school for Miss Ellen but, fortunately, her older brother had had the opportunity of a good primary education in England and he tutored his small sister.

But, as Miss Foster recalled with evident nostalgia, girlhood years on the frontier were not at all dull. The homestead surroundings held all the charms of Nature unspoiled and she found delight in the birds and animals and flowers. Moreover, the young girl had her dog, big, lovable and loyal Bob, and when she was outside, he never left her. He pulled her sled in the snow, hauled eggs to the distant store and hauled groceries back. But one night when the sun was setting, Bob heard a message he could not ignore. Coyotes far away in the direction of the lake were heard to howl and the family dog cocked his ears, barked and wandered into the dusk. Whether he was angry at the howling coyotes, curious or simply lonely for canine companionship, nobody could tell but he never returned and only his bones and bits of his hide were found. Did the wild cousins gang up and kill him or did he adopt the untamed life until he starved? Nobody knew, but the little girl was saddened at the loss of a companion.

Neighbors in that homestead community were friendly people and came together quite often to make music and to dance on kitchen floors. Nobody had a piano but Ellen Foster's father played a violin and had many calls to use it. And while still a small girl, she received violin instruction from her father. That she had special talent became very evident, it was equally evident that she should have the opportunity for the very best in instruction. When she was fifteen years old, mother and daughter moved to Edmonton where the girl could have the benefit of good teachers and pursue her studies in violin. The response was encouraging and Miss Ellen profited from the experience of playing with orchestras and in recitals. With widening recognition, she was invited to play with the Bessie Larcher Company and perform on various Chautauqua circuits in both Canada and the United States. That traveling institution, combining both educational and entertainment features, was modeled after a summer school program at Chautauqua, New York, and enjoyed unsurpassed prestige during the years following the Great War. For Ellen Foster, the Chautauqua experience lasted for seven years and ended only when the advent and acceptance of radio changed public demand for the traveling shows. But after touring extensively and performing in remote parts of the continent, Ellen Foster was glad to settle down in Calgary, there to further her studies in music, teach young people desiring to master the violin, do some painting and write poetry. She never gave up completely the teaching of violin.

There were other events and interests in her life, some romantic, some heartbreaking. People who knew her as a performing musician and a beautiful girl with trim figure and lovely manner wondered why she did not marry. There are some things for which a girl does not need to offer explanation but a certain poem, entitled "Unforgetting," gave a hint of a great secret sadness locked in her heart. It was more, however, than a hint of tragedy in a girl's life; it was an excellent illustration of the tender quality of Ellen Foster's thoughts and words:

You paused beside the gate — How I remember;
You were so shy, your words came with such care,
But oh the magic of your voice grown tender —
It reached my heart and found a temple there.

And high in a tall tower a bird went singing
A mad sweet song of youth and hope and love,
Arcadia's winds blew round us, incense flinging.
We walked as angels walk the realms above.

*You went away to war. I watched you starting
With pomp of martial glory down the street,
The steady march of men — oh God, the parting.
Did you not feel my heart beneath your feet?*

*The years have passed, the temple walls have
    crumbled,
Dead is the bird, its song forever still.
In war's grim ruins youth and hope lie humbled;
Yet love remains, defies the grinding mill.*

*They wonder why I choose the pathway lonely.
Unthinking ones who pass with scornful face.
To me, you were so dear, so brave, mine only,
How could I put another in your place?*

Most of her verses were about birds and animals. Nor was it surprising that her very first attempt at poetry was about cats. Composed at the very tender age of four years, it went like this:

> *Run little kitty,
> Run to your bed
> Or else naughty folks
> On your feet will tread.
> It will hurt you very bad
> And mamma pussy will be sad.*

She possessed the feeling, surely, for poetic greatness. Moreover, she wrote with ease and it took nothing more than a sparrow or a robin to inspire her to verse, as in the following:

Sir Robin Returns

*Good morning, Sir Robin, you've come back, I see,
You want a small bungalow up in a tree?
You were with me last summer, Oh I quite remember
Your tenancy lasted well into September.*

And how is your lady? A new one, Oh dear!
You are slightly fickle, Lord Robin, I fear,
That explains your new coat. That vest I declare
Is the last word in what a smart Robin should wear.

Well, let's get down to business, what kind of a house
Does your fancy dictate for this charming new spouse?
Something high and exclusive, with fashionable gables,
Or something suburban, down near the stables?

This silver birch limb makes a wonderful swing,
The Linnets enjoyed it immensely last spring.
This cradle your lady will find safe and dry,
And round it the winds sing a soft lullaby.

Regarding the terms — well an aria at seven
With a silver-toned carol, perhaps at eleven.
Your wife sings as well! A duet let it be.
And then there is madrigal practice at three.

Concerning the garden, the peas, Robin dear,
Are not in the terms of agreement this year.
The swimming pool's free, and a large hunting ground,
Where insects of almost all species abound.

You'll come in at once, I'm delighted to hear.
If another bird comes — now Robin don't fear,
Bird's-eye villa is yours. I'll announce it to all,
Leased by Sir Robin Redbreast for summer and fall.

    Ellen Foster was not alone in writing about robins but she was almost alone in sensing good character in the lowly sparrows. Perhaps it was the same instinct that made her a friend of stray cats that induced her admiration for sparrows. The little gray birds which received so much human scorn, appeared most frequently in Miss Foster's verses. One of those poems should be noted:

The Sparrow

Across the leaden sky he curves and dips
And from a crystal flake refreshment sips.
He dines off snowy linen, fairy spun
And warms his tiny feet by the pale sun.
Quite undismayed he meets the northern gale,
Content a sparrow's manna will not fail,
A gay adventurer he through stormy days
And yet I wonder why it is he stays.

Now can it be he still regards the words
The Master spoke of him, humblest of birds?
And that is why he has such perky airs,
And such a saucy flit of wing, he dares
Quite boldly on my porch as if he knew
The morsels from my table his just due.

He is a missionary in his way
This lively little ball of brown and grey,
Without the benefit of bell or choir
He chants his litany, a small brown friar,
From leaf-stripped bough to icy roof he hops
And from his cloister mid the chimney tops
His happy creed with chirps he does insist
A most undaunted, small evangelist.

One characteristic never changed, the lady's tender feeling for her animal friends, wild or tame, which could not speak for themselves and were too often made to suffer to satisfy certain human lusts. She was the prime mover in the formation of the Calgary Chapter of the Humane Society For Prevention of Cruelty to Animals on July 11, 1922. Through all the remaining years of her life she served the organization's purposes quietly, consistently, devotedly. Her unfailing loyalty to a cause was recognized most fittingly when, in 1965, the addition to the Society for Prevention of Cruelty to Animals' building in Calgary was dedicated as the Ellen Foster Wing.

Particularly eager to gain the interest of young people, she undertook to form and guide a Band of Mercy within the S.P.C.A. and for many years she conducted educational contests and contributed a Children's Pet Column in one of the newspapers. Ever anxious to do more, she threw her energy behind the Animal Defence League and between 1960 and 1968 operated an educational booth at the Calgary Exhibition and Stampede, passing out literature, talking to people about atrocities on traplines, on the ice where baby seals were being murdered by the thousands, in the laboratories where innocent animals were subjected to terrible suffering in the name of science and medicine, in the fields where the so-called blood sports were popular, and even on the streets where motorists sometimes struck dogs and cats without bothering to stop.

"Yes, a Bill of Rights for animals!" she said. "We need it." She favored a Bill of Rights for humans but a similar statute was needed to safeguard animals from the cruel exploits of the human predators.

Some people said she was a fanatic; some said a nut. But Ellen Foster, to those who knew her, differed mainly in having a more sensitive and admirable conscience than her critics. "If a just and unprejudiced God gave me a soul, he gave His other children the same," she said while patting one of the many homeless cats she had adopted. "And if there is a Heaven for me, there must be the same for my animal friends who by their conduct on earth are certainly no less deserving. Besides, Heaven will be a better place if the birds and animals are there. Wouldn't you agree?"

She wanted to see an animal cemetery in Calgary and when one was finally opened early in 1970, it was named The Ellen Foster Pet Cemetery. On the occasion of the opening, one of Miss Foster's admirers remarked: "If cats and dogs and other animals do qualify for admittance to Heaven, as she chooses to expect, there will sure be a noisy welcome for her when she arrives. And the King of Heaven, who loves mercy, will approve."

Courtesy Orren Jack Turner

HILDA MARION NEATBY:
A PLEA FOR LOVE OF LEARNING

The scholarly and religious Neatbys were from the South London suburb of Sutton in Surrey and about as English as crumpets with tea. In emigrating to Canada in 1906, they stopped at Earl Grey, north of Regina, where the father, a medical doctor, began practicing his profession. Miss Hilda, who would some day win national honors and shake Canadian education to its very roots with good effect, was two years old and one of eight children in the immigrant family.

They remained at Earl Grey only a year and a half; there was the urge to farm and the elder Neatby was leaving his profession and taking his family to a homestead at Renown, driving the last thirty-six miles from Nokomis by team and wagon. In moving to the homestead, the Neatbys were taking little except muscle and faith and a library of good books. It was unusual to encounter such a stockpile of the best English literature and such scholarly tastes in reading far back in homestead country. Anybody who would attempt to read Chaucer or Tennyson while guiding a horse team and two-furrow plow soon gained a reputation for bad plowing and peculiar ways.

The Neatbys, by the standards of the time and place, were the eccentric Englishmen, but in their devotion to good books and good reading, nothing would change them. They loved learning. "Our parents," said Hilda's brother, Dr. Leslie Neatby, "were always ready to discuss what we read. We learned early to dispute on points of morals and literature. I can recall arguing a point of literary criticism with Hilda while we were milking cows in the stable. Study of Dickens, Scott, Macaulay and books of travel and adventure gave us a wide if informal knowledge of history and geography and of human environments very different from our own."[1]

The homestead was twelve miles from Watrous, the nearest point on the railroad at the time, and the fact that there was no public school in the area would have offered the best possible excuse for an escape from formal education. But the Neatbys had no intention of surrendering to such an obstacle. The children were taught at home, and having the benefit of devoted parents and the best in books, they were well taught. The program was religious as well as secular and as noted by Dr. Leslie Neatby: "In a worldly sense, those of us who have taken up authorship owe much to an early and intimate knowledge of that fountain of musical and muscular English prose. the Authorized Version of the English Bible."

When a public school was provided in the district, there was difficulty in accommodating all the pupils of eight grades in a single room and Hilda was one of those who, with help from teacher and parents, continued to do much of her class work at home. She passed Grade VIII in 1916 and Grade X in the next year, having reached that latter standing with a total of only five years of formal schooling. Most farm youngsters of the time were presumed to be needed at home and discontinued their school program at Grade VIII. Not so with the precocious Hilda and her brothers and sisters who were all reading avidly in history and biography. With both brilliance and desire,

[1] Neatby, Leslie, private communication, June, 1975

they were taking advantage of every educational opportunity until it could be wondered if any family in the country could surpass the Neatbys in academic performance.

Because of the flu epidemic in late 1918, Hilda missed the first half of her Grade XI school year but completed the work in the second half and matriculated. After teaching at a rural school for part of 1920, she enrolled at the University of Saskatchewan in the autumn and graduated in 1924 with High Honors in History and French and the recipient of the Copland Scholarship awarded to the graduate with the highest standing in Arts and Science.

Postgraduate studies followed, of course, first a year at the Sorbonne in France on a University of Saskatchewan scholarship, and then back to the Saskatoon campus to instruct in French. Shortly thereafter, she was instructing in history and qualifying for her master's degree. She obtained her doctorate from the University of Minnesota in 1934 and returned to Saskatchewan to teach history at the university's Regina College. There she remained for the next twelve years. From 1958 until her reitrement in 1969, she was the head of the department of history at the University of Saskatchewan. And through the years her extracurricular activities were many and varied, as for example, her service as the only woman on the Massey Royal Commission studying Arts, Letters and Sciences in Canada, between 1949 and 1951.

No doubt the prestige gained by a place on the Royal Commission helped to emphasize the message carried in her almost classical criticism of Canadian education, *So Little for the Mind*, published in 1953. At once she was the object of national attention and showered with commendation and censure. A few people were offended; most agreed with the author. In any case, an analysis was needed and Hilda Neatby with her natural talent, her early training and many years of teaching experience, was the person to write it.

She believed the Canadian school system was failing to challenge young people sufficiently. The idea of training young Canadians without educating them was abhorrent to her. If education failed, society must suffer — and society was already suffering. With all the technical advances, she noted, western society was "dissatisfied, restless and insecure. . . . Ours has become a rootless as well as a faithless society."[1] Education could not escape some responsibility for the "flabby morality" of the time. Had she been writing a couple of decades later, she would have been searching for still stronger terms.

If educationists needed to be jolted, the controversial book proved to be a most effective instrument. But teachers and administrators were divided on principles; some praised the Neatby reasoning while others defended the new or progressive methods of teaching and wished they could "tear the book apart." But even the critics were hard pressed to explain why the best of educational values of other years should not be preserved, meaning particularly, the more liberal studies most likely to enrich the mind. She would order more emphasis on literature, history, languages, mathematics and the arts. That the training of the intellect should be the most important function of the school was a precept with which nobody dared to disagree very loudly.

She was not suggesting that intellectual development stand alone or be isolated from other aspects of the child's needs, emotional, physical and spiritual, but to neglect it would be unfair and unjust. Oh for an "aristocratic revival" in learning, with the things of the mind accorded the place they deserve, she seemed to be saying. Intellectual achievements would be "those which the school as a school delights to honour."[2]

Nor was she objecting to training courses to meet modern demands for technicians and professional workers, but even the growing need did not justify neglect of the liberal or cultural side in a well-rounded education to prepare young Canadians for living during their working years and living in their later years.

[1]Neatby, Hilda, *So Little for the Mind,* Clarke Irwin and Co., 1953
[2]Ibid.

"It is of the utmost importance to remember" she said, "that the stream of pure or liberal learning and the stream of practical knowledge never really mingle, although they flow together."[1]

If she was correct, Canadian education was facing a dilemma and steps had to be taken to change the general direction it was following. Pleading for a cultivation of love for learning such as that which brought greatness to ancient Greece, she expressed confidence that Canada possessed the student resources needed and could provide the "gifted and dedicated teachers who would offer a strenuous kind of education to those who could and would take it."[2]

She felt the challenge keenly and would add: "If this dream or something like it could be fulfilled, I believe we would be on the way to restoring the flickering lamps of Canadian learning to a bright and steady glow."[3]

It was all very well to make educational processes simple and enjoyable but there were, she believed, rich intellectual resources going to waste in young Canadians because instruction had become too easy. Muscular fitness was not achieved without strenuous exercise and intellectual fitness required corresponding application and effort. It would be tragic if cultural development were allowed to suffer because the processes were difficult.

Teachers held the keys to the shape of Canadian lives in years ahead. It was a grave responsibility. Everything possible should be done to hold the good ones in the profession and everything possible should be done to make it easy for the others to get out. Teachers should be allowed to forget, momentarily at least, the problems of the modern world so that they might concentrate on gaining a better perspective of the ills of the whole civilization. Let them see their students, not merely as so many units with emotional drive, but as "heirs of this civilization

---
[1] *Calgary Herald,* May 12, 1959
[2] Ibid.
[3] *Calgary Herald,* May 13, 1959

capable of enjoying it and enriching it." The good teachers would be "evangelists with a genuine love of truth" to be imparted to young Canadians.

Of course, the Hilda Neatby concern went far beyond the schools. Expressing a yearning for a Canadian renascence, she called for a revival of the old art of conversation because "minds need constant exercise." Music and drama should not be neglected and creativeness should certainly be encouraged. Universities must recognize their obligations to the public but should not be allowed to become mere "service institutions of a rather narrowly utilitarian kind with somewhat grudging tolerance for theoretical studies normally in the faculty of Arts . . . It is a nice question whether the intellectual light of the Universities in becoming diffused over an ever widening area may not also be growing correspondingly dim."[1]

The Learned Societies, those key centers for intellectual conversation, must be maintained to do for good Canadian minds what was intended for them, to "fertilize each other and maintain the highest products of scholarship."

Libraries, galleries and museums deserved more attention and support. It was for the daily press, the radio and television to focus more upon the cultural side of Canadian life. "The national radio has served as a most important instrument of general education and culture . . . It has brought music of all kinds, plays, books and even, indirectly, pictures to many who by this means . . . acquired new capacity for enjoyment."[2] Nevertheless, she added, there was no reason for complacency and if broadcasting was considered to be a reflection of the vigor and intensity of our national intellectual life, "we must aim to do much better." "We simply have not enough people who find their chief recreation in intellectual pursuits."

---

[1] Neatby, Hilda, Canadian Culture, condensation of an address to Canada's Tomorrow Conference, *Calgary Herald*, Dec. 4, 1953.
[2] Ibid.

Yes, the warnings and admonitions ruffled a few administrative "feathers" across Canada but led to undetermined numbers of reassessments of education and related matters in all the provinces, and made people generally more conscious of basic values.

And appropriately, many high honors were bestowed upon her. In 1954 she was Saskatoon's Citizen of the Year and in 1967 she was named Woman of the Century by the National Council of Jewish Women and presented with a Centennial Bronze Medal for outstanding service to Canada. The Canadian Women's Press Club presented her with a Centennial Medal for the best historical work written by a woman in Canada in 1968. And honorary degrees were conferred upon her by the University of Saskatchewan and the University of Toronto.

Dr. Hilda Neatby died at Saskatoon on May 14, 1975, age seventy-one, and it was noted at once that Canada had lost one of its greatest teachers, historians and authors, one whose influence was to reinforce the imperfect foundations of Canadian education, one whose rise to national and international fame brought satisfaction and glory to her family, members of her sex, and another pioneer farm home and rural school.

Courtesy Lillooet Publishers, Lillooet, British Columbia

MARGARET "MA" MURRAY: SPEARING FOR THE TRUTH

The *Bridge River-Lillooet News* wasn't like any other newspaper in the world because its editor and publisher, Mrs. Margaret Murray, known across Canada as "Ma" Murray, wasn't like any other person in the business. Rival papers might have bigger circulations and more striking headlines but none carried more forthright and pungent editorials. The editor's language shocked some readers and listeners and her grammar left something to be desired in academic circles, but nobody failed to get the message or understand exactly where she stood on current issues of politics, economics and morals.

In Calgary for a speaking engagement with the District Teachers' Convention in February, 1973 — "sixty years to the day since I came here to help George Fuller sell ads for a special edition of the *Albertan*" — she faced her audience with typical candor, telling the teachers they were losing the dedication they once had; in striking they were renouncing concern about the harm they were doing to the public. "And tenure is no better because it robs teachers of incentive."

If her journalistic style bore some resemblance to that

of Bob Edwards of *Calgary Eye Opener* fame, perhaps it was due to an acquaintance with him which began when she was on her honeymoon in 1913 and grew to admiration. Both editors believed in frankness and honesty in their writings. Both refused to surrender their precious individuality and both had a fine sense of humor. There was one obvious difference in their papers: the *Calgary Eye Opener,* following its editor's unsteady ways, was published "semi-occasionally," while the *Bridge River-Lillooet News* came out on Thursday, as regularly as "weekly choir practice or mealtime for a bottle baby."

Even readers whose main interest was on the sports or comics page found themselves turning first of all to Ma Murray's editorials to get her latest views about the sins of society and see them set down in fire-and-brimstone language they could easily understand. Those eager readers might not agree with her point of view but they knew the editorials would never be dull.

At the paper's masthead, on the upper left-hand corner of the editorial page, was the appropriate introduction: "Bridge River-Lillooet News. Printed in the Sagebush Country of the Lillooet every Thursday, God willing. Guarantees a chuckle every week and a belly laugh once a month or your money back. Subscriptions $5.00 in Canada. Furriners $6.00."

And at the upper right-hand corner of the same page was the statement about circulation with the figure changing from week to week. The announcement on January 7, 1971, as an example, proclaimed: "Circulation 1556, and every bloody one paid for."

When celebrating her eighty-sixth birthday in 1973 and still writing editorials "with lots of salt in 'em," Ma Murray could look back upon an association of sixty years with western journalism. It had been a good life and she wouldn't have changed any part of it. She wouldn't have willingly missed any part of the fun, even for more dollars. "You can miss a lot of good living if you think only of the money; there ain't no pockets in a shroud, you know."

For her introduction to the newspaper business she

gave all credit to her husband, George Matheson Murray, Ontario-born journalist and politican, who died in 1961. She was born at Windy Ridge, Kansas, in 1887, and came to Canada in 1912 "to catch a good-looking cowboy." Correct or not, it was a good story, how she was working for a mail-order store, shipping saddles to western customers, and to one going to Alberta, she attached a personal note and evidently there was a reply and the young lady prepared for a trip to Western Canada. But instead of going to Calgary "to catch a cowboy," she went to Vancouver and worked for a weekly newspaper, the *Vancouver Chinook*, then married the editor, George Matheson Murray. To mark the occasion, the newlyweds had dinner at a Vancouver hotel and the first person they saw when entering the dining room was Bob Edwards and they invited him to join the little party. Bashfully, Bob declined but before many minutes two bottles of champagne were delivered at the Murrays' table with Bob's compliments. "We drank one," said the lady as she reminisced, "and decided to keep the other for the christening." To consume the contents of the second bottle they did not have awfully long to wait because "nine months to the day after our wedding, a daughter was born and we had Bob's bottle for the christening."

In their first year following marriage, the Murrays bought a small magazine, *Country Life*, and went from one publishing venture to another, gaining journalistic fame with passing time. They had their reverses as well as successes, when everything seemed to be going wrong. According to Mrs. Murray's telling: "I'd say to George, 'we've done all we can; we'd better leave the rest to God.' George would caution against leaving too much to God and I'd say 'He's never complained yet.' "

For two years, George Murray was the managing editor of the *Vancouver Sun*. When in 1933 he was elected as Liberal member of the legislature for Lillooet, his wife, left more on her own resources, embarked upon the Lillooet newspaper venture. Her unusual style and talent won immediate attention and the acid in her pen proved strong enough to burn where it touched.

Daughter Georgina and son Dan were interested in journalism and were soon able to assume management responsibilities in other papers the Murrays acquired or started. There was the *Howe Sound News* and the *Cariboo News* and then, when Ma Murray went to inspect the new Alaska Highway under construction in the war period, she sensed a great future for Fort St. John. She resolved to start a paper there, even though the critics were sure that war's end would see the United States engineers and troops withdrawn and Fort St. John shrinking to its former insignificance. But the lady had confidence and on St. Patrick's Day, 1944, she saw the first issue of the *Alaska Highway News* go into the mail. Things were primitive; she could count twenty-eight outdoor privies from her office window, but she set about with characteristic resolution to improve the town and give it the character of permanency. It was a struggle for a while, she confessed, "and we had to raise a lot of hell before St. John shaped up as we had hoped."

George Murray's involvement in public life became greater. After occupying a seat in the provincial legislature for eight years, he was elected in 1949 to the House of Commons, representing the constituency of Cariboo. More and more, Ma Murray was becoming the publishing head of the family and demonstrating her ability. More and more her editorial opinions about human conduct were being read and quoted. Sometimes they offended; often they were entertaining; always they were her own.

Some critics accused her of being old-fashioned and she hastened to say that she was indeed and believed it was time for the revival of certain old-fashioned ideas stressing thrift and vigor and willingness to work. "Preaching what a person believes to be true is never unjustifiably old-fashioned. Canadians have become a pampered people," she said, "and governments are to blame. The state of politics in this country is as low as a snake's belly. We may need a depression to jolt us back to common sense. Never were so many opportunities hitting people right in the face and never was there such a dearth of willing workers. Never did so many people have so much money for so long and do so little with it, and have so little left in the end. What I want to know is just what kind of a society is going to emerge when this nation is finally bankrupt, financially, mentally and morally." Actually she loved politics and would have made an able representative to an elected body. Everybody should be politically involved, she argued.

She wrote much about water policies. The big dam on the Peace River, according to her, "was conceived in egotism and was about 40 years ahead of its time," and "we got too bloody little from the Americans for the Columbia River and you are the ones who are going to be paying through the nose."

"The best damsite is undamned," she told her readers.[1] "The Moran Dam which was mooted immediately after the promotion of the Pacific Great Eastern Railway is the best and safest of all the damned dams and had it been followed with construction in 1924 when the proper survey was handed in at Victoria . . . the Peace River dam could have been skipped for another five decades. . . . The Bennett is the damndest dam of all the dams now proceeding in B.C. The Columbia complex is partially financed by the U.S. It also enslaves Canada as long as the water runs to give them flood control. The Bennett dam is a do-it-yourself deal and the B.C. taxpayer has to dig up every bloody cent of the cost and that's for damshur."

She was impatient with labor unions, just as with governments, and her editorial on August 27, 1970, directed at the mail carriers was rather typical: "So the posties will not strike for three days and isn't that damn white of them, to deliver the old age pension checks. We hope they take a minute and ponder how bloody lucky the posties are to have O.A.P. dependents and thank their lucky stars we

[1] *Bridge River-Lillooet News*, Jan. 14, 1971

and they live in a country where there's enough to pay people who live their lives out — whether it's always enough or not. If the like of the posties and the rest of the rabble who's got the swelled head these days would consider the shakey hold unionism has on the rest of society right now, they should remember that all that goes up, comes down. And thank God for the law of gravity.''

Nor did her own sex escape. "Women are raising a lot of hell these days for liberation,'' she wrote on her editorial page, "If women were smart, talked less, thought more, they'd get liberation. Liberation must come from women themselves, for themselves first. It's 50 years pretty soon since the women by and large on this continent got the franchise. . . . Women have slipped backward since they began to rabble-rouse and covet masculine effect. . . . Women have let style-makers twist them around like a corkscrew. Women permitted shoe manufacturers to practically cripple them by persecutions of narrow, tilted shoes. For five years the style was toothpick shoes, crowding the foot into too long a vamp. Then suddenly shoes switched to a broad toe, clumpy heels, while stockpiles of pointed toes lay unworn at home. Women are a pushover for a lot of things and the more they talk about emancipation, the more they succumb to whims, alibis, substitutes, etc.

"Women have let sex get out of hand. They passively let promiscuity of the male weaken his potency. Women put the kibosh on their best asset when they accepted the pill. Women are now aping men, polishing off their supremacy and hastening the end of an era. They can never be anything but a second sex, but have been too bloody stupid to magnify their greatest asset by making the most of their preferred position in the centre of the family and the ultimate success of mankind.''

Of course her writings irritated some readers, infuriated a few, but when they wrote their brickbats, Ma Murray published the letters, giving them the same prominence as she gave the bouquets. The announcement that Mrs. Murray would receive an Order of Canada award at an investiture in Government House, Ottawa, in 1971, brought countless expressions of congratulations and joy, also a few letters from individuals who believed the honor was misdirected. Among the letters published on February 11, 1971, were two with a diametrically different tone, side by side. One correspondent wrote: "Just heard your bragging session on the radio . . . it was just as sickening as all your so called speeches. . . . Yes, we agree you surely need a medal, but it should be an award for the foul language you use all the time. I must say it's most unbecoming to an old woman. . . . Disgustingly yours, White Rock, B.C."

The other letter, separated by only a line, said: "Would just like to say that if we had a few more Ma Murrays in all our political parties, a lot of things would move a bit faster, or maybe a lot faster, and if these fancy politicians would use less hi-falutin words, the ordinary human being would be a lot more attentive. In politics and every other part of living, we need many more like you, and that's for damshur."

And while Ma's friends were still saying "Congratulations," it was announced that Simon Fraser University would, at the May, 1971, convocation, confer an honorary degree upon her, along with Chief Dan George and Dr. Gordon Shrum. "They must think I'm old enough to quit working," she commented and apparently it did give her the idea because she announced in October of that year a proposal to sell her paper. Yes, if she could find some young fellow "with something to say and willing to spend a year with an old crock like me," she would sell. But after receiving more than a hundred inquiries, she had a change of mind; the eighty-five-year-old had decided to withdraw the paper from the sale list. "I got to asking myself what I'd do if I sold. Besides, it doesn't make any money anyway so why should anybody buy the paper?"

As she prepared for another birthday, she speculated that some people might be inquiring for her recipe for a long life. "If you go by me" she said, "it takes a little bit of everything, a little bit of loving, a little bit of drinking and a little bit of working — and make damned sure you don't slip on a banana skin and break your hip." One of her friends added that it seemed to take "a little bit of cussing too." But whatever the secret, Ma Murray, over many years, made people laugh and made them think and her impact was immense.

Courtesy St. Andrew's College, Saskatoon, Saskatchewan

LYDIA GRUCHY: A LONG WAIT FOR ORDINATION

An October chill was in the air and Moose Jaw people, grateful for anything that would take their thoughts away from depression and drought and drifting soil, suddenly realized that church history was being made in their city. As surprising as if a Catholic priest were being married, a Protestant woman was being ordained into the ministry of her church, the first in all of Canada. Lydia Emelie Gruchy, after having made the highest marks in her graduating class in theology at St. Andrew's College, Saskatoon, in 1923, had waited thirteen long years before the General Council of the United Church of Canada gave authority for the ordination of a woman.

Those churchmen who opposed the full ministerial status for a woman — regardless of how well qualified she might be otherwise — quoted St. Paul in his instructions to the Corinthians: "Let your women keep silence in the churches, for it is not permitted unto them to speak . . . if they will learn anything, let them ask their husbands at home; for it is a shame for women to speak in the church" (First Corinthians 14:34, 35). In saying it again when writing to Timothy, St. Paul was certainly doing nothing to ingratiate himself with modern women, however successful he may have been in convincing those of his generation.

In 1936 a few churchmen continued to shake their heads, asking in tones of frustration: "What's the church coming to?" But for Miss Gruchy and countless members of her sex who believed she was as well qualified to administer the orders of the church as any male, the event of that year was a notable triumph.

It wasn't that she had been idle during the thirteen years; the fact was that she had served the church tirelessly and well in subordinate roles like assistant to the minister. There was nothing in denominational law to prevent her from preaching a sermon, such as even a layman might do, so there was plenty to keep her occupied. But by the terms of authority in her church she could not, any more than an unordained person, administer the sacrament, formally receive new members into the church, or perform baptisms; and she could not be the "Reverend" Lydia Gruchy.

To her friends and supporters, it was neither just nor sensible but that was the way it had been for more than a thousand years and some of the male "pillars in the church" believed it was the way it should remain.

Born in 1895, Lydia Gruchy's birthplace was in the outskirts of Paris where her father — a Jersey Islander — and her mother — an Englishwoman — were making their home. There Lydia received part of her elementary education, with more to follow in Sussex, England. Still at an early age, she, along with brothers and sisters, was left motherless, and at this point, her father resolved to take his growing family — four boys and five girls — to Canada. Acting on impulse, he journeyed in 1913 to Saskatchewan and settled on the fresh soil of a farm at Strasbourg.

It looked like a good place to raise a family but there was one handicap: the completion of education for members of the family could be difficult. The problems were very real, indeed, but by dint of sacrifice all the young people fared well. Lydia completed her high school grades at Nutana Collegiate in Saskatoon and then attended Normal School to qualify for a First Class Teaching Certificate. At this point there was a spell of teaching for the express purpose of financing further studies. In due course she registered at the University of Saskatchewan, to become in time an honors graduate in arts and science and winner of the coveted Governor General's gold medal in 1920.

Now what? Silently, she nursed an ambition.

She was drawn to church work and family circumstances growing out of the tragedy of war seemed to point the way for her. A brother with plans to fit himself for the Methodist ministry enlisted and went overseas early in the First World War — and did not return. Although it brought surprise to many observers within and beyond the church, Miss Lydia's determination was to take the place of her late brother in the church ministry. Accordingly, she applied for entrance to St. Andrew's Theological College, situated on the campus of the University of Saskatchewan, and was accepted. Dr. Walter Murray, as President of the University, and Dr. E. H. Oliver, as Principal of the College, were jointly impressed by this girl's purpose and dedication and both showed personal interest in her progress.

Of course she did brilliantly in theology — as she had done previously — and graduated at the head of her class in 1923. But where could she go from there? Male classmates could go on to ordination while she, with the same degree in theology and a higher academic record, was barred. The ministry was for men only. Her friends were annoyed; some were angry. She was disappointed, but knowing that church law was not easy to change, she accepted the less prestigious roles of service such as assignments in religious education and work among New Canadians in northeastern Saskatchewan, especially among Doukhobors at Verigin and other ethnic groups at Wakaw and Kelvington.

Although small enough in stature to require the extra

elevation afforded by a box or stool when standing behind a pulpit, she possessed boundless energy and won admiration on the mission fields where stamina and vigor rated highly. Dr. John Nicol, who was superintendent of Home Missions in Northern Saskatchewan, could tell of the task of trying to keep up with her in the field.

For all practical purposes she was performing a minister's work in the country and doing it well year after year, but she did not have a minister's status and the protests about this apparent injustice were becoming steadily louder. Eventually, after eleven years of this, Doctor Oliver, a former moderator of the United Church, gave notice of motion to the Saskatchewan Conference of the church for authorization to induct Miss Gruchy. Nobody anticipated much objection at the provincial level and the Conference approved. But gaining the consent of the General Council of the church, on which eastern influence was strong, would be another matter. Everybody knew the motion being sent from Saskatchewan would spark bitter controversy. Approval by the Council would require an amendment to the Basis of Union and presbyteries across the country would have to be polled for their official views. By this time, to be sure, the name of Lydia Gruchy was one of the best known in church circles across Canada. And finally, when the voting tally was known, it showed eighty presbyteries favoring the amendment which would permit the Saskatchewan lady to be ordained, twenty-six opposed and nine which had not registered a vote.

The result was far from being unanimous but it was sufficient to effect the amendment and allow the Saskatchewan Conference to carry out Doctor Oliver's proposal. At the next meeting of the Conference, the president, Doctor Nicol, and four other members were instructed to proceed to induct Miss Gruchy as soon as the General Council acted to remove the technical obstacles. Later in the year, the Basis of Union was amended appropriately and Doctor Nicol's committee lost no time in carrying out its instructions.

A Long Wait for Ordination • 265

The lady concerned was at this time working as the minister's assistant to Rev. Geoffrey Glover of St. Andrew's Church in Moose Jaw. Accordingly, that church was chosen to be the setting for the long-awaited ordination on November 4, 1936. For a change, a church function seemed to enjoy the popularity of a hockey game. Recognizing it as an important moment in ecclesiastical history, many church dignitaries attended and citizens with or without church affiliations crowded into the hall to witness what all knew would be a precedent-shattering ceremony.

Doctor Nicol, as president of the Conference, presided and performed the induction ritual and Dr. George Dorey of Regina delivered the sermon. But the center of attraction was, without question, the little lady with happy expression. They saw her nicely dressed, with streaks of gray showing in her bobbed hair and a boldness in her stride as she walked to the platform. The loud and sustained applause — seldom heard in the church — left no doubt about the local acceptance of the lady's new status. She whispered a confession that it was almost worth waiting thirteen years to experience.

Lydia Gruchy and her friends had gained an objective. It wasn't that she simply wanted the title of Reverend and the privilege of wearing the pastoral gown in her own right, or that she was in a hurry to change the sort of church work she was doing; largely, it was a deep desire to overcome a long-standing prejudice and open the highest offices of the church to members of her sex. She remained for some time at her St. Andrew's Church post in Moose Jaw and then left to become secretary of the Church Deaconess Order for Canada, with office in Toronto. A little later she became acting principal of the United Church Training School in Toronto and then, in 1940, hearing the clear and loud call of the West, she returned to Saskatchewan where she served congregations at various points, Naicam, Simpson, Cupar and finally, Neville, south of Swift Current. They were not large charges but they were the kind she fancied, with pronounced rural character.

Lydia Gruchy was not only the first woman to graduate in theology from St. Andrew's College and the first woman to be ordained into the ministry of the United Church in all of Canada, but she was the first woman to receive the honorary degree of Doctor of Divinity within the United Church. That degree was conferred at the fortieth annual convocation of St. Andrew's College, in February, 1955. Her friends found added reason for pride.

By 1962, the lady who had served the church long and well, and did more than she realized in the cause of women's rights, was retiring. She was leaving her last congregational charge at Neville. As a place for retirement, she had chosen White Rock, overlooking the Pacific. There she would live with her sister, Florence, also a graduate from the University of Saskatchewan, and another who had served the church for many years, working as a nursing sister in both Canada and India.

The Presbytery of Cypress Hills held a special session to express its farewell to Rev. Lydia Gruchy. A special session was most fitting because the Reverend Doctor Lydia Gruchy was a very special kind of person. People of all religious denominations agreed.

Dr. Walter Murray was remembered for having said that "chewing tobacco did more to discourage 'necking' than a hundred years of reform." Another of his sage observations was: "Miss Gruchy did more to improve the role of women than a hundred suffragettes on a window-smashing spree could have done."

Courtesy Ontario Department of Lands and Forests

ANAHAREO:
THE SCREAMS OF SUFFERING ANIMALS

Grey Owl, the colorful English immigrant who adopted an Indian guise and fooled millions of people, won international attention. Anahareo, the Mohawk girl who shared his life for many years and furnished the real inspiration for the conversion from trapper to conservationist which made him famous, was not so well known. While he wrote books, went on lecture tours and became a public figure, she remained in the background, doing nothing to buttress her claim to a fundamental role in his success. There is reason to conclude that without her convictions and influence, the world would not have heard of Grey Owl and he would have remained an obscure trapper in the Canadian backcountry.

It has been said many times that behind every successful man there is an able woman — or an ambitious mother-in-law. Grey Owl admitted that it was Anahareo's ethical regard for wild creatures that led him, first, to be a defender of the beavers and, then, an ardent conservationist with a dislike for all steel traps. It was the trapper-turned-conservationist who became the great popular hero.

She was Mohawk — except for the blood of a Scottish great-grandfather on her father's side. Her mother died when she was four years old and she lived with her father at Mattawa, Ontario. In 1925, when she first saw the man then known as Archie Belaney at Lake Temagami, she was dark and beautiful, with rounded facial features and a graceful figure. She was nineteen but had not abandoned the idea of returning to school.

Grey Owl was thirty-seven years of age at that time, a rollicking fellow, hot-tempered and given to spells of drinking. As he pulled his canoe onto the lakeshore sand on that summer afternoon, she looked up from the book she was reading and found this tall fellow — six feet two inches — staring at her. His long hair hung in braids; his skin was bronzed and his stride was lithe and catlike. He looked like an Indian or at least a part Indian.

Although stunned by the spectacle he presented, she looked away, as proper young ladies were supposed to do. Propriety, however, was not one of Archie Belaney's conspicuous qualities and, with scowl on his face, he advanced toward her. Without a smile, he asked who she was and what she was doing there. She made a pretense of being annoyed — a poor one — by his rude intrusion. They exchanged curt remarks, and when he wheeled to leave, she had the urge to call him back and ask him a few questions. But before being out of range, he wheeled and shouted: "You'll be seeing me again."

Archie Belaney was already a man of mystery in that part — seemed more like the Ojibway Indians with whom he had been living than like the white people in the region, although he spoke with an English accent. Obviously he was at home in the forests where he had trapped, canoed, carried the mail by dogteam, celebrated trapper style when there was reason and sometimes when there was no reason.

Oh yes, he had been wounded and gassed in France during the First World War, then sent to England and discharged from the army. Wherever he went he admitted a dislike for white people and he could not get back fast enough to the Ontario North and the Ojibway friends. It was there that an aged chief adopted him into the tribe, giving him the name, Grey Owl. That settled it; from that moment on he was anxious to forget his English name and English pedigree. Frequently he used the name of McNeil, explaining that his mother was an Indian and his father a Scotsman.

When Anahareo saw him at Lake Temagami, he had just been employed as a guide for the benefit of visitors at the resort, and sure enough, Anahareo saw the fascinating figure again and again. Their second meeting was at a Saturday night dance where he was playing the drums and following her with his dark and penetrating eyes. Next, he appeared unexpectedly at her home and the feeling of strangeness disappeared.

It was her first serious romance but not the first for him, not by any means. Later, when she accepted his invitation to visit him at his trapper's lodge in the northern Quebec wilderness, he told her much about himself, about his meeting with the Indian girl, Angele, and their marriage and the birth of a child; about the wartime affair with the dancing girl in England, followed by marriage and then annulment; about Marie Gerard, whom he met when she was working as a waitress at Bisco, and their escape to his trapping range.

These confessions might have been expected to send her racing home to Father, who was already angry about the prolonged absence with Archie. Instead of feeling upset, she was amused at this amazing man and encouraged him to relate more of his experiences. He told of his arrival at Toronto in 1906, glad to get away from England and the watchful eyes of his two guardian aunts, for one of whom he had developed a genuine hatred.

At his first job in Toronto, he sold men's clothing and found no satisfaction in the work. He heard about a new mineral strike producing a mining rush to Cobalt, far back in the wilds, and resolved to go. He had less than enough money to take him all the way and was obliged to get off the train sixty miles short of the intended destination. He started to walk the remaining distance but, hungry, tired and ill, he collapsed on the trail and might have succumbed had it not been for an Indian who found him and undertook to care for him. With the aid of much beating of tom-toms by a conjuring Medicine Man, and his host's benevolent attention, he revived and discovered that he was at Temagami. It was there that he met the Indian girl, Angele.

Anahareo was fascinated by this man's story and now she was seeing him as a fire ranger, trapper, guide — depending on the season. He was unpredictable and so was she but they were in love with each other and having come for a one-week visit, she never did use the return portion of her railway ticket. They were married in the Indian tradition, a simple and beautiful ceremony performed by the Chief at Simon Lake.

Life with Grey Owl was often difficult but never dull, and having become his wife, she knew she had to accept his failings along with his endearing qualities; also, she would have to be reconciled to trapping as a means of livelihood, even though she had known a lifelong aversion to it. From the time she was a small girl she had had more than the usual Indian respect for animals and although her father had been periodically a trapper, she had developed an intense hatred for steel traps and the cruelty they inflicted. She could not forget the screams of suffering animals held for days until they died from starvation or freezing or exhaustion.

In those first years with Grey Owl, while recognizing the necessity of making a living, she argued with herself and rationalized until March, 1928, when she came upon a lynx in one of their traps. The animal had been held in torture for at least ten days, had gnawed at its entrapped leg until the bone was almost bare of flesh, and had chewed tree bark and eaten snow to stay alive. It was a grisly sight and the girl declared her determination never to trap again.[1] Her husband might continue to trap, but for

---

[1] Anahareo, *Devil in Deerskins,* New Press, Toronto, 1972

her, the cruel business was ended. But how was she to tell the man who had captured her heart how she felt about his occupation? He would probably laugh and dismiss her idea as feminine whim.

It was at this time that two orphan beaver kittens, McGinnis and McGinty, came into her life to reinforce her own convictions and to change Grey Owl. The mother beaver had been trapped and managed to get away with the trap to face a slow death. For the two babies there was no chance of survival unless they received outside help.

"We must save them," Anahareo pleaded. Grey Owl objected to the trouble of taking the kittens to the cabin and trying to feed them but he yielded to his wife's determined wish and the wee things were introduced to canned milk, which was practically forced down their throats at first. But the orphans got the idea and not only survived but captured the heart of the trapper as well as that of his lady. Within a year from the coming of McGinnis and McGinty, Grey Owl announced that he would never set another beaver trap. He might continue to do trapping, but not for beavers. Anahareo said McGinnis and McGinty were responsible for the change. It would have been easy to see her influence as the principal reason; in any case, she was happy about it.

They moved to Temiscouata Lake in eastern Quebec, in the autumn of 1928, taking McGinnis and McGinty with them, of course, because they had become, for all practical purposes, members of the family. With the personally imposed prohibition on the trapping of beaver, the winter ahead was a lean one. Grey Owl and Anahareo might have been hungry had it not been for the sale of his first article on outdoor adventure and then his first public lecture on the same theme, both of which brought demands for more.

The tragedy of the year was the springtime urge on the part of the two young beavers to swim out and see the world. On a day when McGinnis and McGinty seemed to plead with their two human friends to accompany, they answered the call of the wild and were not seen again.

McGinnis and McGinty were missing but another young beaver joined the Grey Owl household, this one to be known as Jellyroll, and still another, Rawhide, no doubt the most widely known beaver people in world history.

Becoming well known, Grey Owl received an appointment as a naturalist at Riding Mountain National Park and Jellyroll and Rawhide and Anahareo moved too. Jellyroll became the mother of four kittens, which didn't make moving any easier. Then, from Riding Mountain, Grey Owl and Anahareo and the beavers moved to Lake Ajawaan at Prince Albert National Park, a location which proved ideal for beavers, and Jellyroll and Rawhide went to work to build a house for themselves, right against Grey Owl's cabin, with the thoughtful provision of a direct entrance from the beaver house to the interior of the cabin. Tables and chairs suffered when the beavers wanted the legs for construction purposes but nobody objected strenuously. At Ajawaan another source of interest and joy occurred in 1932 when baby Shirley Dawn was born. With the blood of two races and distinctiveness in parents, she seemed to inherit personality and charm.

In the course of time, the parents drifted in different directions, Grey Owl taking longer speaking tours and Anahareo going prospecting in the North. But it was back at Ajawaan, on April 13, 1938, that Grey Owl died, to be buried beside his beloved lake. Immediately after the great conservationist's death there was the revelation in headlines across the country that Grey Owl was an Englishman — not an Indian at all. Some writers described him as the Great Deceiver. It was unfortunate that his pedigree should have received so much attention; the important thing should have been his message, a solemn plea for sense and decency in treating Nature's Wild Children. "I realized," he wrote, "what a crime we trappers were committing against Nature that had been so bountiful. I dedicated my life at that moment to conservation of game."

It was a noble and an uncompromising dedication. On

lecture tour in England shortly before his death, he was invited to make a public address for the British Broadcasting Corporation and then certain officials asked him to change the script which was a condemnation of the "blood sports" like fox hunting, but the man who could see nothing good about a so-called sport in which a fox is pursued until torn apart by the dogs, refused to delete or change even a word.

After his death, Anahareo, with no special training, struggled to support herself. She enjoyed the outdoor life of a prospector but it was generally unrewarding. She worked for a time as a park guide at Banff where she was known as Gertrude Bernard. But she was more at home with canoes than with horses and mountains and created a stir by agreeing to shoot Bow Falls for a movie company, a plan which had to be canceled when park authorities refused permission. After leaving the park service, she seemed to disappear from the public view for a few years.

But Anahaero's finest hours came later when she renewed with greater vigor her opposition to cruelty to animals. She singled out the awful trapping by means of leg-hold steel traps and the harsh treatment of domestic animals — even "the way we raise animals for food is unnatural and cruel." She drew convincingly from her memory. Etched on her mind were scenes like that of the female beaver moaning from the pain of one paw held by the wicked jaws of a steel trap but "holding in her good hand one of her young and suckling it."[1] It should have been enough to turn any human against both trapping and furs.

"How ironic," she could add, "that we have now seen fit to make the beaver our national emblem, yet continue to torture this intelligent animal in the leg-hold trap, just as we did 200 years ago. What hypocrisy! We ought to call it our national shame."[2]

---

[1] Anahareo, Letter to the *Albertan*, May 17, 1975
[2] Ibid.

Some of her most pointed criticism was for the so-called sportsmen who maimed and slaughtered animals and wrecked animals' families, "for fun." "They don't even want the meat," she said. "They call that sport and they call us Indians savages."

And the ladies who sought wild furs to satisfy their vanity were no better. "Those lovely ladies clad in their exquisite furs would faint if they were to see the pain and torture suffered by only one of the many creatures whose lives must be taken to make up that fur coat or stole . . . if you must own a fur coat, then buy a ranch-bred fur or better still by far, a lovely fake fur. You will feel much better for it . . . and most assuredly the animal will."[1]

Yes, even in the raising of domestic animals there was much thoughtlessness and cruelty, she noted. "Why can't we live at peace with Nature, in harmony with it as the Indians did. It is an awful greed that leads men to risk destroying the earth for the sake of a few dollars."

She possessed the strongest of convictions. In the words of Daughter Dawn, "this probably comes from her years in the bush; anyone alone in the woods for long periods of time becomes convinced that he or she is right because there is nobody present to offer an argument."[2] At sixty-nine years of age she was becoming more impatient with her fellow humans who would sacrifice everything in Nature's household for the illusive reward of money.

She had an exciting life, colorful and eventful, and at times sad and dangerous. She tasted life's sweetest pleasures and deepest sorrows. The printed story of her life with Grey Owl circulated around the world although her part in making him famous was greater by far than most readers realized. "She has never been given the credit she deserves," her daughter agrees. "Her compassion marked the course." When the turning point in Grey Owl's life, which led to his success, was mentioned to her

---

[1] Ibid.
[2] Bruce, Dawn, Correspondence, June 11, 1975

with the comment, "You did it," she replied, "No, not me, rather McGinty, McGinnis and me."[1]

True, the ways of Anarhareo and Grey Owl parted but he continued to be her hero and she resented in anger anything unkind said or written about him. Was it not that lingering love and loyalty which induced her many years after his passing to make a superb clay model of Grey Owl and Jellyroll, and then to write the book *Devil in Deerskins?* "It is time," she said, "that someone told the true story of the man." She was anxious to correct some false impressions about him. One of the rewards in writing was in reliving all the memorable years spent with the great conservationist and she confessed to Daughter Dawn: "I have fallen in love with your father all over again."[2]

Perhaps that rekindled love explained in part at least how Anahareo's finest contributions came late in life when she was acting alone in taking a bolder and more courageous stand on behalf of the wild creatures which man had so callously mistreated.

---

[1] Ibid.
[2] Ibid.

Grant MacEwan

Author, environmentalist, educator, agricultural scientist, journalist, farmer and politician, **Grant MacEwan** is one of western Canada's most respected and prominent personalities.

From 1946 to 1951, Grant MacEwan was Dean of Agriculture at the University of Manitoba. After terms as a Calgary alderman and an Alberta MLA, he became mayor of Calgary in 1963 and in 1965 was appointed Lieutenant-Governor of Alberta, serving until 1974. He holds honorary degrees from the universities of Alberta, Calgary, Brandon, Guelph and Saskatchewan, and is an honorary chief of the Blood Reserve.

Grant MacEwan has a total of forty-eight titles to his name — an impressive tribute to the prairies and a heartfelt celebration of the land and the people that shaped it. He now resides in Calgary, close to the hills he cherishes.